**This book is to be returned on or before
the last date stamped below.**

21/5/16,
31/5/16

SUTTON LEISURE SERVICES

STEPHEN FRY IN AMERICA

STEPHEN FRY
IN AMERICA

**LARGE
PRINT**

First published 2008
by
HarperCollins Publishers
This Large Print edition published 2009
by
BBC Audiobooks Ltd
by arrangement with
HarperCollins Publishers Ltd

UK Hardcover ISBN 978 1 408 43007 1
UK Softcover   ISBN 978 1 408 43008 8

British Library Cataloguing in Publication Data available

Printed and bound in Great Britain by CPI Antony
Rowe, Chippenham and Eastbourne

CONTENTS

INTRODUCTION

I was so nearly an American. It was *that* close. In the mid-1950s my father was offered a job at Princeton University—something to do with the emerging science of semiconductors. One of the reasons he turned it down was that he didn't think he liked the idea of his children growing up as Americans. I was born, therefore, not in NJ but in NW3.

I was ten when my mother made me a present of this momentous information. The very second she did so, *Steve* was born.

Steve looked exactly like me, same height, weight and hair colour. In fact, until we opened our mouths, it was almost impossible to distinguish one from the other. Steve's voice had the clear, penetrating, high-up-in-the-head twang of American. He called Mummy 'Mom', he used words like 'swell', 'cute' and 'darn'. There were detectable differences in behaviour too. He spread jam (which he called jelly) on his (smooth, not crunchy) peanut butter sand-wiches, he wore jeans, t-shirts and basketball sneakers rather than grey shorts, Airtex shirts and black plimsolls. He had far more money for sweets, which he called candy, than Stephen ever did. Steve was confident almost to the point of rudeness, unlike Stephen who veered unconvincingly between shyness and showing off. If I am honest, I have to confess that Stephen was slightly afraid of Steve.

As they grew up, the pair continued to live their separate, unconnected lives. Stephen developed a mania for listening to records of old music hall and radio comedy stars, watching cricket, reading poetry

1

and novels, becoming hooked on Keats and Dickens, Sherlock Holmes and P.G. Wodehouse and riding around the countryside on a moped. Steve listened to blues and rock and roll, had all of Bob Dylan's albums, collected baseball cards, went to movie theatres three times a week and drove his own car.

Stephen still thinks about Steve and wonders how he is getting along these days. After all, the two of them are genetically identical. It is only natural to speculate on the fate of a long-lost identical twin. Has he grown even plumper than Stephen or does he work out in the gym? Is he in the TV and movie business too? Does he write? Is he 'quintessentially American' in the way Stephen is often charged with being 'quintessentially English'?

All these questions are intriguing but impossible to settle. If you are British, dear reader, then I dare say you too might have been born American had your ancestral circumstances veered a little in their course. What is your long-lost non-existent identical twin up to?

*   *   *

Most people who are obsessed by America are fascinated by the physical—the cars, the music, the movies, the clothes, the gadgets, the sport, the cities, the landscape and the landmarks. I am interested in all of those, of course I am, but I (perhaps because of my father's decision) am interested in something more. I have always wanted to get right under the skin of American life. To know what it *really* is to be American, to have grown up and been schooled as an American; to work and play as an American; to romance, labour, succeed, fail, feud, fight, vote, shop, drift, dream and drop out as an American; to grow ill and grow old as an American.

For years then, I have harboured deep within me the desire to make a series of documentary films about 'the real' America. Not the usual road movies in a Mustang and certainly not the kind of films where minority maniacs are trapped into making exhibitions of themselves. It is easy enough to find Americans to sneer at if you look hard enough, just as it is easy to find ludicrous and lunatic Britons to sneer at. Without the intention of fawning and flattering then, I did want to make an honest film about America, an unashamed love letter to its physical beauty and a film that allowed Americans to reveal themselves in all their variety.

*   *   *

Anti-Americanism is said to be on the rise around the world. Obviously this has more to do with American foreign policy than Americans as people. In a democracy, however, you can't quite divorce populace from policy. Like any kind of racism there are the full-frontal and the casual kinds.

I have often felt a hot flare of shame inside me when I listen to my fellow Britons casually jeering at the perceived depth of American ignorance, American crassness, American isolationism, American materialism, American lack of irony and American vulgarity. Aside from the sheer rudeness of such open and unapologetic mockery, it seems to me to reveal very little about America and a great deal about the rather feeble need of some Britons to feel superior. All right, they seem to be saying, we no longer have an Empire, power, prestige or respect in the world, but we do have 'taste' and 'subtlety' and 'broad general knowledge', unlike those poor Yanks. What silly, self-deluding rubbish! What small-minded stupidity! Such Britons hug themselves with the thought that they are more cosmopolitan and sophisticated than Americans because they think they know more about geography and world culture, as if *firstly* being cosmopolitan and sophisticated can be scored in a quiz and as if *secondly* (and much more importantly) being cosmopolitan and sophisticated is in any way desirable or admirable to begin with. Sophistication is not a moral quality, nor is it (unless one is mad) a criterion by which one would choose one's friends. Why do we like people? Because they are knowledgeable, cosmopolitan and sophisticated? No, because they are charming, kind, considerate, exciting to be with, amusing . . . there is a long list, but knowing what the capital of Kazakhstan is will not be on it. Unless, as I repeat, you are mad.

The truth is, we are offended by the clear fact that so many Americans know and care so very little about us. How *dare* they not know who our Prime Minister is, or be so indifferent as to believe that Wales is an island off the coast of Scotland? We are quite literally not on the map as far as they are concerned and that hurts. They can get along without us, it seems, a lot better than we can get along without them and how can that not be galling to our pride? Thus we (or some of us) react with the superiority and conceit characteristic of people who have been made to feel deeply inferior.

I do not believe, incidentally, that most Britons are anti-American, far from it. Many are as fascinated in a positive way by the United States as I am, and if their pride needs to be salvaged by a little affectionate banter then I suppose it does little harm.

4

So I wanted to make an American series which was not about how amusingly unironic and ignorant Americans are, nor about religious nuts and gun-toting militiamen, but one which tried to penetrate everyday American life at many levels and across the whole United States. What sort of a design should such a series have? What sort of a structure and itinerary? It is a big country, the United States, and surely . . .

The United *States!* America's full name held the clue all along, for America, it has often been said, is not one country, but fifty. If I wanted to avoid all the clichés, all the cheap shots and stereotypes and really see what America was, then why not make a series about those fifty countries, the actual states themselves? It is all very well to talk about living and dying, hoping and dreaming, loving and loathing 'as an American', but what does that mean when America is divided into such distinct and diverse parcels? To live and die as a Floridian is surely very different from living and dying as a Minnesotan? The experience of hoping and dreaming as an Arizonan cannot have much in common with that of hoping and dreaming as a Rhode Islander, can it?

So, to film in every state. I had a structure and a purpose. It suddenly seemed so obvious and so natural that I was amazed no British television company had ever done it before. But how would I get about? I often drive around in a London taxi. The traditional black cab is good and roomy for filming in and perhaps the sight of one braving the canyons, deserts and interstate highways of America could become a happy signature image for the whole journey. A black cab it would be.

There is no right tempo for a project like this. The whole thing could be achieved in two weeks by someone who just wanted to tick off the states like a train-spotter, or it could be done over the course of years, with great time and attention given to the almost infinite social, political, cultural and physical nuances of each state. The pace at which my taxi and I zipped along provided me not with definitive portraits but with multiple snapshots of experience, which I hope when taken together will cause a bigger picture of the country and its fifty constituent parts to emerge.

* * *

Between these pages I have been more anxious to convey the experience than to interpret it—in other words, while this is a book about a journey, it does not presume to draw conclusions. I would not dare to suggest that my trip, though as exhausting and exhaustive as we could make it, has granted me a definitive insight into so complex and gigantic a nation as America, nor even a definitive insight into each state. I do hope however, that it will communicate the scale of the nation, the diversity, depth of identity and wealth of pride that prevails in every one of its fifty distinct states. I hope too that it will fill in some gaps for those of you, who—like me—might have been rather unsure where Wisconsin, say, or Nebraska exactly fitted on the map, who wanted to know a little more about the Deep South, the Heartland, New England, the Pacific Northwest, the Delta and the Great Lakes, the Rocky and the Smoky Mountains, the wide Mississippi and High Plains and the people who live out their lives in these remarkable places. You can, of course, use this book as a quick reference when you need to remind yourself where Vermont is, or what the state capital of Kansas might be and you can try your hand at the little quiz I have included at the end of the book. If you use a gentle pencil to fill in your answers, then others can have a go too . . .

*   *   *

Having said that this book presumes to draw no conclusions, I will offer this: the overwhelming majority of Americans I met on my journey were kind, courteous, honourable and hospitable beyond expectation. Such striking levels of warmth, politeness and consideration were encountered not just in those I was meeting for on-camera interview, they were to be found in the ordinary Americans I met in the filling-stations, restaurants, hotels and shops too.

If I were to run out of petrol in the middle of the night I would feel more confident about knocking on the door of an American home than one in any other country I know—including my own. The friendly welcome, the generosity, the helpfulness of Americans—especially, I ought to say, in the South and Midwest—is as good a reason to visit as the scenery. Yes, Americans are terrible drivers (endlessly weaving between lanes while on the phone, bullying their way through if they drive a big vehicle, no waves of thanks or acknowledgement, no letting other cars into traffic), yes, they have no idea what cheese or bread can be and yes, strip malls, TV

7

commercials and talk radio are gratingly dreadful. But weighing the good, the kind, the original, the enchanting, the breathtaking, the hilarious and the lovable against the bad, the cruel, the banal, the ugly, the crass, the silly and the monstrous, I see the scales coming down towards the good every time.

If you are an American you will, I hope, accept my apologies for such statements of the obvious, such errors of fact and judgement, such generalisations and misapprehensions as will be painfully evident to you, privileged as you are with that almost unconscious knowledge and instinctive understanding of your native state and nation that comes with citizenship. Human nature, after all, dictates that you turn straight to the entry in this book that covers your own state, and you will doubtless find that your home town has been ignored and that I have passed over all the ingredients you regard as essential in the make-up, character and identity of your state, and this might poison your mind against my judgement. My eyes, those of an outsider looking in, are bound to miss and to misinterpret. As it happens, I enjoy reading impressions of Britain written by visitors to our shores; the mistakes and misreadings only add to the pleasure and often make me think about my country in new ways, so perhaps my sweeping inaccuracies and dumb failures to grasp the essentials can be taken in that light, as revealing rather than obscuring. Sometimes the spectator sees more of the game. In any event, few if any Americans I met in my travels had ever visited all fifty states, or anything close to that number, so perhaps even you will find something new here.

There is one phrase I probably heard more than any other on my travels: 'Only in America!'

If you were to hear a Briton say 'Tch! Only in Britain, eh?' it would probably refer to something that was either predictable, miserable, oppressive, dull, bureaucratic, queuey, damp, spoil-sporty or incompetent—or a mixture of all of those. 'Only in America!' on the other hand, always refers to something shocking, amazing, eccentric, wild, weird or unpredictable. Americans are constantly being surprised by their own country. Britons are constantly having their worst fears confirmed about theirs. This seems to be one of the major differences between us.

*   *   *

We began filming the series in Maine in late September 2007 and finished in Hawaii in the first week of May, 2008.

At 6.45 a.m. on my very first morning I was sitting in the WaCo Diner, which styles itself 'America's eastmost dining-room'. Marvelle prepared a Seafood Scramble for me while her colleague Darna replenished my coffee cup for the third time. Endless free refilling or 'bottomless coffee' as they call it is the norm in diners all across the United States. How outraged Americans are when they come to Europe and find themselves charged for each cup. Anyway, the television at the end of the counter was running a commercial for a local telecoms company. And that is where I heard a refrain that, *mutatis mutandis*, followed me over the next eight months as I travelled from sea to shining sea: 'In Maine we don't always follow the rules. We sometimes make our own. In Maine we think different.'

Those words, surely somewhat overblown in the context of a television advertisement for a local phone

9

network, confirmed my suspicions about American statal pride. 'We think different in Tennessee', 'South Dakotans march to a different drum', 'We don't follow the pack in New Mexico', 'I guess you can call us Missourians mavericks'. . . and so on.

We all like to think ourselves different, 'I'm unconventional like everybody else,' as Wilde once almost said, but it seems particularly important to Americans to remind themselves of their separateness, their uniqueness, their rebel spirit and they do it, not so much as a nation, but state by state.

And which of the states is my personal favourite? I have been asked that a great deal and I have yet to come up with a smart, snappy answer. A combination of Montana, northern California, Arizona, Maine and Alaska would be pretty impressive. But I have left out Utah, Wyoming and Massachusetts and where are Vermont and Kentucky? Am I saying I didn't like Pennsylvania and South Carolina? Oh dear. Without the loyalty that comes from being actually born in one of the states it seems impossible to choose between them. I could live in most of them perfectly happily. Living the life I do, I would have to make my choice according to conveniences like proximity to a major American city. Thus to have Chicago, Boston, New Orleans, San Francisco or New York within reach would tilt the balance away from Montana, Arizona and Maine, for example. Yet I could live happily in any of those three if I were to retire from the kind of work that makes access to a large urban centre necessary.

As the taxi and I travelled around America I pictured myself in an adobe on the edges of the Saguaro Park outside Tucson, Arizona, in an artfully luxurious beachfront shack on the New England coast, in a Colorado condo in the shadow of the Rockies, in an Italianate villa in the Napa Valley, in a gracious antebellum residence in the lowlands of South Carolina, in a modern glass-fronted creation built into the hillside overlooking Puget Sound in Seattle, Washington, in a Ted Turner-style ranch house in Montana, in an elegant townhouse in a historic square in Savannah, Georgia or in a traditional clapboard, clinker-built home with a view over Chesapeake Bay, Maryland. Any one of those would suit me fine.

Damn, I was lucky to be able to do what I did. I hope you find in the pages to come information and experience which will encourage you to think again about America. Maybe you will even consider following in my tyre-treads on your own trip of a lifetime.

Take your own cheese.

SF—June 2008

NEW ENGLAND AND THE EAST COAST

MAINE
KEY FACTS

Abbreviation:
ME

Nickname:
The Pine Tree State

Capital:
Augusta

Flower:
White pinecone

Tree:
Eastern white pine

Bird:
Black-capped chickadee

Motto:
Dirigo ('I lead')

Well-known residents and natives:
Edward Muskie, Dorothea Dix, Winslow Homer,
Henry Wadsworth Longfellow, Harriet Beecher
Stowe, Edna St Vincent Millay, Artemis Ward,
E.B. White, Stephen King, John Ford,
Patrick Dempsey, Jonathan Frakes, Liv Tyler,
Judd Nelson.

MAINE

'I can assure you of this. If I find a friendlier, more welcoming and kinder set of people in all America than Mainers I will send you film of me eating my hat.'

Squeezed by Canada on two sides and connected to the rest of America by a straight-line border with New Hampshire, Maine is home to a million and a quarter citizens who roam roomily around a land larger than all of Scotland.

The southeast half of the state is where the urban action is. Portland and Bangor are the big towns; the former is the birthplace and home town of Stephen King, the novel laureate of Maine, whose prolific output has stayed loyal to the state for over thirty years. But I'm heading north, passing through Portland, Augusta and Bangor, getting used to how much of a head-turner my little London taxi will be. Augusta, with one of the lowest populations of any of the fifty state capitals, seems small, depressed and depressing. I hurry through on my way Down East. 'Down', in Maine-speak, means 'Up'.

With the exception of Louisiana and Alaska whose administrative districts are called parishes and boroughs respectively, all the American states are divided into counties. These are much like their British counterparts, but with sheriffs who are real live law-enforcement officers rather than our ceremonial figureheads in silly costumes. Every US county has its chief town and administrative headquarters, known as the County Seat. The number of counties in each state will vary. Florida, for example, has 67, Nebraska 93 and Texas 254. Maine has just 16 and at the top right of this topmost, rightmost state you will find Washington County, the easternmost county in all America. My destination is Eastport, the easternmost town in that easternmost county.

DOWN EAST

The most obvious physical features of the Down East scenery are forest and ocean. But then this is true of the whole state. Mainers will tell you that if you were to straighten every wrinkle and crinkle of their coastline it would stretch out wider than the whole breadth of the United States—into three and half thousand miles of inlets, creeks, coves, bays, promontories, spits, sounds and headlands. As for the land—well, there is only ten per cent of Maine that is *not* forest and much of that is lake and river. Water and wood, then—water and wood everywhere.

They will also tell you that Eastport was once

16

famed for its sardine-packing industry. 'Fame' is an odd thing in America. There cannot be many towns with a population of more than ten thousand that do not make some claim to it. It usually comes in the form of a burger: 'Snucksville, NC—home of the world famous Snuckyburger', a dish that will never have been heard of more than five miles from its originating diner. But 'back in the day' Eastport genuinely was famous for sardines. An industry, that, if the Eastporters are to be believed, was effectively wrecked by The Most Trusted Man In America.

The doyen of news anchors, Walter 'and that's the way it is' Cronkite liked apparently to sail in the waters around Eastport and was disturbed one day to see a film of oil all over the water, staining the trim paintwork of his yacht. He made complaints. A government agency looked at the fish oil coming from the cannery and imposed regulations so strict that the economic viability of the business was compromised and the industry left Eastport for good. That at least is the story I was told as gospel by many Eastporters. Certainly the deserted shells of the old canneries still brood over the harbour awaiting their full regeneration. The body of water that dominates the harbour is Passamaquoddy Bay and the land on the other side is, confusingly, Canada. A line straight down the middle of the bay forms the border between the two countries.

Before the British, before the French, before any Europeans came to Maine there were the tribesmen, the 'First Nations' or Native Americans, as I expected I should have to be very careful to call them. Actually the word 'Indian' seems inoffensive to the tribespeople I speak to around town. The federal agency is still called The Bureau of Indian Affairs and there are Indian Creeks and Indian Roads and Indian Rivers everywhere. It is true that the word was wrongly applied to the native tribes by Columbus and his settlers who thought they had landed in India. But the word stuck, misnomer or not. Sometimes political correctness exists more in the furious minds of its enemies than in reality, which gets on with compromise and common sense without too much hysteria.

Anyway, the indigenous peoples of the Maine/New Brunswick area are the Passamaquoddy, a European mangling of their original name which meant something like 'the people who live quite close to pollock and spear them a lot from small boats', which may not be a snappy title for a tribe but can hardly be faulted as a piece of self-description.

My first full day in Eastport will see me on Passamaquoddy Bay, not spearing pollock, but hunting a local delicacy prized around the world.

LOBSTERING

The word Maine goes before the word lobster much as Florida goes before orange juice, Idaho before potato and Tennessee before Williams. Three out of four lobsters eaten in America, so I am told, are caught in Maine waters. There are crab, and scallop and innumerable other molluscs and crustaceans making a living in the cold Atlantic waters, but the real prize has always been lobster.

Angus McPhail has been lobstering all his life. He and his sons Charlie and Jesse agree to take me on board for a morning. 'So long as I do my share of work.' Hum. Work, eh? I'm in *television* . . .

'You come aboard, you work. You can help empty and bait the pots.'

The pots are actually traps: crates filled with a tempting bag of stinky bait (for lobsters are aggressive predators of the deep and will not be lured by bright colours or attractively arranged slices of tropical fruit) that have a cunning arrangement of interior hinged doors designed to imprison any lobster that strays in. These cages are laid down in long connected lines on the American side of the border. Angus, skippering the boat, has all the latest sat nav technology to allow him to mark with an X on his screen exactly where the lures have been set. To help the boys on the deck, a buoy marked with the name of the vessel floats on the surface above each pot. Americans, as you may know, pronounce 'buoy' to rhyme not with 'joy' but with 'hooey'.

How is it that work clothes *know* when they are being worn by an amateur, a dilettante, an interloper? I wear exactly the same aprons and boots and gloves as Charlie and Jesse. They look like fishermen, I look like ten types of gormless arse. Heigh ho. I had better get used to this ineluctable fact, for it will chase me across America.

It is extraordinarily hard work. The moment we reach a trap, the boys are hooking the line and hauling in the pot. In the meantime I have been stuffing the bait nets with hideously rotted fish which I am told are in fact sardines. The pot arrives on deck and instantly I must pull the lobsters from each trap and drop them on the great sorting table that forms much of the forward part of the deck. If there are good-looking crabs in the traps they can join the party too, less appetising specimens and species are thrown back into the ocean.

19

Lobsters of course, are mean, aggressive animals. But who can blame them for wanting a piece of my hand? They are fighting for their lives. Equipped with homegrown cutlery expressly designed to snip off bits of enemy, they don't take my handling without a fight.

As soon as the trap has been emptied I'm at the table, sorting. This sorting is important. Livelihoods are at stake. The Maine lobstermen and marine authorities are determined not to allow overfishing to deplete their waters and there is fierce legislation in place to protect the stocks. Jesse explains.

'If it's too small, it goes back in. Use this to measure.'

He hands me a complicated doodad that is something between a calibrated nutcracker and an adjustable spanner.

'Any undersized lobsters they gotta go back in the water, okay?'

'Don't they taste as good?'

A look somewhere between pity and contempt meets this idiotic remark. 'They won't be full-grown, see? Gotta let them breed first. Keep the stocks up.'

'Oh, yes. Of course. Duh! Sorreee!' I always feel a fool when in the company of people who work for a living. It brings out my startling lack of common sense.

'If you find a female in egg, notch her tail with these pliers and throw her back in too.'

'In *egg?* How do I . . . ?'

'You'll know.'

How right he was. A pregnant lobster is impossible to miss: hundreds and hundreds of thousands of glistening black beads stuck all round her body like an over-fertile bramble hedge thick with blackberries.

'Notch her tail' is one of the things that takes a second to say and three and a half minutes of thrashing, wrestling and swearing to accomplish. The blend of curiosity, amusement and disbelief with which I am watched by Jesse and Charlie only makes me feel hotter and clumsier.

'Is this strictly necessary?'

'The inspectors find any illegal lobsters in our catch they'll fine us more'n we can afford. They'll even take the boat.'

'How cruel!'

'Just doing their job. I went to school with most of them. Go out hunting in the woods with them weekends. That wouldn't stop them closing us down if they had to.'

'Done it!' I hold up one properly notched pregnant female. Jesse takes a look and nods, and I throw her back into the ocean.

'Good. Now you gotta band the keepers.'

'I've got to what the which?'

The mature, full-sized, non-pregnant lobsters the crew don't have to throw back are called 'keepers' and it seems that a rubber band must be pulled over their claws and that I am the man to do it.

Charlie hands me the device with which one is supposed to pick up a band, stretch it and get it round the lobster's formidably thick weaponry in one swift movement. Charlie demonstrates beautifully: this implement however marks me down as an amateur as soon as I attempt to pick it up and in a short while I am sending elastic bands flying around the deck like a schoolboy at the back of the bus.

'Otherwise they'll injure each other,' explains Charlie.

'Yes, fine. Of course. Whereas this way they only injure me. I see the justice in that.' I try again. 'Ouch. I mean, quite seriously, *ouch!*'

21

It transpires that lobsters, if they had their way, would prefer not to have elastic bands limiting their pincers' reach, range and movement and they are quite prepared to make a fuss about it. The whole operation of sorting and banding is harder than trying to shove a pound of melted butter into a wildcat's left ear with a red-hot needle in a darkened room, as someone once said about something. And what really gets me is that just as I finish sorting and am ready to turn my mind to a nice cup of tea and a reminisce about our famous victory over the lobsters, Charlie and Jesse send down a fresh pot, Angus moves the boat on and another trap is being pulled aboard.

'You mean one has to do more than one of these?' I gasp.

'We make about thirty drafts a day.'

A draft being the pulling-up, emptying and re-baiting of a trap.

Oh my. This is hard work. Gruellingly hard work. The morning we make our run is a fine sparkling one with only the mildest of swells. The McPhails go out in all weathers and almost all seas.

You have probably seen TV chefs like Rick Stein spend the day with fishermen and pay testament to their bravery and fortitude. We can all admire the bold hunters of the deep, especially these artisanal rather than industrial fishers like the McPhails, crewing their small craft and husbanding the stocks with respect, skill and sensitivity. But until you have joined them, even for one morning, it is hard truly to appreciate the toil, skill, hardiness and uncomplaining courage of these men, and yes it is exclusively men who go out to sea in fishing boats.

They do it for one reason and one reason only. Their families. They have wives and children and they need to support them. There are not many jobs going in Down East Maine, not much in the way of industry, no sign of Starbucks, malls and service-sector employment. This is work on the nineteenth-century model. This is labour.

Given how hard their days are you might think they end each night in bars drinking themselves silly. Actually they need to be home in time for a bath and bed, for the next morning they will be up again at four. It is perhaps unsurprising to hear Jesse tell me that he wants his own sons to do any work other than this. Maybe we should prepare for the price of lobster to go up in our restaurants and fishmongers. Whatever these men make, it surely isn't enough.

FROM THE SEA TO THE TABLE

Lobsters, it seems to me, are simply giant marine insects. Huge bugs in creepy armour. Look at a woodlouse and then a lobster. Cousins, surely? And look at the flesh of a lobster and then at a maggot. Exactly. Cover them in mayonnaise and Frenchify them all you will, lobsters are insects: scary scuttling insects.

None of which stops them from tasting de-mothering-licious of course. And it is with lip-smacking anticipation that I jump off Angus's lobsterman and prepare to feast on our catch at Bob del Papa's Chowder House right on the quayside. Bob del Papa is . . . well, he is as his name leads you to hope he might be, big, amiable, powerful-looking and hospitable. He came up from Rhode Island many years ago having served his country and learned his seamanship with the United States Coastguard. There doesn't seem to be much in Eastport that Bob doesn't own, including the lobsters themselves. He buys them from the fishermen and sells them on to whoever then gets them finally to the restaurant kitchens of America. Bob is far from your typical desk and chair entrepreneur however—he drives the forklift, hauls the crates, cooks the food and sweeps the yard. He is very determined that I should enjoy a Maine lobster properly served with all the correct accoutrements and habiliments traditionally associated with a Maine lobster dinner and takes great pleasure in preparing a grand feast.

We eat right out on the dockside. A big pot is hauled onto a gas ring and a long trestle table laid against the wall and under a canopy to protect it from the rain that is beginning to fall. Bad weather instantly sends the British inside, but in Maine they seem to be made of hardier stuff. An al fresco banquet was prepared and an al fresco banquet we shall all have. One by one Bob's friends and neighbours start to arrive; everyone is grinning and rubbing their hands with pleasurable anticipation.

Before tossing each lobster to its boiling fate it is possible to hypnotise them, or at least send them into a strange cataleptic trance. Bob teaches me how to place one upright on a table and firmly stroke the back of its neck: after a surprisingly short while it freezes and stays there immobile. It is to be hoped that this state will deprive it of even a millisecond of scalding agony when finally into the pot it falls. While dozens of them boil away in the cauldron for nine or ten minutes, turning from browny-bluey-coral to bright cardinal red, I sit myself down and allow Bob's staff of smiling waitresses to serve the first course.

We start with cups of Clam Chowder, the

celebrated New England soup of cream, potatoes, onions, bacon, fish stock and quahogs. These last, now made immortal in the name of the home town in *Family Guy*, are Atlantic hard-shelled clams, a little larger than the cherrystone or little-neck clams which also abound in these fruitful waters. From Maine to Massachusetts a cup of chowder is traditionally served with 'oyster' crackers, small saltine-style biscuits crumbled into the soup to thicken it further. A little white pepper makes the whole experience even more toothsome, but don't even *think* of adding tomato. This is actually illegal in Maine, thanks to a piece of 1939 legislation specifically outlawing the practice. It may be good enough for 'Manhattan Chowder', which I am told is no more than Italian clam soup rebranded, but the real New England deal must be creamy white and tomato free. Like so many enduring local dishes, chowder has an especial greatness when consumed in its land of origin. We all know how delicious *retsina* is sipped on a Greek island and yet how duff it tastes back home. Well, I don't think Clam Chowder is ever duff, but eaten on a quayside in Down East Maine, even in the driving rain, it is to my mind and stomach as close to perfect as any dish can be. Until the lobster arrives, that is.

Each of us is given a pair of crackers, a pot of coleslaw, a bib, a tub of melted and clarified butter and a great red lobster. I recognise mine as one who gave me an especially painful nip earlier in the day so it is with regrettable but understandable savagery that I tear him to pieces, dipping his maggot-flesh with frenzied delight into the ghee and fully justifying the bib, which—I notice—I am the only one wearing.

Bob del Papa claps me on the shoulder. 'Dunt get much bedder 'n this, does it?'

25

I take another sip of the supernacular wine and swallow another piece of the sensational blueberry pie that Bob himself baked. The late afternoon sun pushes through the clouds on its way down west where all the rest of America lies.

'No, Bob, it doesn't. It truly does not.'

But I was wrong.

LEFT RIGHT CENTER

That night Bob takes me to the Happy Crab, a magnificent eatery run by two expat Britons from Leicester, where he initiates me into Left Right Center (the American spelling of centre is, one feels, obligatory), a dice game of startling simplicity and fun. He even gives me a set of dice. I plan to make it the latest gaming sensation in London.

It was inexpressibly touching to discover how much the Mainers want me to love their state. An easy wish to grant. At one point Bob even speculates on which states I might prefer, as if this grand tour was a competition. 'I'm worried about Montana. Ve-e-ery beautiful. Nice people. Hell, if it had a coastline I might even live there myself. Yep, I'm worried you might like Montana more than Maine. But you think we'll be in the top ten?'

I do not laugh, for I see how seriously the issue concerns him.

'There are no top tens,' I say, 'but I can assure you of this. If I find a friendlier, more welcoming and kinder set of people in all America than the Down East Mainers I will send you film of me eating my hat.'

NEW HAMPSHIRE
KEY FACTS

Abbreviation:
NH

Nickname:
The Granite State

Capital:
Concord

Flower:
Purple lilac

Tree:
White birch

Bird:
Purple finch

Motto:
Live Free or Die

Well-known residents and natives:
Josiah Bartlett, Daniel Webster, Horace 'Go West,
Young Man' Greeley, Mary Baker Eddy,
Brooke Astor, Robert Frost, Grace Metalious,
J.D. Salinger, John Irving, P.J. O'Rourke,
Ken Burns, Adam Sandler.

NEW HAMPSHIRE

'What is it with Americans and cinnamon?'

If the word lobster is forever yoked to Maine then who can separate from New Hampshire the word 'primary'? But what the heck is a primary, let alone a New Hampshire one? Something to do with politics one is almost certain but what, precisely?

Primaries in the USA are election races for the presidential nomination. There are, as I expect you know, two parties in American politics: the Democrats (symbol, a donkey or jackass) and the Republicans (the Grand Old Party, symbol an elephant). When the time for presidential elections comes, each party must field a candidate: and who that candidate might be is decided by the outcome of primaries (and caucuses and conventions, but we'll leave them for the time being). Only registered members of the Republican Party can vote for Republican candidates and only registered Democrats for theirs. Like many American institutions it makes sense, is very democratic, transparent and open but comes down, fundamentally, to race, religion, media and—most of all—money.

And why is the New Hampshire primary so important? Because it is traditionally the first of the cycle to be held. The primacy of the New Hampshire primary derives primarily from its prime position as the primary primary. To lose badly here can dish a candidate's chances from the get-go, as they like to say, while to win first out of the traps can impart valuable momentum. Huge amounts of money and effort are expended by all the runners and riders here.

The people of New Hampshire, one of the smallest states in physical size and population, although also one of the most prosperous, are treated every four years to more political speeches, sincere promises, sunny compliments and rosy blandishments than any other citizens in America . . . in the world possibly.

The presidential election takes place every four years, 2004, 2008, 2012 and so on. The primaries begin in the preceding years, 2003, 2007, 2011. I arrive in Manchester, New Hampshire in October, 2007—just as the primary season for the 2008 elections is hotting up. We now all know who won, of course, but as I knock on the door of a certain campaign office, I am certain of nothing other than that it appears to be a close race for both parties. The Democrats are going to have to choose between Hillary Clinton, Chris Dodd, John Edwards, Barack Obama and Bill Richardson. The Republicans have Rudy Giuliani, Mike Huckabee, John McCain, Mitt Romney and Fred Thompson. So the next US President could be a woman, a Mormon, a Latino, an

African-American, a Baptist minister or a television actor . . . there are certainly plenty of firsts on offer.

ON THE ROAD WITH MITT

I am welcomed to the office by a very pretty young girl called Deirdra, the name and the red hair offering picture-book testament to her Irish ancestry. She is one of the many hundreds, indeed thousands, of students and young people who dedicate their time at this season to helping their chosen candidate. Her guy, and for this day my guy too, is Republican Mitt Romney.

'I just love him. He's awesome.'

'What's different about him?' I wonder.

'I saw him last year, just about like before he announced? Just listening to him speak, his charisma and such is mindboggling.'

Whatever my own political views, and they happen not to coincide strikingly with those of Governor Romney, I am touched to be trusted so much by the campaign team, who leave me free to follow Deirdra around, handing out fliers, badges (Americans call them buttons) and posters and attending to the low-level but necessary grunt work that devolves to a young campaign keenie.

As a matter of fact, my production team and I had also approached Clinton's and Obama's people on the Democratic side who, true to their donkey nature, were obstinate and would not budge: no behind the scenes filming. Both Giuliani's and Romney's teams were only too happy to help us out, no strings attached. I was simultaneously impressed and disappointed by the laid-back, friendly and calm

30

atmosphere of the campaign office. I had expected and rather looked forward to the frenzy, paranoia and brilliant, fast-talking, wise-cracking repartee of the TV series *The West Wing*.

Deirdra and I watched Mitt make a speech at a hospital and then at a family home. These 'house parties' are 'Meet Mitt' events where local people turn up and are encouraged to 'just go ahead and ask Mitt anything'. A tidy lower-middle-class home in Hooksett, NH, has been chosen complete with standard Halloween garden decorations and an aroma of cinnamon. What *is* it with Americans and cinnamon? The smell is everywhere; they flavour chewing gum with it, they ruin wine and coffee with it, they slather it over chicken and fish . . . it is all most peculiar.

Deirdra and I turn up armed with pamphlets only minutes before the Governor himself arrives. The excitement is palpable: the householders, Rod and Patricia, are so proud and pleased they look as if they might burst; all their friends and neighbours have gathered, video news crews are lined up pointing at the fireplace whose mantelpiece is replete with miniature pumpkins, artfully stuffed scarecrows and dark-red candles scented with, of course, cinnamon.

With a great flurry of handshakes and smiles Mitt is suddenly in the house, marching straight to the space in front of the fireplace where a mike on a stand awaits him, as for a stand-up comedian. He is wearing a smart suit, the purpose of which, it seems, is to allow him to whip off the jacket in a moment of wild unscripted anarchy, so as to demonstrate his informality and desire to get right down to business and to hell with the outrage and horror this will cause in his minders. British MPs and candidates of all

31

stripes now do the same thing. The world over, male politicians have trousers that wear out three times more quickly than their coats. And who would vote for a man who kept his jacket on? Why, it is tantamount to broadcasting your contempt for the masses. Politicians who wear jackets might as well eat the common people's children and have done with it.

Romney is impressive in a rather ghastly kind of way, which is not really his fault. He has already gone over so many of his arguments and rehearsed so many of his cunningly wrought lines that, try as he might, the techniques he employs to inject a little life and freshness into them are identical to those used by game-show hosts, the class of person Governor Romney most resembles: lots of little chuckled-in phrases, like 'am I right?' and 'gosh, I don't know but it seems to me that', 'heck, maybe it's time' and so on. In fact he is so like an American version of Bob Monkhouse in his verbal and physical mannerisms that I become quite distracted. Rod and Patricia beam so hard and so shiningly they begin to look like the swollen pumpkins that surround them.

'Hey, you know, I don't live and die just for Republicans or just for whacking down Democrats, I wanna get America right,' says Mitt when invited to blame the opposition.

A minder makes an almost indiscernible gesture from the back, which Mitt picks up on right away. Time to leave.

'Holy cow, I have just loved talking to you folks,' he says, pausing on the way out to be photographed. 'This is what democracy means.'

'I told you he was awesome,' says Deirdra.

In the afternoon we move on to Phillips Exeter Academy, one of the most famous, exclusive and prestigious private schools in the land, the 'Eton of America' that educated Daniel Webster, Gore Vidal, John Irving, and numerous other illustrious Americans all the way up to Mark Zuckerberg, the creator of Facebook as well as half the line-up of indie rockers Arcade Fire. The school has an endowment of one billion dollars.

In this heady atmosphere of privilege, wealth, tradition and youthful glamour Mitt is given a harder time. The students question the honesty of his newly acquired anti-gay, anti-abortion 'values'. It seems he was a liberal as Governor of Massachusetts and has now had to add a little red meat and iron to his policies in order to placate the more right-wing members of his party. The girls and boys of the school (whose Democratic Club is more than twice the size of its Republican, I am told) are unconvinced by the Governor's wriggling and squirming on this issue and he only just manages, in the opinion of this observer at least, to get away with not being jeered. I could quite understand his shouting out, 'What the hell you rich kids think you know about families beats the crap out of me', but he did not, which is good for his campaign but a pity for those of us who like a little theatre in our politics.

By the time he appeared on the steps outside the school hall to answer some press questions I was tired, even if he was not. The scene could not have been more delightful, a late-afternoon sun setting the bright autumnal leaves on fire; smooth, noble and well-maintained collegiate architecture and lawns and American politics alive and in fine health. I came away admiring Governor Romney's stamina, calm and good humour. If every candidate has to go through such slog and grind day after day after day,

33

merely to win the right finally to move forward and *really* campaign, then one can at least guarantee that the Leader of the Free World, whoever he or she may be, has energy, an even temper and great stores of endurance. I noticed that the Governor's jacket had somehow magically been placed in the back of his SUV. Ready to be put on in order to be taken off again next time.

BRETTON WOODS

New Hampshire is more than just a political Petri dish, however; it is also home to some of the most beautiful scenery in America. The White Mountains are a craggy range that form part of the great Appalachian chain that sweeps down from Canada to Alabama, reaching their peak at Mount Washington, the highest point in America east of the Mississippi, at whose foothills sprawls the enormous Mount Washington Hotel at Bretton Woods. Damn—politics again.

I never studied economics at school and for some reason I had always thought that the 'Bretton Woods Agreement' was, like the Hoare–Laval pact, the product of two people, one called Bretton and one called Woods. No, the system that gave the world the International Monetary Fund, the World Bank and stable exchange rates based on a decided value for gold was the result of a conference in 1944 here in Bretton Woods, attended by all the allied and non-aligned nations who knew that the post-war world would have to be reconstructed and developed within permanent and powerful institutions. The economic structure of the world since, for good and ill, has

34

largely flowed from that momentous meeting—if structures can be said to flow.

The hotel is certainly big enough to house such a giant convention. It is hard not to think of Jack Nicholson and *The Shining* as I get repeatedly lost in its vast corridors and verandas. I sip tea and watch the huge vista of a misty, drizzly afternoon on the mountains recede into a dull evening. If fate is kind to me, the next day will dawn bright and sunny. Perfect for an expedition to the summit. Unlikely, for Mount Washington sees the least sunshine and the worst weather of anywhere in America. That is an official fact.

Fate is immensely kind, however. Not only does she send a day as sparklingly clear as any I have seen, but she also makes sure that the train and cog line are in prime working order so I can make my way up the 6,000 feet in comfort and without the expenditure of a single calorie, all of which—thanks to my American diet—have far too much to do swelling my tummy to be bothered with exercise. A steam locomotive—nuzzle pointing cutely down ready to push us all up the hill—puffs gently at the foothills. This rack and pinion line has been taking tourists and skiers to the top of Mount Washington for over a hundred and forty years. I join a happy crowd of people on board. The 'engineer' (which is American for engine driver) does something clever with levers at the back of the train and after enough clanking and grinding we are off. Up front, the grimy-faced brakeman tells me a little about the locomotive.

'This was the first,' he says proudly.

'What the first in the world?'

'Yep.'

It wasn't actually, but I haven't the heart to tell him.

35

The world's first cog railway was in Leeds, England, but the Mount Washington line was the first ever to go up a mountain, and that's what counts.

Up we go, pushed by the engine at no more than a fast walking pace. You can almost hear the locomotive wheeze 'gonnamakeit, gonnamakeit, gonnamakeit!' And make it we do.

New *Hampshire?* The highest point in Old Hampshire that I have ever visited is Watership Down, a round green hillock famous for its bunny rabbits. The great granite crags of the White Mountains are a world away from the soft chalk downs of the mother country. The sheer scale is dizzying. I feel as if I have visited two huge countries already and all I have done is take a look round a couple of America's smaller states.

The Appalachians and I have a long way still to go before we reach the south. I gaze down as they march off out of view. What a monumentally, outrageously, heart-stoppingly beautiful country this is. And how frighteningly big.

MASSACHUSETTS

KEY FACTS

Abbreviation:
MA

Nickname:
The Bay State

Capital:
Boston

Flower:
Mayflower

Tree:
American elm

Bird:
Chickadee

Motto:
Ense petit placidam sub libertate quietem
('By the sword she seeks peace under liberty')

Well-known residents and natives:
Paul Revere, John Adams (2nd President),
John Quincy Adams (6th), Calvin Coolidge (30th),
John F. Kennedy (35th), George H. W. Bush (41st),
John Hancock, Benjamin Franklin, Susan B.
Anthony, Oliver Wendell Holmes, Robert Kennedy,
Edward Kennedy, Michael Dukakis, John Kerry,
Mitt Romney, John Harvard, Eli Whitney, Elias
Howe, Samuel Morse, Alexander Graham Bell,
James McNeill Whistler.

MASSACHUSETTS

'By twelve o'clock it's all over and everyone is in bed. There's more true Gothic horror in a digestive biscuit, but never mind.'

Massachusetts prides herself on being a commonwealth rather than a state. It is a meaningless distinction constitutionally but says something about the history and special grandeur of this, the most populous of the New England states. Cape Cod, Martha's Vineyard, the Kennedys, Harvard University, Boston . . . there is a sophisticated patina, a ritzy finish to the place. It has its blue-collar Irish, its rural poor but the image is still that of patrician wealth and founding history. And a quick glance up at the list of notable natives shows that American literature in the first two hundred years of the nation would not have amounted to much without Massachusetts. Maybe having to learn how to spell the name of the state inculcated a literary precision early on . . .

WHALING

Much of the prosperity of nineteenth-century Massachusetts derived from the now disgraced industry of whaling. The centre of this grisly trade was the island town of Nantucket, now a neat and pretty, if somewhat sterile, heritage and holiday resort. It is a pompous and priggish error to judge our ancestors according to our own particular and temporary moral codes, but nonetheless it is hard to understand how once we slaughtered so many whales with so little compunction.

I am shown round the whaling museum by Nathaniel Philbrick, the leading historian of the area, a man boundlessly enthusiastic about all things Nantuckian.

'The whaling companies were the BPs and Mobils of their day,' he says as we pass an enormous whale skeleton. 'The oil from sperm whales lit the lamps of the western world and lubricated the moving parts of industry.'

'But it was such a slaughter . . .'

Nathaniel hears this every day. 'Can't deny it. But look what we're doing now in order to get today's equivalent. Petroleum.'

'Yes, but . . .'

'The Nantucket whalers depredated one species for its oil, which I don't defend, but we tear the whole earth to pieces, endangering hundreds of thousands of species. We fill the air with a climate-changing pollution that threatens all life, including all whales.'

The awful devastation to the whale on the one hand and the unquestionable courage, endurance and skill displayed by the whalers on the other has been Nathaniel's theme as a writer for many years now.

'How will our descendants look at us?' he wonders, as we look down on Nantucket from the roof of the museum. 'Only a sanctimonious fool could deny the valour and hardiness of the New England whalers. But will our great-grandchildren say the same about the oil explorers and oil-tanker crews?'

A petroleum-burning ferry takes us away from Nantucket, past Hyannisport, the home to this day of the Kennedy compound: 'Yeah, saw old Ted sailing just yesterday afternoon,' the ferry captain tells me. 'Gave me a wave, he did.'

THE PILGRIMS

I drive along the coast to Plymouth, Massachusetts where they keep a replica of the *Mayflower*, the ship that carried a boatload of Puritans from Plymouth, Devon to the coast of America in 1620–21. These Pilgrim Fathers have been given, almost arbitrarily one might think, the iconic status of nation-builders; it is almost as if Plymouth Rock is the very rock on which America itself was built. The turkeys those pilgrims killed for food and the sour cranberries they ate with them in their first hard winter are annually memorialised on the third Thursday of every November in the great American feasting ritual known as Thanksgiving. Those who can trace their ancestry back to the pilgrims count themselves almost a kind of aristocracy.

I enjoy a morning clambering about the boat listening to the heritage talk and watching parties of American schoolchildren having the legend of the Pilgrim Fathers reinforced in their young minds.

'I be John Harcourt, out of Plymouth, Hampshire,'

declaims a bearded man in a leather jerkin.

'No you baint,' I tell him firmly. 'You be an actor, out of New York City.'

Only I say no such thing because I am too polite. The ship is crewed by Equity members in smocks and leather caps whose idea of an English accent is to say 'thee', 'thou' and 'my lady' and trust to luck.

'Do thee hail from the Old Country?' I am asked.

'No, no, no!' I am once more too polite to say. 'You mean "Dost thou"—"Do thee" makes no sense.'

The idea that the Puritans came to New England to avoid persecution is lodged firmly in the American psyche. Gore Vidal's view that they came, 'not to be free from persecution, but on the contrary, to be free to persecute' while heretical to America's vision of itself is to some extent born out in the literature of Hawthorne and the decidedly murky regimes of tyranny, bigotry and intolerance under which the citizens of the New World were forced to live in the early days. Quakers, for example, were persecuted, suppressed, tortured and discriminated against in much of New England throughout the early years of the colonies. But I suppose the tortuous alteration of real history and the elevation of the Pilgrim Fathers to heroic status was important for America, which needed to create a vision of itself consonant with its lofty aims. I dare say Robin Hood was a greedy cut-throat and Boadicea a cruel tyrant—all nations twist history and cleanse their heroes in order to express an ideal to live up to.

Nowhere in America is the religious intolerance and fanaticism of the early colonies more apparent, or more weirdly celebrated, than in the small town of Salem, MA.

THE WITCHES

Halloween is the first of America's great winter festivals of celebration and commerce, followed by Thanksgiving and completed by Christmas (or the Holidays, as they are usually called, in deference to non-Christians) and New Year. Children across America go trick-or-treating dressed up as ghosts, monsters, gore-spattered zombies or, somewhat inexplicably, superheroes. For weeks before the actual day houses and gardens ('yards') are decorated with scarecrows, gravestones, pumpkins and autumn fruits creating a weirdly pagan mélange of Wicker Man Celtic, Transylvanian Gothic and Parish Harvest Festival.

In the late seventeenth century an attack of mass hysteria in Salem, Massachusetts resulted in a series of witch trials, judicial torture and hangings. Arthur Miller's play *The Crucible* famously used the episode as a metaphor for the Communist 'witch-hunts' of his own time. The shameful, primitive and disgusting events of the 1690s have receded into jokey folk lore and Salem now embraces its position as the Halloween and Olde Puritan capital of America, abounding with Publick Houses and Crafte Shoppes. Indeed there are now real witches in Salem, witches who are Out and Proud.

'Can you feel the positive energy here?'

'Er, well, since you mention it, not really . . .'

I meet High Priestess Laurie Cabot in her occult shop 'The Cat, The Crow and The Crown', the first of its kind, she claims, anywhere in the world. She and her co-religionists have fought long and hard for 'the Craft' to be treated as any other faith under the constitution. Laurie is the 'Official Witch of

Massachusetts', a title granted by Governor Dukakis in the seventies. She is not to know that I am entirely allergic to anyone using the word 'energy' in a nonsensical, New Age way. A hundred years ago it would have been 'vibrations'. I am determined not to be surly and unhelpful, however, so I plough on.

'Big day for you, today, Laurie. Halloween.'

'Today is not Halloween,' she says, putting me right, 'it is the ancient Celtic festival of Samhain. The Christians took it over, along with so much else.' There is no black cat perched on her shoulder, but there might as well be. 'The Christians went from persecuting us to scorning us for what they call superstition.'

I murmur sympathy, which is genuine. To me, all religions are equally nonsensical and the idea that Christians, with their particular invisible friends, virgin births, immaculate conceptions and bread turning into flesh, could have the cheek to mock people like Laurie for being 'superstitious' is appalling humbug.

Laurie invites me to a great Samhain meeting (I forbear from using the word 'coven' for I have an inkling it might offend); it is to be held not naked and out of doors, leaping through flames and around pentacles, but in the ballroom of The Hawthorne Hotel. No black candles, no reciting of the Lord's Prayer backwards. This is not Hammer House of Horror but a kind of syncretic New Age mixture of Druidism, Celtic folklore and much vague talk about 'energies'.

The meeting itself is a very charming party in which the Cabot-style witches who have come from all over the world to be here dress up, dance (to seventies and eighties pop mostly) and then come

43

forward for a 'circle' in which a sword is waved, incantations are made and 'energies' invoked. It is all over very quickly and then Laurie and I get on with the business of judging the best costume of the evening.

Meanwhile outside, the entire town of Salem has turned into a huge horror and gore theme park. The smell of donuts and burgers, the sound of rock music, the sight of murder, mayhem and death. By twelve o'clock it's all over and everyone is in bed. It seems to me that there is more true Gothic horror in a digestive biscuit, but never mind. Tomorrow I shall be immersed in the comforting sophisticated grandeur of the state capital.

BOSTON AND HARVARD YARD

I spend a morning in the city of Boston, 'Cradle of the Revolution', filming around the docks where the Boston Tea Party took place and searching (in vain) for Paul Revere's house. Revere was the patriot and hero whose midnight ride from Boston to Lexington shouting 'The British are coming!' is still celebrated in legend and song. The apparent address of his house defeats the taxi's satellite navigation system and after driving around Boston's Chinatown asking puzzled citizens for 'the Revere House' I find myself in desperate need of a cup of tea.

It so happens that I have heard of a place across the water in Harvard Yard where, almost uniquely in America, a proper cup of tea can be had. If you can pronounce 'Harvard Yard' the way the locals do, you can speak Bostonian. It's more than I can manage—I contrive always to sound Australian when I try. The 'a's are almost as short as in 'cat', even though they are followed by 'r's. Impossible.

Harvard University is America's Cambridge. So much so that the town it is in, over the water from Boston, is actually called Cambridge.

Those who like good old-fashioned English 'afternoon tea', with proper sandwiches and proper cakes, and tea that isn't the etiolated issue of a bag dangled in warm water, those who like to meet pert young students and trim graduates and twinkly, stylish professors, all congregate gratefully at the weekly teas held by Professor Peter Gomes, theologian, preacher and a natural leader of Harvard society. He dresses like a character from the pages of his favourite author. When asked to offer his list of the Hundred Best Novels in the English Language for one of those millennial surveys in 1999 he lamented, 'But any such list will always be four short! P.G. Wodehouse only wrote ninety-six books.'

Black, gay, intensely charming, a connoisseur and an anglophile, Gomes is not what you expect of a Baptist minister, a Baptist minister furthermore who (though now a Democrat) was something of a chaplain to the Republican Party, having led prayers at the inaugurations of both Ronald Reagan and George Bush Snr.

'I was a Republican because my mother was a Republican and her mother before her. That nice President Lincoln who freed the slaves was a Republican and our family chose not to forget that fact.'

The downstairs lavatory in his beautifully furnished house is filled with portraits of Queen Victoria at various stages of her life, from young princess to elderly widow. I emerge from it murmuring praise.

45

'Ah, you like my Victoria Station!' beams Gomes, 'I'm so happy.'

'You're obviously gay,' I say to him. 'But some people might be surprised to know that you are also openly black . . . no, hang on, I've got that the wrong way round.'

He bellows with laughter. 'No, you got it entirely right, you naughty man.'

'Your command of language, your love of ornament, literature and social style . . . is that regarded by some as a kind of betrayal?'

'Someone once called me an Afro-Saxon,' he says. 'It was meant as an insult, but I take it as a compliment.'

*   *   *

I am sorry to leave the elegance and charm of Harvard, but there is plenty more elegance and charm awaiting me up ahead in Rhode Island.

RHODE ISLAND
KEY FACTS

Abbreviation:
RI

Nickname:
The Ocean State

Capital:
Providence

Flower:
Violet

Tree:
Red maple

Bird:
Rhode Island red chicken

Drink:
Coffee milk

Motto:
Hope

Well-known residents and natives:
General Burnside, Dee Dee Myers, H.P. Lovecraft,
S.J. Perelman, Cormac McCarthy,
George M. Cohan, Nelson Eddy, Van Johnson,
James Woods, the Farelly Brothers,
Seth 'Family Guy' MacFarlane.

RHODE ISLAND

'I do not especially mind being asked as a guest onboard a boat, so long as I do not have to do anything more than sip wine.'

Wedged between Massachusetts and Connecticut and very much the smallest state in the union, the anchor on Rhode Island's seal and its official nickname of the 'Ocean State' tell you that they take nautical matters seriously here . . .

THE CLIFF WALK

From about the middle of the nineteenth century wealthy plantation families from the South began to build themselves 'cottages' along the clifftops of Newport, where they could escape the insufferably humid heat of the Southern summer and enjoy the relatively bracing and comfortable breezes rolling in from the Atlantic. Over the next few decades rich Northern families began to do the same as the Gilded Age of Vanderbilts and Astors reached its imponderably wealthy, stiflingly opulent and dizzyingly powerful zenith. These cottages were in fact vast mansions, some of seventy rooms or more, designed to be lived in for only a few months of the year, but all displaying the incalculable and overwhelming riches and status that the robber barons and industrialists of post-Civil-War America had heaped up in so short a time. Never in the field of human commerce, I think it is fair to say, had so much money been made so fast and by so few.

Today the cliff walk between Bellevue Avenue and the sea is a tourist destination and many of the grander cottages are owned and run, not by their original families, but by the Newport County Preservation Society and other trusts and bodies dedicated to keeping these gigantic fantasies from crumbling away.

There are still some survivors living around Bellevue Avenue, however, and I have tea with one of them, the great Oatsie Charles, a wondrous wicked twinkling *grande dame* of the old school. The first president she ever met was Franklin D. Roosevelt, she attended the wedding of JFK to Jacqueline Bouvier and her talk is a magnificent *tour d'horizon* of high-born American family life—Hugh Auchincloss, Doris Duke, Astors, Mellons, Radziwills, parties, disputed wills, feuds, marriages, divorces and scandals:

'She was a Van Allen, of course, which made all the difference . . . Bunny Mellon and C.Z. Guest were there *naturally* . . . Heaven knows what he saw in her, she can't have had more than two hundred million which *these days* . . . she married the Duke of

49

Marlborough. Calamitous error, we all saw that it would never do . . .' All spoken in a luxurious and old-style Alabama accent elegantly mixed with an international rich aristocrat's amused drawl.

'I can't tell you how beautiful even ugly people looked back then.'

'Was it quite formal?'

'Well, we dressed for dinner every night and all the houses were formally staffed. Handsome footmen in divine livery. We certainly never saw anyone looking like you . . .' Oatsie wrinkles her nose in apparent disgust at the film crew who are dressed in the standard grungey outfit of shorts, t-shirts and sandals. 'A man's neck can be a thing of beauty,' she adds, rather startlingly. 'And yours,' she indicates the sound recordist's, 'has all the qualities. Even yours, darling,' she turns to me, 'though yours is higher than most.'

The tea has turned rapidly to claret, served by a devoted butler, whose duty is also to transport his mistress around her messuage in a golf cart, upon which entirely silly conveyance Oatsie somehow managed to bestow the air and dignity of a fabulous Oriental litter. We go next door to the Big Mansion, for Oatsie now makes do in a converted chauffeur's house which is big and beautiful enough in its own right, being full of her paintings, furniture and exquisite knick-knacks. 'Land's End', the Big Mansion, built by the novelist Edith Wharton, the supreme chronicler of the Gilded Age, has been given by Oatsie to her daughter Victoria and son-in-law Joe.

A little gilt may have come off the Age and a little guilt may have been added, but from where I stood it was pretty Gilded still.

50

I AM SAILING

Aside from the eye-popping, jaw-dropping, bowel-shattering wealth on display along the cliff walk, there is class of a trimmer, more elegant kind still flourishing in Newport. This is a wonderful place to sail and has been a centre of regattas and races for over a hundred years.

The greatest prize in sailing is of course the America's Cup, 'the oldest active trophy in international sport', the great dream, the Holy Grail— The One. It was offered as a prize by the British Royal Yacht Squadron of Cowes, Isle of Wight in 1851, and was won by a boat called *America*, which is how the cup gets its name, though it might just as well have been because yachts from the United States have won it so consistently and for so long . . .

Enormous fortunes have been poured into chasing the cup and for 132 years it remained in America, for much of that time in Newport. Poor Britain, that great sailing nation, has won the trophy precisely zero times. The United States held it for the longest winning streak in history, testament to the remarkable qualities of American seamanship, marine savvy, nautical engineering skills and sheer damned money.

Most would agree that the Golden Age of America's Cup racing was the late forties, fifties and sixties, the days of the 12-metre class yacht. In 1962, winning by 4–1 and watched by President and Mrs Kennedy, was the graceful *Weatherly*. She kept the cup in Newport, where it had been since 1930 and where it would remain until Alan Bond of Perth, Australia finally broke that winning streak in 1983. The *Weatherly* is now one of only three surviving wooden America's Cup defenders in the world, the only yacht to have won the cup when not newly built. She is beautiful. My, she is yare, as Grace Kelly says about her boat the *True Love* in the film *High Society,* which is set, of course, in Rhode Island. The *Weatherly* is as yare as they come. She is now owned by George Hill and Herb Marshall who manage to keep her in tip-top racing condition and to make money from her by charter.

George, a fit and trim fifty-year-old with silver hair and a lean, outdoors face, watches me clamber aboard, pick myself up, trip over a sticky-up thing that had no right to be there, pick myself up again and fall down in a heap, gasping.

'Welcome aboard,' he says.

A crew of three barefoot limber girls and a barefoot limber youth are tying knots with their toes, hauling on winches and, without trying, outdoing Tommy Hilfiger and Ralph Lauren models for looks and style. Within a few minutes sails have been unfurled and ropes uncleated and we are under way. I take up a position next to George, who is manning the wheel and calling out mysterious commands.

This is real sailing, the power, speed and excitement is hard to convey. I have always been a physical coward in sporting endeavours, sailing not excluded. Being shouted at to 'turn about', having to duck as great beams swing round to bang you on the head, leaning over precipitately, simply not understanding what is going on, having words like 'tack', 'jib', 'sheet' and 'cleat' hurled at you . . . my childhood was full of such moments, growing up as I did in a nautical county like Norfolk and I long ago decided that sailing was for Other People. I do not especially mind being asked as a guest on board a boat, so long as I do not have to do anything more than sip wine.

George has other ideas. If I am to go on board the *Weatherly* then I am to pay my way by crewing. He is very kind but very firm on this point as he steps aside for me to steer.

'You're luffing,' he says.

'Well, more a bark of joy at the blue sky and the crisp . . .'

'No, not laughing, luffing. The canvas is flapping. Steer into the wind and keep the sail smooth.'

'Oh right. Got you.'

George is a proud Rhode Islander. 'Rhode Island is known to most Americans as a unit of size,' he says. 'You hear news stories like "an iceberg broke off Antarctica bigger than the state of Rhode Island" or "So and so's ranch is bigger than Rhode Island". Try to come up just a little bit. Once you're on the breeze like this just little small slow adjustments. That's good, just there and no higher. The Rhode Island charter of 1663 is an amazing document. It contains all of the concepts of freedom of speech and freedom of religion at a time when—you're luffing again . . . when she loads up like that, just straighten her out.'

Strangely I enjoy myself. I enjoy myself very much indeed. I will go further. I have one of the most pleasurable days of the 18,330 or so I have spent thus far on this confusing and beguiling planet. The speed, the precision, the astounding power bewitched me: it was a glorious day, Newport Sound and Narragansett Bay sparkled and shimmered and glittered, the great bridges and landmarks around Newport shone in clean, clear light. You would have to be sullen and curmudgeonly indeed not to be enchanted, intoxicated and thrilled to the soles of your boat-shoes by this fabulous (and fabulously expensive) class of sailing.

Farewell, Rhode Island. Farewell too any lingering belief that America might be a classless society . . . I luff myself silly at such a thought.

CONNECTICUT
KEY FACTS

Abbreviation:
CT

Nicknames:
The Constitution State, The Nutmeg State

Capital:
Hartford

Flower:
Mountain laurel

Tree:
Charter white oak

Bird:
American robin

Motto:
Qui transtulit sustinet ('He who is transplanted, still sustains'—Hm, loses in translation I suspect)

Well-known residents and natives:
Aaron Burr, Dean Acheson, George W. Bush (43rd President), Benedict Arnold, Ethan Allen, Noah Webster, Samuel Colt, P.T. Barnum, J.P. Morgan, Charles Goodyear, Charles Ives, Al Capp, Benjamin Spock, William Buckley, John Gregory Dunne, Ira Levin, E. Annie Proulx, Rosalind Russell, Katharine Hepburn, Robert Mitchum,

Ernest Borgnine, Ed Begley, Paul Newman, Joanne Woodward, Glenn Close, Meg Ryan, Christopher Walken, Christopher Lloyd, Seth McFarlane, Gene Pitney, Dave Brubeck, Karen and Richard Carpenter, Jose Feliciano, Michael Bolton, Moby.

CONNECTICUT

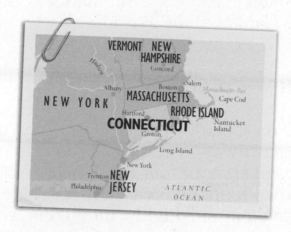

'My travels so far have already taught me that Nature did not fashion Stephen Fry to serve in submarines . . .'

Only Delaware and neighbouring Rhode Island are smaller than the Constitution State. As it happens, the seven smallest states in mainland America are all in New England and most, like Connecticut, make up in history, wealth, population density and dazzling scenery what they lack in size.

The name derives from the Mohican word *quinnitukqut*, which Scrabble-winning entry apparently means 'place of long tidal river'. This doesn't quite satisfactorily explain the silent second 'c' in my opinion. Never mind. It all adds to the mystique.

The whole of Connecticut's shoreline faces Long Island and the body of water is therefore Long Island Sound rather than open Atlantic Ocean. This geography leads to a calm and balmy climate and a strategically ideal situation for submarine pens.

My taxi and I are headed for Groton, CT, where on the River Thames in New London can be found the United States Navy's Submarine Base, 'the Submarine Capital of the World'.

THE *SPRINGFIELD*

I am led on board, well, shoved down a tight, clambery hatchway and here I am, in a nuclear submarine, all six foot four and a half of me.

I am shown round by Petty Officer James Poton, a shy, soft-spoken and highly intelligent young man who answers my footling questions with grace and humour.

'And here, Stephen,' Americans like to use first names as much as possible, 'is the control room. This is where we dive and drive the boat from. We have a helmsman and a planesman who controls the rudder and bow planes, then over here you have the stern planes on the back of the ship.'

'Wow. And this is the weapons station is it?' I point at a collection of screens and controls.

'Stephen, this is exactly where the solutions for the weapons are plotted. Fire control takes bearings from Sonar and they plot solutions on the contacts.'

'It's like a gaming arcade.'

'Actually, Stephen, this weapons lodge console is a little more expensive than a typical arcade game.'

I suppose James is used to visitors asking what the various buttons and screens are for and, in particular, he must be accustomed to hearing them beg to be allowed to use the periscope. This is a big moment for me: countless films and TV series can't prepare one for the actual feeling of that device under one's control, with its fluid hydraulic hiss and gently insistent physical pull. I spin it around, pulling on its motorcycle throttle zoom and burbling a mixture of Royal Navy (*Above Us the Waves*) and US (*Crimson Tide*) Navy jargon. 'Now hear this. You have the conn, Number One. Steady . . . steady . . . up 'scope, chaps . . .' and so on.

We are aboard the *Springfield*, a hunter-killer nuclear submarine built for the great Cold War game that was played out across the oceans of the world between the US and the USSR for more than forty years. Nowadays the *Springfield* is mostly deployed for . . . oh, I am so sorry, I am not allowed to tell you or I would have to hunt you and kill you. Let us just say there are still uses for a nuclear submarine in today's volatile world.

Actually, PO Poton does attempt to explain to me what the strategic purpose of the nuclear submarine fleet in the post-Cold-War era is, but it seems all a bit vague and jargon-rich for me to grasp. Either that or I am too obsessed with the quotidian detail of life on one of these cramped tubes. Everywhere I bump my head. Everywhere I am in the way. There is nowhere to sit down unless you are eating or operating some fearsome communication, navigation or weaponry technology. Every single spare inch of wall and ceiling (though where one ends and the other begins is a moot point) is taken up with wiring, ducting, piping, lagging and strange snaking coils of nameless substance that terminate every now and again in a switch or control panel. For all the astounding quantities of money these babies cost, they are severely, but severely functional. Not one penny appears to have been expended in the service of aesthetics or fun. Which is, I suppose, as it should be.

The sleeping quarters or 'racks' are cruelly Spartan. The only concession to privacy a thin curtain, the only offering to spare time an LCD screen screwed into the rack above, fed by a Sony PlayStation, so that DVDs and games can be enjoyed lying on one's back.

On the wall of the mess, which is in reality like a small traditional roadside diner, hangs an original Springfield Rifle, in honour of the town of Springfield, Massachusetts, even though the vessel is in fact named for Springfield, Illinois (it being a naval tradition to name submarines after state capitals)— otherwise, aside from the obligatory ketchup and hot-sauce bottles, there is not much to see. No exterior view of course, no portholes.

It seems to me inconceivable that men (and only men can be submariners in the United States Navy) could spend any length of time in one of these without being sent entirely mad. I cannot imagine myself 'under way' for more than two days without screaming to be let off.

'What's the longest tour of duty?' I ask.

'Stephen, it's about six months.'

'Good Lord. Any more and I suppose you'd all go mad?'

'Actually, Stephen, the only consideration that limits how long we can be under way is the amount of food we can carry. We could stay out indefinitely if we could carry enough provisions.'

James and all the other submariners I speak to say that they cannot wait to be under way again. Aside from missing their families, they love it, life below the waves.

I can't even console myself with the thought that it is because they are all short enough to nip about

60

without banging their head every five minutes, for I meet an officer who is at least two inches taller than me.

'What's your greatest fear when you're under way?'

James looks at me. 'In a word, fire, Stephen.'

That was two words, but I let it go.

FIRE TRAINING

I say my goodbyes to the crew of the *Springfield* and am escorted to the fire-drill training centre on the base.

Fire is as great an enemy as the one a submarine crew may be tasked to hunt down. So much so that every submariner who goes to sea must take a fire-fighting course. I am to join a fire crew in the position of rookie submariner and be taught how to put out various different kinds of conflagration.

Once more I am made to look like ten types of doofus: all dressed up in hood, gloves, helmet, boiler suit and goggles, I loom and stagger about the place, a powerful hose in my hands, a liability to all.

Petty Officer McDade has been assigned the dread task of being my mentor for this drill. He recites to me, by heart, an explanation of the 'Training Time Out' or TTO which might be called at any time if there is an emergency:

'A TTO may be called in any training situation when a student or instructor expresses concern for personal safety or need for clarification of procedures or requirements exists. TTO is also an appropriate means for a student experiencing undue pain, heat stress or other serious physical discomfort to obtain relief.'

Mm. Undue pain and heat stress, eh? I begin to sweat under my goggles.

'TTO shall be called verbally and/or using the hand signal, a raised fist accompanied by a waving motion as necessary to attract attention. The exercise shall be stopped, the situation shall be examined . . .'

The idea is for me to rush into a replica of the submarine engine rooms which will be on fire. PO McDade will be in front of me and a guy called Ralph behind. Between us we will be carrying the hose.

'Don't kneel, make sure you sit on your haunches,' says Ralph.

'Oh. Why's that?'

'The radiation of heat to the metal deckplates could burn your knees.'

'Fair enough.'

'I will start,' says McDade, 'then, at a signal from me, you will take your right hand to the front of the hose . . .'

'Which will be bucking like a bronco,' adds Ralph, helpfully.

'You will grab the pistol grip and we will swap places. I go to the back of the line, while you take over fire-fighting duties.'

'I will be behind you supporting you to make sure you don't fall over,' says Ralph.

'Which way is the pressure of the water likely to impel me, back or forward?'

'Yes.'

My travels so far have already taught me that nature did not fashion Stephen Fry to serve in submarines, to race yachts, to hunt the wild lobster or to run for political office—to that list I can now confidently add 'to fight fires'.

I have a feeling, however, as I leave Connecticut

and point the taxi back north to the state of Vermont
that something awaits me there that will suit me right
down to my socks.

VERMONT
KEY FACTS

Abbreviation:
VT

Nickname:
The Green Mountain State

Capital:
Montpelier

Flower:
Red clover

Tree:
Sugar maple

Bird:
Hermit thrush

Motto:
Freedom and Unity

Well-known residents and natives:
Chester Arthur (21st President),
Calvin Coolidge (30th), John Deere,
Joseph Smith, Brigham Young, Sinclair Lewis,
Pearl S. Buck, Jamaica Kincaid, John Irving,
David Mamet, Rudy Vallée, Elizabeth Perkins,
William H. Macy, Felicity Huffman,
M. Emmet Walsh, KT Tunstall.

VERMONT

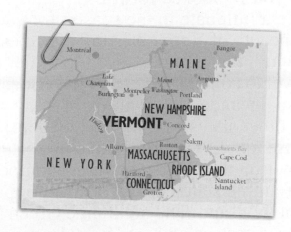

'Stephen, you created an ice-cream flavour. And it was good. Now you may rest.'

Vermont, Vermont, how beautiful you are.

Not the absolute last place in which you would imagine Rudyard Kipling writing 'Gunga Din' and *The Jungle Book*, but surely not the first, either. Yet he did. And 'Mandalay' too, 'where the flyin'-fishes play', in Battleboro, VT, the home of his American wife, Carrie.

I reckon that if you ask the average American what they know of Vermont, the first thing they will mention is maple syrup. You will notice that the sugar maple is the State Tree of Vermont—it is also more or less the state industry. The maple brings tourists who come to marvel at the blazing colours of the autumn leaves and it brings cash dollars in the form of the unctuous, faintly metallic syrup that Americans like to pour all over their breakfast, on waffles and pancakes certainly, but on bacon too. Sounds alarming to English ears, but actually it is rather delicious. Like crack, crystal meth and Chocolate HobNobs, one nibble and you're hooked for life.

I am here a little late in the season for catching the legendary beauty of Vermont's fall. The best days for 'leaf peeping' have gone and the time of maple tapping is yet to come. However, I have seen plenty of fiery reds, incandescent yellows and screaming oranges in other states so I do not feel deprived.

What else does Vermont have to offer? Not a thrusting metropolis, that is for sure. Montpelier is the smallest of all the state capitals, with a population of barely eight thousand. The nickname Green Mountain State suggests pastureland, and pasture suggests cows and sheep and goats, and cows and sheep and goats suggest dairy produce—milk, cream and cheese. There is a bastard concoction that dares to call itself 'Vermont Cheddar' but that we will ignore, presenting it with the coldest of British shoulders. No, I am in search of a product altogether more desirable, a world more indulgent and disgraceful, wholly addictive and dreadful and proudly American: it is the prospect of this which has me hurtling northwest with the intense concentration and merciless swiftness of a shark streaking towards blood in the water. Except that sharks don't drool and shout 'Come to mama!'

It was in 1978 that the two sainted hippies, Ben Cohen and Jerry Greenfield opened their first ice-cream parlour in Burlington, Vermont's largest town. After many adventures, tribulations and law-suits against Häagen-Dazs they established themselves as just about the best-known brand in ice-cream. Their eco-friendly pint pots, chatty labels and jokey punning flavour names ('Vermonty Python', 'Cherry

66

Garcia', 'Karamel Sutra', etc.) have established them as the prototypical anti-suit corporation, and a great influence on other food companies who want to present a healthy, cheery, laid-back image. There is a question as to whether or not the company, which has since been sold to the giant Unilever Corporation, behaved with just as much restrictive meanness when it came to distribution as their original rivals Häagen-Dazs, but they certainly won the branding wars. Everyone loves Ben and Jerry's. They're so like 'hey!' and they chat to you on the labelling and they're your friend.

The factory in Waterbury, VT, is about thirty miles southeast of Burlington and constitutes Vermont's single biggest tourist attraction. The moment I arrive I feel like Veruca Salt standing at the gates of Willy Wonka's Chocolate Factory. With golden ticket clutched in fist I want it and I want it *now*.

I am to be given the freedom of the ingredients cabinet, a chance to mix my own flavour. This is an honour rarely bestowed. It is as if Château Margaux asked me to blend their cabernet sauvignon and merlot for this year's vintage. Well, all right, it's nothing whatever like that, but it is a great honour nonetheless.

'Welcome, Stephen, we're very excited that you're here!' says Sean, the flavourologist. 'But if you're gonna mix like a pro, you'd better dress like a pro.'

He hands me a white lab coat while I ponder the task before me.

The base, I decide, should be of good vanilla-bean ice-cream, nothing more fancy than that. To hand are spatulas, spoons and little pots and bags of semi-frozen ingredients: cookie dough, biscuity substances, chocolate in the shape of a cow and so forth. I try to stay calm. I mustn't be too childish about this, as what little dignity I have left is at stake. The temptation to produce a pink confection filled with marshmallows, strawberries and cake mix is strong, but I feel the need to fly the flag for British style and discretion. I find an ingredient called English toffee and swirl it into the vanilla base. Good. Not the kind of hard black toffees Kensington nannies gave children in their prams to keep them quiet while they kissed the footman, but a good start. To this promising base I add chocolate fudge, a gloopy substance that freezes when added to the ice-cream, like a lava flow meeting water. A granulated texture is added with which I feel well pleased.

Very fine—strong, adult, not too sweet, but there's something missing . . . I rootle and scrabble, searching for the magic extra ingredient that will transform my mixture into a true flavour, my rough prototype into a working masterpiece. The clock is ticking, for a tour party is about to come in at any moment and I am to feed them and then stand with bowed head to receive their judgement.

Just as I am about to give up and offer my acceptable but now to my mind rather lame decoction my fingers curl around a bag of knobbly somethings. I have found it! It adds crunch, a hint of sophisticated bitterness and a rich musty, nutty centre around which the other flavours can play their unctuous, toffee-like, chocolaty games. Walnuts! I stir them in with my spatula and Sean helps me transfer the giant mixture into small tourist-sized tubs. This is done by squeezing a kind of piping bag. Within seconds I have lost all feeling in my hands.

'It's very cold,' I observe.

'Many are cold,' says Sean, 'but few are frozen.'

Before I have time to throw something at him, the tour party enters.

'Welcome everybody,' beams Sean. 'This is a special occasion. You will be trying a new flavour, mixed by our Guest Flavourist, here. His invention is called . . .?'

'Er . . . I . . . that is . . . um . . .'

'. . . is called "Even Stephens"!' extemporises Sean happily.

I stand meekly, submissively, hopefully while the tourists surge forward to begin the tasting. Despite my humble demeanour, I *know*, I really know that I have struck gold. There have not been many moments in my life when I have been quite so sure of success. But here, I am convinced, is a perfect blend of flavours.

The tourists agree. Once the filming stops and the camera crew have dived in too there is nothing left of Even Stephens but my memory of a solid-gold vanilla-based triumph.

Stephen, you created an ice-cream flavour. And it was good. Now you may rest.

Vermont seems even more beautiful on a full stomach. This is a state I will most certainly return to one day. It is the first landlocked state I have visited, but what it lacks in coastline it makes up for in mountains, valleys and lakes. I am leaving by ferry across Lake Champlain, through which runs Vermont's northern border. At the prow of the boat my taxi points proudly towards the gigantic majesty of our next destination—New York State.

NEW YORK STATE
KEY FACTS

Abbreviation:
NY

Nickname:
The Empire State

Capital:
Albany

Flower:
Rose

Tree:
Sugar maple
(I know: same as Vermont—copycats, eh?)

Bird:
Eastern bluebird

Motto:
Excelsior!

Well-known residents and natives:
That would be unfair on the other states:
there are thousands.

NEW YORK STATE

'One of the most diverse adventure playgrounds on earth; where else can you meet deer-hunters and a man who raised money for the IRA?'

New York State is bigger than England. Despite this, it is only the twenty-seventh largest state in America, not even halfway up the list. The truth of how stupendously, absurdly large this country is has still failed properly to penetrate my brain. I have driven over a thousand miles and I have done no more than wander around an area on the map smaller than the nail of my little finger.

I cross Lake Champlain from Vermont into upstate New York. The lakes and wilderness here are all part of the Adirondack mountain chain. New York State also contains the Appalachians and the Catskills, with the Rivers Hudson, Allegheny, Susquehanna, Niagara and Delaware too. This is one of the most remarkable and diverse adventure playgrounds on earth. And that

71

is before you even consider the delights of Broadway, Central Park, Greenwich Village and Long Island.

New York is nearly always called New York State, so as to distinguish it from New York City. This is true of Washington State too. Where I am now, Montreal, Canada is only eighty miles north, while Fifth Avenue, NYC is at least five and half hours away by fast car. The accents all around me are much closer to Canadian than to Brooklyn. The plaid shirts, the antlers, and the gun shops tell me that this is Hunting Country.

Somewhere along the line the American love affair with wilderness changed from the thoughtful, sensitive isolationism of Thoreau to the bully, manly, outdoorsman bravado of Teddy Roosevelt. It is not for me, as an outsider, either to bemoan or celebrate this fact, only to observe it. Deep in the male American psyche is a love affair with the backwoods, log-cabin, camping-out life.

There is no living creature here that cannot, in its right season, be hunted or trapped. Deer, moose, bear, squirrel, partridge, beaver, otter, possum, raccoon, you name it, there's someone killing one right now. When I say hunted, I mean of course, shot at with a high-velocity rifle. I have no particular brief for killing animals with dogs or falcons, but when I hear the word 'hunt' I think of something more than a man in a forage cap and tartan shirt armed with a powerful carbine. In America it is different. Hunting means 'man bonding with man, man bonding with son, man bonding with pick-up truck, man bonding with wood cabin, man bonding with rifle, man bonding—above all—with plaid'.

INTO THE WOODS

I am to be the guest of a group of friends who have built themselves a cabin deep in the woods some ten or twenty miles from the town of Saranac, NY. Bill and Tom are nice guys, ordinary guys. Hunting for white-tail deer, which is the game they are mostly after, is like fishing for bass, a mostly blue-collar pastime in America. Think of that Michael Cimino film *The Deer Hunter* and you will get the idea. Bill and Tom are not, I am relieved to discover, machismo alpha-male show-offs, bullies or bigots. They are working men (sheet metal, transport, warehousing, that kind of thing) who pour all of their spare time into maintaining and enjoying their life in the woods.

'Welcome to camp,' says Tom.

The cabin is surprisingly warm and snug when I arrive at six o'clock on a bitterly cold morning. The taxi has never had to negotiate such rough tracks before and I am terribly afraid that I will suffer the humiliation of being towed by one of the enormous pick-up trucks that usually roam these pathways. One of the group's number, Craig, has cooked just about the most fabulous breakfast I have ever, ever eaten. Bacon, sausage, French toast and lots and lots of home-tapped and home-refined maple syrup. All around the cabin are maple trees with pipework stuck into them, like hospital tubes and drips. Round the back is the machinery needed to transform the liquor from the tree into breakfast syrup.

'Now, let's get you kitted up . . .' Tom holds up a plaid jacket and an enormous pair of woollen trousers.

Naturally. Of course. It wouldn't do for me to look dignified or sensible.

73

'This hat is rather a sudden orange, isn't it?' I complain, dropping a day-glo foraging cap on the table.

'Hunting orange, they call it. Other huntsmen know not to shoot you.'

'Mm. Yes.' I pick the cap up again. 'I like it. Goes with my complexion.'

I make it very plain as we head for the trails that I would rather not hold a rifle and certainly prefer not to watch anything being killed. My sentimental Bambi-loving self is not keen on the idea of seeing a deer felled. The antlers on the wall of the cabin tell me that these guys, charming as they are, have done a good deal of killing in their time. They are perfectly okay about my reluctance to kill; I think they had sized me up for a cissy the moment I stepped out of the cab.

My role then is to skip along with them prattling about life and nature.

'The American relationship with the outdoors,' I say, 'the Thoreau ideal. It's deep in the American psyche isn't it? Man and nature. The great paradox of a nation that invades and degrades the wilderness and yet treasures it above all else.'

'Guess so.'

'New York State contains this, the great outdoors, the American dream of the woods and wilderness but also the industry, the suburbs, the great urban sprawl and of course Manhattan. Maybe New York State is symbolic of all America, embodying both the call of the wild and the call of the street.'

'Maybe.'

'You're right. I'm talking drivel. I'll shut up now.'

I am happy to say that no deer were killed in the making of our scene. In fact we didn't even see a deer, which suited me. Instead I enjoyed wonderful hospitality, warm companionship and a good walk in beautiful woodland. I berated myself for having been so afraid.

But, after a cup of coffee, it was time for a three-hundred-and-thirty-mile drive: I was due to meet another group of potentially terrifying men.

Italian Americans.

Taps side of nose.

Wise guys.

Winks conspiratorially.

GoodFellas.

Bad-a-bing!

THE MIDDLE VILLAGE SOCIAL CLUB

Middle Village is an area of Queens, New York mostly inhabited by Irish and Italian Americans, two ethnic groups which traditionally get along with each other pretty well.

I have been invited to say hello to the boys of a particular social club. I have seen these places before, in gangster pictures like *Donnie Brasco*, *GoodFellas* and *Casino*. Not to mention in real footage of FBI stings and wiretappings on the Gambino family clubs of John Gotti and Sammy 'the Bull' Gravano. Am I really going to hang out with organised crime hoods, with mobsters? Is that an ethical thing to do? To contribute to the glamour and status of violent criminals?

Well, this social club is largely different. It is—how can I put it nicely?—a home for failed gangsters. For guys who didn't quite make it. Possibly because they were too nice. The old ones are really very old indeed and the young ones, like Mikey who wears a

Godfather t-shirt under the obligatory leather jacket, have earned more money from doing bit-parts in *The Sopranos* than from anything illegal.

At least *so I am led to believe*.

I am welcomed inside this little two-room house by Mikey and the boys. The back room is given over to card games; the front room has a big screen TV, sofa, a bar and walls that are covered with sporting photographs and posters. Betting seems to play a large part in the life of this club.

I am not surprised Mikey has found work in TV and movies, he has a central-casting low hairline and a 'you talking to me?' posture and gait. He cannot stop smiling. He cannot stop telling stories. He cannot stop *talking*. I have not been in there half an hour before he tells me a story he has already told. The others all meet my confused gaze and roll their eyes. 'Good old Mikey, he don't know when to shut up,' an old boy whispers to me. I suppose that is why he has failed to make it as a button man or whatever the phrase is. That and the fact that he just seems too, well, too good-natured, too lacking in guile. He is like a great puppy. He tells twice a story about chasing a thief through the neighbourhood, tackling him and punching his lights out before the police arrived, so perhaps I am being a little naïve. He is anxious for me to know that he would only ever show violence to someone 'nasty'. The thief had stolen a child's bicycle. 'And dat,' he says, 'youse do not do.' You will think 'youse' is a bit old hat, a bit Damon Runyon, but I promise you that is how he said it.

I sit down on the sofa with Dave, who tells me tales about 'da old days'. An immensely complex story about cocking up a horse-nobbling takes ten minutes and is filled with the kind of colour and splendour that fiction cannot match. Some time back in the forties, when Dave was young, he had 'a sure ting', he had inside knowledge of a horse which would win a race 'on account of how he had dis drug, dis whatchercallit'.

I am stared at through Dave's one good eye and nudged quite violently to provide the name of this drug, as if I am an expert. This puzzles me. I had no idea that there was a drug which could guarantee a horse winning a race. 'Um, a stimulant of some kind maybe . . .'

'Dat's it! Stimu- like you said.'

I get an even sharper dig in the ribs for having solved the mystery of what the drug might have been. I am beginning to revise my opinion of the non-violent nature of these people. Anecdotal Assault may not carry a heavy sentence, may not even be recognised in law as a crime against the person, but by the time I rise from the sofa I am more or less black and blue. Dave told me tales of his days running numbers, laying bets and serving time in prison (only on-track betting, OTB, is legal in America, so all street bookies are liable to arrest). 'We always ordered dinner from Giovanni's restaurant to be delivered to our cell. The sergeant would let us make the call so long as we included a linguini for him. It was a good arrangement. Worked well for twenty years till they rebuilt the station house and moved the sergeant to another precinct. What are you gonna do?' All his stories seemed to feature him in a disastrous situation where, as a small-time bookie's runner, he lost money for someone, forgot to lay off a bet, got in trouble, ended up in prison. The speed with which he can still shade odds and rattle through the 13–5, 11–4-type ratios made my head spin. He may have liked to present himself as one of nature's losers, but he was clearly not a fool.

Whenever I press these old boys and use words like 'Mafia' or 'cosa nostra', they smile and raise their hands in innocent bewilderment. I am beginning to think they are simply charming senior citizens who just happen to have the same accents and ethnicity as Mafiosi.

Then I spot the bullet holes.

You can see one in the group photograph, in the metal door upright, just next to the Star-Spangled Banner. There are more inside.

'Yeah, that was a drive-by. We was playing cards. A bullet just missed Don's head. So much.' Mikey brings his forefinger and thumb very close together.

'But why?' I ask.

'Sheeesh. What are you gonna do?'

Which is no kind of answer.

The guy who really owns and runs the club turns up. A barrel-chested fellow about five foot tall. There is something in his eye which compels me to stop asking questions. He too is friendly, but it is impossible not to notice when the mere presence of someone in a room shuts everyone else up.

He has the extraordinary ability to silence Mikey. I smell power.

JOHN THE CABBIE

My guide in New York City has been a cabbie called John. He lives round the corner from the Italian social club and he is the one who effected my introduction. John is of Irish stock; indeed he quite proudly tells me how he had worked hard for Noraid,

78

the 'charity' that funded the IRA, back in the days of the Troubles.

As we drive to his yellow-cab garage, which is like a scene out of the seventies sitcom *Taxi*, I ask him how he feels about the new accord in Northern Irish politics.

'I fought for thirty years to let Ian Paisley rule?' he says. 'How do you think I feel?'

Mm. In a short while I have met deer-hunters, Mafia criminals and a man who raised money for the IRA. And I liked them all. I saw their points of view.

What is happening to me?

NEW JERSEY
KEY FACTS

Abbreviation:
NJ

Nickname:
The Garden State

Capital:
Trenton

Flower:
Common meadow violet

Tree:
Northern red oak

Bird:
American goldfinch

Shell:
Knobbed whelk (honest)

Motto:
Liberty and Prosperity

Well-known residents and natives:
Grover Cleveland (22nd and 24th President),
Thomas Alva Edison, Alfred Kinsey, William
Carlos Williams, Allen Ginsberg, Philip Roth,
Andrea Dworkin, Martha Stewart, Abbott and
Costello, Jerry Lewis, Jack Nicholson, Meryl Streep,

Danny DeVito, Joe Pesci, John Travolta, Ray Liotta, Bruce Willis, Kevin Spacey, David Cassidy, James Gandolfini, Count Basie, Frank Sinatra, Bruce Springsteen, Jon Bon Jovi, Whitney Houston, Shaquille O'Neal.

NEW JERSEY

'And so I find myself driving into hell.'

New Jersey is, let's be honest, the Essex of America. Jersey girls and Jersey boys will forever be mocked in jokes and songs for their dumbness, illiteracy, vulgarity and sexual availability. The industrial ugliness of much of the state where it borders the Hudson and looks across the river to Manhattan is hard to deny: Jersey City, Newark, Brunswick, Elizabeth and the chemical factories and choking pollution they bring have conferred great prosperity, but also a damningly negative image. It can call itself 'The Garden State' as much as it likes but it makes no difference; for all the beauties of Princeton and much of the coastline, Jersey will always, it seems, suffer from being looked on as something of a dump. About as far from Newport, RI as you can get, culturally and demographically.

My taxi and I are on our way to a place that has

hammered its own nails into the coffin of Jersey's reputation for refinement. Atlantic City.

Best known in the nineteenth and twentieth centuries for its boardwalk, all seven miles of it, Atlantic City on the south Jersey shore was one of the most prosperous and successful resort towns in America. After the Second World War it freefell into what seemed irreversible decline, until, as a last-ditch effort in 1976, the citizens voted to allow gambling. Two years later the first casino in the eastern United States opened and ever since Atlantic City has been second only to Las Vegas as a plughole into which high and low rollers from all over the world are irresistibly drained.

And so I find myself driving into hell.

TRUMPERY

The weather does not help; heavy bruised skies brood over grey Atlantic rollers and on the beach the tide leaves a line of scummy frothing mousse and soggy litter. The signs advertising 'Fun' and 'Family Rides' on the vile seaside piers tinkle and clang in the sharp wind, a forlorn and spindly Ferris wheel squeaks and groans. Styrofoam coffee cups and flappy burger containers are rolled and tossed along the deserted boardwalk—New Jersey's urban, eastern reinterpretation of the mythic tumbleweed and sagebrush of the West. Above tower the hotels, the 'resort casinos', blank façades in whose appearance and architectural qualities the developers have taken a precisely double-zero interest.

Would it not have been better to let this seedy resort town, the home of Monopoly and remnant of another way of holidaying, simply fall into the sea? Instead we are given this obscene Gehenna, a place of such tawdry, tacky, tinselly, tasteless and trumpery tat that the desire to run away clutching my hand to my mouth is overwhelming. But no, I must brave the interior of the most tawdry and literally trumpery tower of them all . . . The Trump Taj Mahal. For taking the name of the priceless mausoleum of Agra, one of the beauties and wonders of the world, for that alone Donald Trump should be stripped naked and whipped with scorpions along the boardwalk. It is as if a giant toad has raped a butterfly. I am not an enemy of developers, per se; I know that people must make money from construction and development projects, I know that there is a demand and that casinos will be built. I can pardon Trump all his vanities and shady junk-bonded dealings and financial brinkmanship, I would even forgive him his hair, were it not that everything he does is done with such poisonously atrocious taste, such false glamour, such shallow grandeur, such cynical vulgarity. At least Las Vegas developments, preposterous as they are have a kind of joy and wit to them . . . oh well, it is no good putting off the moment, Stephen. In you go.

The automatic doors of the black smoked-glass entrance hiss open and I am inside. I see at once that the exterior, boardwalk side of Atlantic City is deliberately kept as unappealing as possible, just to make sure people stay inside. All you need is within, mini-streets complete with Starbucks and burger outlets, there is even a shop devoted entirely to the personality of Donald Trump himself, with quotes from the great man all over the walls: 'You've got to think anyway, so why not think big?' and similar comforting and illuminating insights that enrich and nourish the hungry human soul. Everything sold here is in the 'executive' style, like bad eighties Pierre Cardin: slimy thin belts of glossy leather, notepads, cufflinks, unspeakable objects made of brass and mahogany. There is nothing here that I would not be ashamed to be seen owning. Not a thing. Oh, must we stay here one minute longer?

Perhaps I am just in a bad mood. At the top of the main staircase that leads to the gambling hall I meet up with the PR lady who has arranged for me to be trained as a blackjack dealer. She is perky and charming and seems to love her work.

'You're so very welcome indeed to this facility,' she breathes. 'If there is anything I can do to make your visit with us more pleasurable . . .?'

It would be churlish to suggest a flame-thrower and bazooka, so I grin toothily and follow her to the servants' quarters, the backstage area.

TRAINEE DEALER FRY

Down we travel, by service elevator and stairway, through numberless corridors until we reach the zone where the staff uniforms are kept. Thousands and thousands of tunics are held on rails which, at the touch of a button leap to life. Great circulating loops of human-shaped shirtings process around like flapping zombies in a spooky dumb show reproduction of the gamblers above, the same robotic gestures—animated but with all the flesh sucked out.

I am given a 'butter'-coloured chemise (a new colour line which has just come in to replace the 'garnet' still widely in use) and a strange black thing edged in gold that goes around my waist. Where a

85

purse would be if I were an Austrian café waiter. A name tag tells the world that I am 'Stephen Fry: Trainee'.

Blackjack is universally referred to as BJ without a trace of humour or even any apparent awareness that those initials have another common application. A girl called Kelly has been deputed to initiate me into the mysteries of BJ and she is fierce. Really fierce. I am familiar with blackjack as a player and think myself reasonably competent with a pack of cards. But Kelly's impatience and contemptuous astonishment at my inability to work out the 3–2 insurance coverage on aces dealt to the dealer, my use of the right hand instead of the left hand to collect money from the left-hand side of the table, my slowness in payout calculation . . . all these conspire to make me feel more than usually clumsy and behave more than usually ham-fistedly.

Slap. 'No, no. You get it wrong!'

'Sorry, but . . .'

'No "but", no "sorry". Not difficult.'

By the time a group of real players come along I am feeling hot, bothered and nervous. Kelly, originally a Vietnamese 'boat person', is happy to let me sink or swim.

Slowly, after a few mistakes, gently pointed out by the seasoned pros sitting opposite me, I start to get the hang of things.

Above my head glitter the chandeliers that for some reason Trump is so proud of. '$14 million worth of German crystal chandeliers, including 245,000 piece chandeliers in the casino alone, each valued at a cost of $250,000, and taking over 20 hours to hang,' trumpets the publicity.

'An entire two-year output of Northern Italy's

Carrera marble quarries—the marble of choice for all of Michelangelo's art—adorn the hotel's lobby, guest rooms, casino, hallways and public areas.' Yes, it may well have been the marble of choice for Michelangelo's art. English was the language of choice for Shakespeare's, but that doesn't lift this sentence, for example, out of the ordinary. And believe me the only similarity between Michelangelo and the Trump Taj Mahal that I can spot is that they've both got an M in their names.

'$4 million in uniforms and costumes outfit over 6,000 employees.' Including one butter-coloured shirt as worn by me.

'Four and a half times more steel than the Eiffel Tower.'

'If laid end to end, the building support pilings would stretch the 62 miles from Atlantic City to Philadelphia.'

'The Trump Taj Mahal Casino Resort can generate enough air conditioning to cool 4,000 homes.'

You see, all this mad boasting says to me is 'Our Casino Makes A Shed Load Of Money'. They can afford to lavish a quarter of a million bucks on each chandelier, can they? And where does this money come from, we wonder? From profits from their 'city within a city' Starbucks concession? From sales of patent leather belts and onyx desk sets? No, from the remorseless mathematical fact that gambling is profitable. The house wins. The punter loses. It is a certainty.

This abattoir may be made of marble, but it is still a place for stunning, plucking, skinning and gutting sad chickens.

Hey, but it's *fun*, Stevie! It's *gaming*. People want to play, don't be such a Savonarola.

Well, perhaps I am a bit of a grumpy guts today. I am treated very well and I do enjoy the dealing part of the game. The players facing me are grown-ups. They know what they are doing. Who am I to pee on their parade?

Still, it is with real pleasure that I leave Atlantic City behind me, certain that I shall never return.

South we drive, the taxi and I, towards Cape May and the Delaware Bay.

DELAWARE
KEY FACTS

Abbreviation:
DE

Nickname:
The First State

Capital:
Dover

Flower:
Peach blossom

Tree:
American holly

Bird:
Blue hen chicken

Macroinvertebrate:
Stonefly

Motto:
Liberty and Independence

Well-known residents and natives:
The du Pont family, Howard Pyle,
R. Crumb, Elizabeth Shue, Judge Reinhold,
Susan 'The Producers' Stroman,
Sean Patrick Thomas, Ryan Phillippe.

DELAWARE

'A policeman I met in Lewes where the ferry lands told me that "soft and slow" is the Delaware way.'

Poor old Delaware. I don't know why I say this. She is a beautiful state. Only Rhode Island is smaller, but Delaware can make greater claims to history. Being the First State to ratify the US constitution is her proudest boast. Being home to the DuPont empire another. DuPont invented nylon, polymers and Teflon and is still the second-biggest chemical company in the world.

For most Americans the word Delaware conjures up the painting by Emanuel Leutze, 'Washington Crossing the Delaware'. It commemorates an important moment in the colonial wars—or the Revolutionary Wars as Americans prefer to call them.

On Christmas Day 1776 Washington led his army, which had been twice defeated by the British, across the river and, making landfall in Pennsylvania, led

90

them up to Trenton, New Jersey where they surprised the British and won a famous victory.

It is one of those fine historical moments of generalship on which reputations rest. General Wolfe scaling the Heights of Abraham to win Quebec, Horatius on the bridge, Hannibal passing through the Alps. Washington crossing the Delaware.

Unfortunately for Delaware none of this took place within the state itself. Washington crossed from New Jersey into Pennsylvania. Only the name of the river has any connection with the state of Delaware. He would today have taken the Delaware Memorial Bridge, the longest twin-span suspension bridge in the world.

A policeman I meet in Lewes where the ferry lands with considerably less hoopla and ice than Washington's boats, tells me that 'soft and slow' is the Delaware way and now, as I rattle hard and fast up the main road towards the state capital Dover, I feel a bit of a heel for betraying the state philosophy quite so brutishly and insensitively.

I drive along, humming the words of the Perry Como song, 'What did Della wear?' I think about where exactly we are.

Delaware is in a kind of middle area. This is not yet the South, but nor am I any longer in New England, that much is clear. The countryside is beautiful and one or two trees still sport bright fall colours, but the architecture and the landscape have subtly changed. Less dramatic in terms of crags, valleys and hills, less clapboard and slate in terms of housing. Dutch barns, Dutch gabled houses, softly rounded hills.

Dover comes and goes, then I pass Wilmington, the biggest town in the state. I am already very nearly in Pennsylvania.

Well aware, Delaware, that I did not give you much attention. Another time.

PENNSYLVANIA
KEY FACTS

Abbreviation:
PA

Nicknames:
The Keystone State, The Quaker State

Capital:
Harrisburg

Flower:
Mountain laurel

Tree:
Eastern hemlock

Bird:
Ruffed grouse

Toy:
Slinky (I'm not making this up)

Motto:
Virtue, Liberty and Independence

Well-known residents and natives:
Benjamin Franklin, Gertrude Stein, Wallace
Stevens, John Updike, August Wilson,
James A. Michener, Dean Koontz, John O'Hara,
Thomas Eakins, Pearl S. Buck, Man Ray,
Andy Warhol, Marilyn Horne, W.C. Fields,

the Barrymores, David O. Selznick, Gene Kelly,
Jayne Mansfield, Grace Kelly, Henry Mancini,
Charles Bronson, Richard Gere, Kevin Bacon,
Sharon Stone, Will Smith, M. Night Shyamalan,
Perry Como, Bill Haley, Chubby Checker,
Keith Jarrett, Hall and Oates, Christina Aguilera.

PENNSYLVANIA

'There is something in the hope and idealism of this frustrating and contradictory nation that still makes my spirits soar.'

The Commonwealth of Pennsylvania is the only state to be named after a person. Oh, apart from Washington of course. And New York, because that was named not after the city of York, but after James, Duke of York. Oh, and the Carolinas were named after King Charles I. And Virginia after Elizabeth, the Virgin Queen. And Maryland after Henrietta Maria, wife of Charles I . . . all right. All *right*. So actually *lots* of states have been named after people. Pennsylvania is just one. It gets its name from William Penn, the Quaker who was the founder and absolute controller of what was in its day the largest of the colonial states. Although in strict fact it was named after his father, Admiral Sir William Penn, who had lent Charles II a great deal of money and received in return the rights to the land west of the Delaware River on behalf of his son. The Admiral himself was not a Quaker (you cannot really have a Quaker with a military rank, it doesn't compute) and did not like the fact that his son was, but William Jnr, a remarkable man who had braved much contempt, imprisonment and persecution for his pacifist, heterodox beliefs, used the family money, his father's favour with the King and his own intelligence and natural leadership skills to carve out this great tract of land, which functioned independently under a democratic constitution long before independence came.

Philadelphia (an adaptation of the Greek for 'brotherly love') is the chief city, although not the capital. Here can be found Independence Hall and the famously, and perhaps proleptically, cracked Liberty Bell amongst other tourist attractions.

Although America was consecrated, if that is the right word (and you will soon see why I chose it) on July 4th, 1776 in Philadelphia when John Hancock became the first to append his name (one's 'John Hancock' in America is to this day one's signature) to the Declaration of Independence, for me and for many the moment America grew up was when it was re-consecrated 'four score and seven' years later on a battlefield 140 miles to the west of Philadelphia, towards which I am now driving, under heavy clouds and through torrential rain.

GETTYSBURG

The weather improves with dramatic suddenness the moment I pass the sign that tells me I have arrived in

Gettysburg. The clouds depart, a clear autumnal sun lights the still bright leaves of the trees around the cemetery and makes the puddles glint and flash as I pass.

I am welcomed by Abraham Lincoln. Well, by an actor, historian and lookalike called Jim. Jim conducts me around the cemetery, contriving to stay in character in a way that is not irritating or twee.

It might seem something of a puzzle that a nation born out of such high ideals, such humanitarian vision and such intellectual clarity and rational enlightenment as America should have descended, by the 1860s, into the bloodiest war that humanity had ever recorded. Man for man, no conflict has ever been more attritional and deadly than the American Civil War of 1861–65.

Jim offers the view that it is perhaps only in the clear light of history that one can argue the war *had* to happen. America's written constitution, with its lofty air of permanence and marmoreal splendour, had not addressed what America might be in the modern world. To us all now the Civil War was, or should have been, about the evils of slavery and that is how most will think of it. But many of the Northerners who fought so bitterly, and with such ample funding, were fighting because their paymasters and political leaders looked across the Atlantic at the Industrial Revolution that was propelling Britain to unimagined heights of prosperity and they saw that their own country, with its two economies, one powered by slavery and the other not, was at a huge disadvantage. Slavery was outlawed across Europe, whose countries would not trade with America—not so much out of moral repugnance as annoyance at the unfair advantage a labour bill of zero gave the plantation owners. The North wanted to create

97

conditions for a modern industrial state, an enterprise economy, and to do that it had to bid an enforced goodbye to the plantations. It was no good having two Americas: a neighbour with a slave economy was never going to allow the kind of commercial equity the North demanded. So it was, *au fond*, an economic and commercial war. Nothing new there. Are not most wars? Ironically, Britain, the mother country, the old tyranny, the stuck-in-the-mud monarchy, had in many respects become a more modern and democratic country than America. Without one United States, a democracy founded on fairness, America could never prosper in the way Britain did: the true meaning of democracy was at stake.

This, Jim tells me, is an important part of the background to Abraham Lincoln's shining moment of oratory.

THE ADDRESS

In July of 1863 the Union forces had won a great victory over Lee's Confederate army at Gettysburg, PA, a victory that was believed at the time to be a potentially decisive turning point. The losses were staggering, the largest number of any battle in that war: over 50,000 casualties in two days of dreadful fighting.

It was decided that a great and grand National Cemetery should be created to house the dead of both sides. A dedication ceremony was planned for November and, almost at the last minute, Abraham Lincoln was asked to say a few words, as President. The main oration was to be made by one Edward Everett.

Came the day and Everett spoke for two hours. Lincoln then rose to deliver a ten-sentence address in his 'high-pitched Kentucky accent'. When he sat down it is unlikely he knew that he had delivered one of the greatest speeches in political history, a speech memorised by generation after generation of American schoolchildren. A speech whose final sentence is so well known it is in danger of landing on one's ears like an inelegant cliché. I am keen to hear it again. Jim naturally knows it by heart and gives me a private performance.

'Four score and seven years ago . . .' Jim's voice is sharp and clear. He is speaking the words in exactly the same place where Lincoln first spoke them. The gravestones have heard them before. '. . . our fathers brought forth on this continent a new nation, conceived in Liberty, and dedicated to the proposition that all men are created equal.

'Now we are engaged in a great civil war, testing whether that nation, or any nation, so conceived and so dedicated, can long endure. We are met on a great battle-field of that war. We have come to dedicate a portion of that field, as a final resting place for those who here gave their lives that that nation might live. It is altogether fitting and proper that we should do this.

'But, in a larger sense, we can not dedicate—we can not consecrate—we can not hallow—this ground. The brave men, living and dead, who struggled here, have consecrated it, far above our poor power to add or detract. The world will little note, nor long remember what we say here, but it can never forget what they did here. It is for us the living, rather, to be dedicated here to the unfinished work which they who fought here have thus far so nobly advanced. It is rather for us to be here dedicated to the great task

99

remaining before us—that from these honored dead we take increased devotion to that cause for which they gave the last full measure of devotion—that we here highly resolve that these dead shall not have died in vain—that this nation, under God, shall have a new birth of freedom—and that government of the people, by the people, for the people, shall not perish from the earth.'

I am in tears by the time Jim finishes. The speech is moving on any occasion, but here amongst the buried dead, on the very ground that 'we cannot hallow' it is charged with even greater power. Jim tips his hat and walks slowly off, that unmistakable gait and profile heading towards a group of schoolchildren who, it seems, want his autograph.

The 'new birth of freedom' that Lincoln described is what the Civil War somehow, for all its horrors, achieved. It was a necessary war. Heaven knows there was pain and persecution and intolerance after it. But just look at America's economy in the fifty years before that war and in the fifty years *after*. As I wrote when looking at the Newport cottages from the Gilded Age, 'Never in the field of human commerce . . . had so much money been made so fast and by so few.' If the Vanderbilts and their ilk were the most prominent beneficiaries of the Civil War, the rest of America waxed fat too. It took the emancipated slaves and their descendants a long time, a shamefully long time, to benefit from the 'new birth of freedom' and many might argue they still have not, but without the Civil War, it seems hard to believe that America could ever have risen to her world pre-eminence in power and prosperity.

There is something in the American project, something in simple American oratory, something in the hope and idealism of this frustrating and contradictory nation that still makes my spirits soar and my heart leap with optimism and belief. If only they understood how to make a cup of tea.

MARYLAND

KEY FACTS

Abbreviation:
MD

Nickname:
The Old Line State

Capital:
Annapolis

Flower:
Black-eyed Susan

Tree:
White oak

Bird:
Baltimore oriole

Motto:
Fatti maschii, parole femine
('Manly deeds, womanly words'—I mean, what?)

Well-known residents and natives:
Spiro Agnew, Carl Bernstein, James M. Cain,
Tom Clancy, Dashiell Hammett, H.L. Mencken,
Ogden Nash, Edgar Allan Poe, Upton Sinclair,
Leon Uris, Tori Amos, Toni Braxton,
David Byrne, Cab Calloway, Philip Glass,
Billie Holiday, Frank Zappa, David Hasselhoff,
Goldie Hawn, Jim Henson, Spike Jonze,
Edward Norton, John Waters, Johns Hopkins,
George Peabody.

WASHINGTON D.C.
KEY FACTS

Abbreviation:
D.C.

Nickname:
The District

Motto:
Justitia omnibus ('Justice for all')

Well-known residents and natives:
Helen Hayes, Samuel L. Jackson, Chita Rivera,
Frank Rich, Duke Ellington, Marvin Gaye,
Kate Smith, John Philip Sousa,
John Foster Dulles, Al Gore, Edward Albee,
Pat Buchanan, J. Edgar Hoover,
Robert F. Kennedy Jnr.

MARYLAND
(& WASHINGTON D.C.)

'So neat, so pretty. Even the horse that took me about the streets had nail varnish and an expensive coiffeur. I feel I could live here.'

Maryland (pronounced something like 'murlan') is, like Delaware, a Middle State, not quite South and certainly not Yankee.

If ever there was a silly name for a town it is surely that of Maryland's elegant and graceful capital city Annapolis. I hope Queen Anne, after whom it was named, wasn't too hacked off about it. What would have been wrong with Anneville? Oh, it sounds like a blacksmith's iron. Of course. Incidentally, one of the minor but interesting linguistic differences that one meets along the way in America is that they say 'named for' where we would say 'named after'. So they might say Annapolis was named for Queen Anne and Baltimore, Maryland's biggest town, was named for the English peer Cecil Calvert, Lord Baltimore, who, as it happened, married one Anne Arundell, after whom, or for whom, Annapolis was originally named Anne's Town before, in a fit of sycophancy, the city fathers dedicated it to the then young Princess Anne, later of course the last of the Stuart monarchs. One might say all that and then be left both out of breath and holding the loose end of a conversational thread.

Annapolis, 'Nap Town' (from the 'nap' in the middle of its name), would argue with Newport, RI over which is the sailing capital of America. Indeed Annapolis styles itself the sailing capital of the *world*. The approach, over the gorgeous Chesapeake Bay, makes for one of the most attractive arrivals imaginable. Water is everywhere, the perfect place to sail and to train naval cadets, really. And there, sure enough, stands the United States Naval Academy, the navy's equivalent of West Point.

With a main street which is the closest to an English country town High Street I have ever seen in America, flower-bedecked shop-fronts, a graceful State House and handsome naval cadets strolling about wherever you look, Annapolis strikes me as one hundred per cent charming. So neat, so pretty. Even the horse that took me about the streets had nail varnish and an expensive coiffure. I feel I could live here. The urban excitements of Baltimore and Washington D.C. are not too far away, should one miss bright city lights. And it is towards Washington, thirty-five miles to the west, that I next turn my attention.

CHICKEN MARYLAND

Firstly, however, I have to get to the bottom of

Chicken Maryland, or Maryland Chicken. Driving towards Annapolis and feeling faint from hunger, at least an hour having passed since I savaged a blueberry muffin, I stop off at a diner for a late lunch.

'Do you know?' I decide, 'I think I shall have Chicken Maryland.'

'Say what?'

'Maryland Chicken? You know, Chicken Maryland.'

'Ain't never heard of that, honey.'

'I am still in Maryland, aren't I?'

'You sure are.'

'Hm. And, forgive me, are you yourself from Maryland?'

'Born 'n' raised.'

Well! Not wishing to humiliate this fine young waitress by exposing further ignorance of her own home state, nor wanting to rob her of my custom, I order a hot-dog and a root beer.

The next diner was supervised by an elderly waitress. Surely she would know her state dish?

'Chicken Maryland? Never did hear of such a thing. Whass in it?'

'Well, er . . . fried chicken, I think. Banana and pineapple fritters, gammon, that sort of thing.'

'You say *banana?*'

Several hours later I had eaten three burgers, two more hot-dogs, a plate of chilli and four ice-creams. The news everywhere was the same. Chicken Maryland: Not Known At This Address.

The last diner I try hasn't heard of the dish either, but I notice they offer a free wi-fi internet service, so I turn to trusty old Wikipedia:

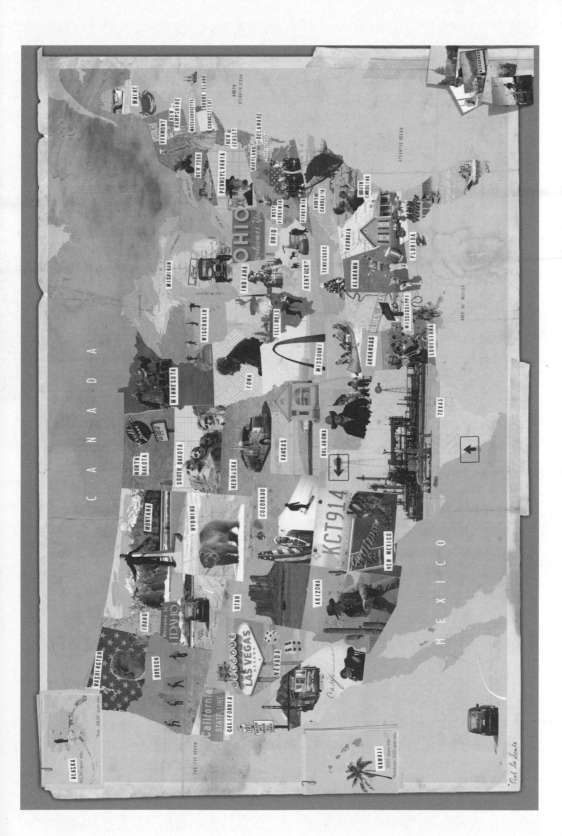

MAINE
Dawn in Eastport: the first light to strike America.

Englishman with a bib.

NEW HAMPSHIRE
Mount Washington's Cog Railway. 'This was the first,'
says the brakeman. Wrongly.

MASSACHUSETTS

Salem: by twelve o'clock it's all over and everyone is in bed. There's more true Gothic horror in a digestive biscuit, but never mind.

With Professor Gomes in his humble Baptist shack.

RHODE ISLAND
The Weatherly: George and SF correcting a luff.

CONNECTICUT
My travels so far
have already
taught me that
Nature did not
fashion
Stephen Fry to
serve in
submarines . . .

NEW YORK STATE
Wise Guys.

Relaxing after 'just about the most fabulous breakfast I have ever, ever eaten'.

VERMONT
Lake Champlain with New York State on the horizon.

WASHINGTON D.C.
Skimming around D.C. like a . . .

PENNSYLVANIA
Shooting the breeze with Abe.

Chicken Maryland or **Maryland Chicken** is a dish with various interpretations, depending on the country of origin. It is not necessarily known in the U.S. state of Maryland, and is not considered a native dish thereof.

Well, that explains it. Curse those school-dinner ladies. But thank you, internet. Which reminds me, I am late for an appointment with Wikipedia's founder, Jimmy Wales. We are due to meet in the lobby of the Willard Hotel, Washington D.C.

WASHINGTON D.C.

THE WILLARD

The Willard Hotel is a grand Washington institution. Martin Luther King wrote his 'I have a dream' speech in one of its bedrooms, in 1963. Abraham Lincoln stayed here before his inauguration and Ulysses S. Grant used to retreat to the hotel lobby for tea and nibbles when he was President. He is said to have grown so annoyed with those hanging around and begging him for favours that he cursed them as 'those damned lobbyists'. Now I happen to know that this explanation of the origin of the word 'lobbyist' is untrue, but I arrive for a meeting with Jimmy Wales hoping to catch out his remarkable creation.

Wales, as is fairly well known, made his first fortune in the options market in Chicago and his second with an 'adult-oriented' web portal called Bomis. With his editor-in-chief Larry Sanger he created Nupedia. To feed this gargantuan and ambitious online encyclopaedia idea, they created a

115

wiki-based site whose aim, originally, was to service and feed the Nupedia project. Well, Wikipedia, as the world knows, has grown and grown into the most popular reference source in the history of the planet. It is mocked for mistakes, but in reality, who could possibly deny its value, reach, depth and importance? On top of this it is free, open, wholly funded by volunteer donations and entirely non-profit making.

The neat friendly fellow who meets me in the lobby of the Willard seems to me to symbolise much of what America has given the world in business and entrepreneurialism. On the one hand we have a man who did a master's degree in finance and copped a bundle in the raw capitalist world of options trading and then repeated the trick with, if not pornography, certainly a trade which no one could regard as idealistic and on the other, we have a philanthropist the third act of whose career involves the creation of something wholly new, idealistic and (allowing for the natural flaws all human creations are likely to suffer from) good.

I sit with laptop perched atop lap as tea is brought. 'Did you know,' I say, 'that "laptop machines" is an anagram of "Apple Macintosh"?'

'Yes,' says Jimmy Wales.

'Oh. Anyway. Hope you don't mind, but I thought we'd test your creation?'

'Go right ahead.'

Wikipedia leaps the first hurdle straight away. Did the terms 'lobbyist' and 'to lobby' originate here?

... this is probably false, as the verb to lobby is found decades earlier and did not originally refer to Washington politics.

Good one, Wikipedia.

'Phew!' breathes Jimmy.

I show him the entry under 'Stephen Fry', not an article I am prone to gaze at fondly, but every now and again I have become used to people asking me how I enjoyed myself at the public school Gresham's. Whenever I protest that I did not go there, they assure me that I did because it says so in Wikipedia.

'Okay, let's change it,' says Jimmy with the patient ease of one who has had to do this many times at parties. He shows me how to register, log in and edit the article. 'Wikipedia is organic, self-healing. Mistakes are put right.'

'But sometimes not before journalists have embarrassed themselves by quoting from an erroneous entry,' I point out.

'If Wikipedia can add to its public service role by embarrassing journalists . . . why then . . .' Jimmy downs his tea. 'Gotta rush. Great talking to you.'

He leaves for the airport and I walk over to the Ronald Reagan Conference Center (there appear to be more institutions, streets and buildings named for that president than almost any other) to catch a performance by the Capitol Steps, a satirical revue troupe who use well-known songs with changed lyrics to poke fun at the political establishment, 'How do you solve a problem like Korea?', that sort of thing. All very good fun and excellently performed. Capitol Steps has become almost as much of a Washington institution as Grant's Tomb and the Lincoln Memorial. I meet Bari, one of the performers, and she promises to show me those and other sights tomorrow.

SEGWAY

And when the morrow dawns a new potential way for me to make an arse of myself is discovered. I drive Bari in the cab while she points out the sights and tells me where the bodies are buried.

'I used to come here as a girl,' she says as we zoom past the Capitol. 'If people knew what went on—all the sexual scandals.'

'Oh do tell!'

'Imagine the worst and double it,' is all she will say. 'There must be something in the air. Washington is built on a drained swamp, after all . . .'

I drop Bari off and pop in to the Segway hire company to be given a lesson in controlling one of their strange electric conveyances, half bicycle, half tennis-court white-line roller. Apparently George W. Bush fell off one and caused great embarrassment to himself and the manufacturers. George W. may have his faults but I suspect he is more coordinated and physically able than me, so I entertain real doubts as to whether the Segway and I are going to be friends.

Extraordinarily we hit it off from the first and I am soon skimming around D.C. like a . . . well it isn't easy to know what I skim like. A hippo figure-skating, I suspect.

As I whizz past the Jefferson and Lincoln Memorials I see the American flags fluttering against a lilac sunset and I realise that tomorrow is November 11th. Armistice Day. Just five hundred yards further on is the state line and beyond it, Virginia and Arlington Cemetery. Another state beckons.

SOUTH EAST AND FLORIDA

VIRGINIA
KEY FACTS

Abbreviation:
VA

Nickname:
Old Dominion, Mother of Presidents

Capital:
Richmond

Flower:
Dogwood

Tree:
Dogwood

Bird:
Cardinal

Bat:
Virginia Big-eared bat

Motto:
Sic semper tyrannis ('Ever thus for tyrants')

Well-known residents and natives: George Washington (1st President),
Thomas Jefferson (3rd), James Madison (4th),
James Monroe (5th), William Henry Harrison (9th),
John Tyler (10th), Zachary Taylor (12th),
Woodrow Wilson (28th), Patrick Henry,

General Robert E. Lee, General Douglas MacArthur,
General George Patton, George Marshall,
Edgar Allan Poe, William Styron, Tom Wolfe,
Cy Twombly, Ella Fitzgerald, Pearl Bailey,
Patsy Cline, June Carter Cash, Jim Morrison,
Warren Beatty, Shirley MacLaine, Sandra Bullock.

VIRGINIA

'If I tried to count how many Stars and Stripes I see if I drive a hundred miles along an average highway, I lose count or end up in a ditch.'

It is appropriate that the Commonwealth of Virginia (as with Massachusetts and Pennsylvania the title is not constitutionally significant), named for the Virgin Queen, should claim perhaps the most impressive roll of female achievers of any state so far. American music would be a great deal poorer without Ella Fitzgerald, Patsy Cline and Pearl Bailey. The brother and sister combo of Warren Beatty and Shirley MacLaine is a proud boast for any state, but if we look at the top of the list we see eight presidents, and three of the most important generals in American history. The first three presidents were also Founding Fathers (signatories of the Declaration of Independence), a title also usually conferred upon James 'Doctrine' Monroe and Patrick 'Give me

Liberty or give me Death' Henry, Virginia's first Governor under independence. So this state, this Old Virginny Home, could regard herself as the Cradle of the Revolution, the Birthplace of the Republic. And she does. The three great heritage sites of Colonial Williamsburg, Jamestown and Yorktown form one of the most popular tourist destinations in the world. Much dressing up in tricorn hats and shouting of 'Oyyez' goes on there daily. It is all very distressing, but things must be, I suppose.

Virginia, like Maryland, snuggles right up to Washington D.C. So much so that it is a relatively short walk from the White House to Arlington, VA, where the National Cemetery has its home.

I cross over the Potomac River and point the cab down the long straight drive to Arlington. It is November 11th, Armistice Day and Remembrance Sunday for the British, Veterans Day for the Americans. As it happens today is a Sunday and a beautiful one at that. Not a cloud in the sky, the sun glinting off the dazzling uniforms of the cadets and young soldiers who usher visitors to their places for the ceremony. For it is on this day at Arlington that the nation publicly commemorates and honours its veterans: tickets are hard to come by, but I have slipped in on a press pass. This is not quite the same as our Cenotaph ceremony, for Veterans Day is dedicated to the survivors, the 'vets'—there is another day, in May, which is dedicated to the fallen. All around me, streaming into the amphitheatre where the ceremony will be held, I see men (and some women) with medals swinging from their chests.

On the way in I notice the fields surrounding the amphitheatre, filled with white tombstones in rows so regular that they play strange games of parallax and perspective with the eye, making a cat's cradle of their symmetry. Diagonals become ranks and files which, as you walk past, become long diagonals again. Each white point in the line a life. No crosses, crescents or stars of David, just simple white tablets. The latest tombs commemorate lives lost in Iraq and Afghanistan.

I get into my press place and survey the scene before me. Veterans of every description and in every kind of weird tunic, jacket, beret, cap and trousering, each offered in different colourways and textures, are filling the amphitheatre. There are purple silk blousons with gold lettering, light blue tunics with silver—it is all very bewildering. I head for a group of grizzled fifty and sixty-year-olds, mostly bearded, long-haired and dressed in leather: they look scarily like bikers. They proudly announce themselves to be a Hell's Angels chapter of veterans. One of them, an ex-army chaplain, explains to me that the Hell's Angels 'movement' started out as a group of Second World War vets. I wonder that such a counter-cultural grouping should be so faithful to mainstream America.

'Do you approve of where the government sends its soldiers and how it treats them?' I ask.

The chaplain starts to answer with a fairly damning view of the way the military is run by its political masters when his eye freezes at a point somewhere above my left shoulder. He stops speaking.

'Er . . . you were saying?'

He smiles but says nothing. Someone behind him, inside the knot of Hell's Angels, has signalled to him not to speak any further. He quite literally says not one word more to me. Whether this is military discipline or Hell's Angels' discipline I cannot be sure: either way it frightens me.

124

A startlingly well-presented young officer with blazing epaulettes, white gloves and dazzling sword is more prepared to talk, albeit in a rather rattled-out 'sirry' kind of style. His cap is so low down over his eyes that I never quite manage to meet his gaze.

'Lieutenant Payne, *sir*. I am a serving member of the US Navy, but I do have a special role. My shipmates and I are part of the US Navy ceremonial guard, sir.'

'I can't help noticing your sword. A shine like that doesn't come about by accident.'

'There's a lot of hours that go into that, sir. Behind the scenes. I estimate ten to fifteen man-hours, sir.'

'Right. Well, it's a big day, of course.'

'I understand, sir, you have the same thing in England as well, sir. Which is a . . . could you explain, Poppy Day . . . is it poppy?'

I am not sure my explanation makes much sense to him, but he is too polite to snort derisively.

Meanwhile the ceremony has got under way with the sound of a military band. This is something Americans do very much in their own style, thanks to the distinctive sounds created for them by John Philip Sousa. 'The Washington Post', 'Liberty Bell' (used by Monty Python as their theme tune and impossible to listen to without expecting a giant raspberry sound to cut it off), 'Stars and Stripes for Ever'—all the classics are played to us with just the required pizzazz as, behind the amphitheatre and out of sight, the Distinguished Party lays a wreath on the Tomb of the Unknown Soldier.

Next tune up is the rousing Marine Hymn, 'From the Halls of Montezuma, To the shores of Tripoli'. I am beginning to get into the mood. When a young girl in military uniform sings 'America the Beautiful', I feel a lump rising in my throat. As the Distinguished Party comes on stage and everyone rises for a lusty verse of 'The Star-Spangled Banner' I feel wetness in the eyes. It is preposterous to be moved by the patriotic paraphernalia and national iconography of another country, but I cannot help it.

The Distinguished Party is no less a figure than Dick Cheney, the Vice-President. He surveys us with that peculiar distant, yet triumphant look of humorous disdain he shares with Soviet leaders saluting their military parades. Grey-suited and pasty-faced, he makes a speech about freedom. It is very hard I should imagine, even if you think Cheney and his war are justified, not to picture the newly buried bodies lying in the earth all around while he reels off his mind-numbing clichés. This would be true whatever one thought of any war—it would be true for example at this same ceremony during the Second World War—but it is especially difficult to listen to a speech which keeps using *that word* again and again and again and with such little justification other than the twisted logic of formulaic patriotism. I register thirty uses of 'free' and 'freedom' before I give up counting.

I believe most Americans fully and honestly believe that they live in the freest country in the world. There is perhaps justification for that. In pure libertarian terms America is certainly freer and less encumbered than most nations. Freedom is the national given here. In America they like to talk about 'the taste of freedom', and 'the smell of freedom' a great deal. It seems to follow therefore, in the minds of politicians at least, that everything America does must automatically be 'in the name of freedom'. The United States of course, like any country, acts in her own interests, as she should. But a certain kind of

126

batty logic assumes that as 'the beacon of freedom' America's own best interests must also always naturally coincide with the best interests of freedom. Not just America's freedom, but Freedom with a big 'F', Freedom as a kind of abstract entity, a goddess, Lady Liberty. Therefore to invade a country and pound it into dust and leave it in anarchy and ruin is done 'in the cause of freedom'. Likewise anyone who dislikes American foreign policy is 'an enemy of freedom'. It is a most peculiar formulation and an upsetting abuse of reason. It is very like the way, in a communist country, everything is done 'in the name of the people' and anyone who opposes it is 'an enemy of the people'. Well, it follows, doesn't it? Hum. True freedom, surely, would include freedom from this kind of windy tyranny of ideas.

And then there's the flag. If I tried to count how many Stars and Stripes I could see driving a hundred miles along an average highway, I would lose count or end up in a ditch. Here in Arlington it is easier to count the number of patches of space that are *not* occupied by Old Glory.

In Britain we are so very different. Our flag faintly embarrasses us. I do not believe we would be any less patriotic if it came to a fight for our liberty and our sovereign independence, and I am sure most of us can get a bit weepy at the Last Night of the Proms or when listening to a Churchill speech or contemplating our landscape, traditions and history, but it really is not done to go on about it. Rudyard Kipling, regarded by many as the quintessential British patriotic writer, actually shows the heroes of one of his books, *Stalky & Co*, hissing and booing at a politician who goes on about the flag. You don't talk about it. You feel it, if you do, but you don't share it or write about it or make

127

florid speeches about it. In America it is proudly different. The flag is everywhere. Americans seem to feel the need to give colour, shape and dimension to their sense of nationhood so that they can exhibit it and in doing so exhibit their patriotism and their belief in the values that made America the country it is. Only sneering liberal elitist atheist scum like me would raise an eyebrow at this outward and visible form of an inward and spiritual creed. And anyway, I am not American, so I don't understand. And perhaps that is true. I do not scorn patriotism, and I do not think those who hoist the flag outside their homes are necessarily dumb white trash or right-wing yahoos. I know it is far from the case. But the two F's, Freedom and the Flag, reinforce my sense of how different it is to be an American.

After an unbelievably wearisome reading out of the names of important members of various staggeringly specific veterans' affairs committees (committees for Disabled Jewish Tennessee Marines, Catholic Naval Veterans of New Mexico, etc., etc.) I also come to the conclusion, with a rare fierce stab of my own patriotism, that ghastly, doomed and mediocre as much of Britain may well be, when it comes to pageant, display, pomp, ceremony, precision and processional style we still have something to teach the New World.

WEST VIRGINIA
KEY FACTS

Abbreviation:
WV

Nickname:
The Mountain State

Capital:
Charleston

Flower:
Rhododendron

Tree:
Sugar maple

Bird:
Cardinal

Motto:
Montani semper liberi
('Mountain men are always free')

Well-known residents and natives:
General Stonewall Jackson, Pearl S. Buck,
Bill Withers, Brad Dourif, Morgan Spurlock,
Jennifer Garner, Booker T. Washington,
Chuck Yeager.

WEST VIRGINIA

'I find myself in the middle of nowhere, about a hundred miles from the back of beyond.'

I drive my taxi along dirt tracks and through woods in search of a legendary entity which looms so large as a symbol in America that it is easy to forget that it actually does exist as a physical reality. I am in search of the Mason–Dixon Line.

But first I cross another line, this time it is the Eastern Continental Divide. A continental divide is a ridge of land which separates two watersheds. I really did not know this until it was explained to me. My knowledge of geography, as I have said, is pathetically shallow, so forgive me if I am relating the obvious. To be perfectly honest I did not really know what a watershed was either, except in the sense of a time after which you can safely say 'tits' on national television.

MASON–DIXON

I look out of the cab window. The dramatic Appalachian scenery does not seem any different, but here is the big sign by the side of the road: 'Eastern Continental Divide'. Any drop of water that falls on the eastern side of the divide, I am told, will eventually drain into the Atlantic Ocean, any water that falls on the western side will drain into the Gulf of Mexico. Further west lies the Great Continental Divide, to the west of which all waters flow into the Pacific, to the east of which all waters flow into the Gulf of Mexico, and therefore, in reality, into the Atlantic. I think I have got that right. Anyway, it puts me in the mood for dividing lines.

In the popular imagination the Mason–Dixon line is what separates the North from the South. In reality it is a boundary line that was created before Independence by two British surveyors, Charles Mason and Jeremiah Dixon, in order to settle a border dispute between Pennsylvania, Delaware, Maryland and West Virginia (although actually at the time there was only one Virginia). The line was marked by stones every mile and 'crownstones', in honour of King George, every five. They still exist and I am keen to find one. I have always taken pleasure in the strange properties of boundaries, frontiers and lines of demarcation. They are powerful, be they ever so notional and arbitrary. The equator of course is not arbitrary, but the meridian is, and the Mason–Dixon line could not be more so. And yet to this day people talk of affairs 'south of the Mason–Dixon line' as if it has real meaning.

After a struggle with maps and in-car sat nav devices I find myself in the middle of nowhere, about a hundred miles from the back of beyond outside a small house in the garden of which a man is exercising his rather fierce-looking dogs.

'I wonder if you can help me?' I call to him from the fence. 'This sounds a daft question, but what state am I in?'

'Pennsylvania.'

'Thank you,' I say, and turn to leave.

'West Virginia.'

I turn back. 'Excuse me?'

'Pennsylvania.'

'I'm sorry?'

'You're stepping on the state line, son.' The man, whose name is Bill, agrees to take me to a place where he thinks we may be able to find evidence of the almost 250-year-old line.

Under forest litter not a hundred yards from his house we do find a genuine Mason–Dixon milestone. It is no more than a big boulder with a date carved in it. Worn and mossy. But it tells me that from now on I shall be travelling in a different America.

With my back to Bill and Pennsylvania I point the taxi south, down the Appalachians and towards West Virginia's capital, Charleston. Dixie here I come.

KANAWHA EAGLE MINE

I know what some of you may be thinking. Charleston. Gracious residential squares, tree-lined avenues, Spanish moss, gentlemen called Beauregard handing mint juleps to ladies called Beulah? Well, I fear you have Charleston, South Carolina in your mind. Charleston, West Virginia is quite another kettle of ballparks.

132

Abe Lincoln announced that the upper west part of Virginia had been successfully integrated back into the Union in 1863, right plumb spang in the middle of the Civil War. As a reward he granted it separation from Virginia and new independent statehood for itself. The Union armies needed the one thing they still have here in abundance and which I am about to meet quite literally face to face. Coal.

I meet Bob from the Kanawha Eagle Mine the night before I am due to make the descent with the morning shift. He is anxious to show me plans, outline safety procedures and prepare my mind for the colossal underground city I shall be exploring. And truly the mine is a kind of city. The whole area is divided, like Manhattan, into streets and avenues. I pass a sleepless night unable quite to imagine what it will be like. Images of Davy lamps and pickaxes and canaries in cages revolve in my mind like the montage of a school information film on the history of mining.

The day begins with the obligatory 'let's humiliate Stephen by dressing him up' moment. A white newbie suit, gloves, boots, goggles and a Batman-style utility belt offering oxygen and a battery pack to power the miner's lamp which is built into the helmet. For once I am not so concerned with how I look, for everything I put on is a safety feature. Safety is of the first importance to Bob and, to be honest, it's pretty high up in my list of priorities too. The mocking of Health and Safety that is so fashionable suddenly seems a lot less clever and funny.

Nonetheless, I do look a dick, obviously.

Bob leads me to where the miners, almost all of them moustached, are smoking their last cigarettes and downing their last coffees before the descent. They greet me cheerfully enough. What they must think of this large Englishmen babbling questions at them at six in the morning I can only imagine, but they respond to all my excited enquiries politely and with dry wit.

'This is Ron,' one of them says, 'he's new.'

'Good Lord,' I say. 'He doesn't have a moustache. Is that allowed?'

'I'm gonna grow one over the weekend,' says Ron. 'Then I'll fit in.'

'Go safe,' they call as one as into the elevator and down we go. When the doors open at the bottom a huge rush of cold air billows towards us. I am told to make the most it, for as we penetrate the mountain it will only get warmer and warmer. The coal face is actually about two miles away but we do not have to walk. A train awaits. Actually, it is called a manbus which sounds like a rude Australian euphemism, but Americans don't do that sort of humour, so manbus it is. It runs on rickety rails and reminds me of the conveyance used in *Indiana Jones and the Temple of Doom*. 'Ha, ha, ha, Doctor Jones! Very funny, Doctor Jones!'

The walls of the tunnel glisten palely. 'Everything's white!'

'That's what we call rock dust,' says Bob. 'Pulverised limestone. Coal dust is combustible, so we spray it. Decreases the combustibility of the coal so it doesn't have the likelihood to ignite by itself. Plus it keeps it out of the miners' lungs. People always expect a coalmine to be black and then the first thing they see is this.'

I watch the walls flash by on this ghost ride. What a strange commute these men have. Every now and again I see black patches that glisten as if wet, the prize that has brought us down here.

134

We come to the end of the line, dismount (which I am not able to do very nimbly much to everyone's amusement) and walk towards the face. Well, not so much walk as bow, stagger, crouch, squat and limp. I find progress unbelievably uncomfortable. The floor is rutted, pitted and puddled and the roof so low that my neck has constantly to be dropped to one side. I am shown that I might find it easier if I grasp my hands behind my back and stoop, which does help but I am hating this. I want to escape, NOW, right this minute please, but I am too much of a coward to let anyone see what a coward I am. Every now and then the height of the ceiling increases enough for me to stand. What I finally understand is that we are of course walking through an already excavated seam; sometimes when they are mined out the seams are shallow, sometimes—rarely—they are deep enough to allow a man of six foot four to stand upright.

The shift stops at an assembly point for prayers. This might sound very peculiar to us but Americans do not seem in the least embarrassed about this kind of thing. Given too the danger lurking around every corner I suppose the faithful reckon they could do with a little help from above, further above even than management. An average of seven West Virginian miners a year die in accidents, though last year was an especially bad one. The Sago Mine Disaster further upstate claimed twelve lives all on its own. Down here they do not say 'Goodbye' or 'See you later' when they leave for their various individual work stations, they say to each other 'Work safe' or 'Go safely'. I have been in places before where safety is said to be paramount, but never where it was quite so clearly meant. Bob is very proud that his mine has an unimpeachable record, but he knows that he cannot rely on that. Every day is the first day and every day is dangerous. Aside from the possibility of a structural collapse there is the ever-present danger of explosion, which will in itself trigger a fall. There is high-voltage electricity down here, there are huge hydraulic vehicles, there are the manbus railways and miles and miles and miles of conveyor belt that carry the coal to the surface, there is the mining machinery itself. All of these can generate sparks. An atmosphere impregnated with methane and coal dust, the notorious firedamp that caused so many deaths in British mines, is a permanent potential hazard that has constantly to be monitored.

'. . . most gracious heavenly Father . . . please watch over us, heavenly Father, keep us safe, watch over our children as we're here . . . please bring our service people home cos they need us so dearly. We ask all these things in His holy name. Amen.'

'Amen,' echoes Bob. 'Guys, be safe. Be safe, Franchise.'

'Franchise?'

'Most of the miners got a nickname,' says Bob. 'This here's Trigger, and Franchise . . .'

'Trigger, yes, but *Franchise?*'

'It's too long of a story . . .' says Franchise. 'Work safe.'

When we arrive at the face itself I am astonished to find that the whole mining operation is carried out by one man with a PlayStation-style game controller in his hand.

'This is Brian.'

'I thought you said all miners had nicknames?'

'That's right. His real name is Tim.'

Brian stands just to one side of a colossal snaking, spitting, thrashing, grinding machine, which looks

136

horribly alive, like something out of a dystopian science-fiction movie. It tears with ferocious grinding claws at the face, up and down, up and down, a frenzied systematic gnawing directed by Tim with his joysticks; the water that sprays like saliva from its tubes to calm the dust only reinforces the image of a giant armoured insect drooling as it feasts. The machine feeds by hurling the coal back into itself while a docking procedure at its rear mates it with another long, long hydraulic vehicle which transfers the coal into its own violently shaking, rolling interior and then roars off to the internal belt system half a mile away. In this way coal is being torn from the mountain and conveyed to the surface at all times. Always, twenty-four hours a day, seven days a week.

I gulp in the fresh air with gratitude when at last I can escape to the top without looking like too much of a wimp.

I add miners to the list of people I tremendously admire but would rather die than emulate.

Bob shakes me by the hand.

'Thanks,' I say. 'Hell of a tour.'

'Go safe,' says Bob.

KENTUCKY
KEY FACTS

Abbreviation:
KY

Nickname:
The Bluegrass State

Capital:
Frankfort

Flower:
Goldenrod

Tree:
Tulip poplar

Bird:
Cardinal

Instrument:
Appalachian dulcimer

Motto:
United We Stand, Divided We Fall

Well-known residents and natives: Zachary Taylor (12th President), Abraham Lincoln (16th), Jefferson Davis (President of the Confederacy), Kit Carson, Judge Roy Bean, Robert Penn Warren, Hunter S. Thompson, Larry Flynt, D.W. Griffith, Tod Browning, John Carpenter, Gus van Sant,

Victor Mature, Patricia Neal, Warren Oates,
Ned Beatty, Harry Dean Stanton, George Clooney,
Tom Cruise, Johnny Depp, Rosemary Clooney,
Billy Ray Cyrus, Colonel Harland Sanders
(yes, that Colonel Sanders. Who else?).

KENTUCKY

'To be honest, by the time I've inhaled all those fumes from the vats and tasted the liquor in its various stages of ageing nothing much sinks in.'

The Commonwealth of Kentucky (the last of the four Commonwealths we shall meet on our travels) seems to be bordered by more states than any other. You might say the Kentucky spirit is part Missouri, part Illinois, part Indiana, part Ohio, part West Virginia, part Virginia and part Tennessee. In other words as much Midwest as Southern. Of course the Kentucky spirit is really bourbon whiskey and I am on my way to find some.

Mind you, the state's split personality does seem crucial to understanding Kentucky. You might look at the Civil War as a dispute between the two opposing sides of her identity: Kentucky-born Abraham Lincoln, President of the Union, versus Kentucky-born Jefferson Davis, President of the Confederacy.

When I ask a Kentuckian if Kentucky is the South, they reply, somewhat gnomically, 'Kentucky is a southern state, but we are not in the South.' Hm.

WOODFORD RESERVE

First, I must go to Versailles, which as everyone knows, is just outside Paris. Only this Versailles is pronounced 'Vairsails' and lies about thirty miles west of Paris, KY, the county seat of Bourbon County. Hidden off Route 60, behind white rail fences and tucked low down in a valley beneath the green rolling fields of prime Kentucky horse country I finally discover a charming grey stone building that reminds me instantly of the many Scotch whisky distilleries I have happily visited in the past. This is Woodford Reserve, the place where sour-mash fermentation was invented by one Dr James Crow back in the 1820s.

Chris Morris, the present-day Master Distiller, shows me round. Everything here is done the old-fashioned way—the traditional copper stills were custom-built in Glasgow; the barrels are coopered, charred (for colour and flavour), labelled, filled and bunged by hand. Bourbon differs from Scotch in that it must by law be made mostly from maize—corn as they call it here—with barley, rye and wheat making up the rest if desired. Sour mash refers to a fermentation process in which the pH value of the yeast enzymes is regulated by the addition of acid, as in the making of sourdough bread. Something like that anyway: to be honest, by the time I've inhaled all those fumes from the vats, drilled some weep-holes, sucked in my portion of the angel's share in the cellar

141

and tasted the liquor in its various stages of ageing nothing much sinks in. I look down at the bubbles coming up from the vat.

'That's carbon dioxide,' Chris explains.

'CO_2? Not very environmentally friendly of you.'

Chris laughs moderately.

A cat wanders past.

'Do you think that cat might be alcoholic?' I ask. 'All those fumes.'

'He's an employee, one of our mousers. So he better not be drinking.'

I laugh immoderately. The fumes are definitely getting to me.

'Time,' says Chris, 'to do some tasting.' He makes it sound as if a terrible chore awaits us.

I add branch to my first glass. I have heard this called for in bars up and down America. 'Gimme a bourbon and branch.' Branch actually just means plain water, but it once meant water from a branch, or tributary stream, of a river. A tiny amount just takes the hottest peak of fire from the drink.

While I rapidly neck three glasses of the 1995 Chris talks about the spectrum of flavours: apricot, cinnamon, burnt coffee, vanilla and dusty oak.

'You see raspberry juice is just raspberry juice, but the action of yeast in bourbon creates over 200 separate flavour elements.'

'Nobody really understands me . . .'

'So the number of actual flavour combinations possible is 200 times 199 times 198 and so on. Billions. Many of them beyond human sensory reach of course . . .'

'My mummy understands me. My teddy bears understand me.'

Chris offers me a handkerchief. The uncontrollable

142

sobs turn to uncontrollable giggles and I am led away hiccoughing.

Woodford Reserve is proud to be the 'official bourbon' of the Kentucky Derby, America's most prestigious, glamorous and celebrated horse race. In fact, Lexington, where I am taking my drunken self to bed, is the capital of America's racing industry. In many ways it can be regarded as the racing capital of the world. If my hangover doesn't prevent me, I shall find out more tomorrow.

BRANDING

You have to admire the branding people—you know, those advertising PR professionals who are paid fortunes to come up with slogans and logos for corporations, councils and other institutions. Kentucky is best known for bourbon whiskey and for horses. I think you'll agree with me that for once the design and branding people earned their money. This is what they came up with:

Kentucky: unbridled spirit.

You've got to hand it to them. Genius. Just two words, but they say it all.

PRETTY RUN AND KEENELAND

Nursing a gently nagging head, I head out for Pretty Run, a very well named brood mare farm owned and (prettily) run by Tom van Meter in the heart of Bluegrass Country. I pick that bone with him straight away. The grass is green. Green as anything.

'From a distance in the spring,' says Tom in a heart-melting Kentucky drawl, 'the blue seed heads of the poa grass give a kind of azure tinge to the fields.'

I take his word for it, but cannot help feeling let down. I was so looking forward to seeing genuinely blue grass.

I have noticed the name van Meter just about everywhere in the Lexington area and it turns out he is one of a family that have lived and worked here for eight or nine generations. I watch spirited mares, all of them pregnant, frisking and skittering about the fields, tossing their manes, shivering their flanks and acting as thoroughbreds will—leaping in eye-rolling panic at the sight of just about anything in other words. Especially Stephens. I can spook a dead donkey. I don't know what it is that our four-hoofed friends see in me, but whatever it is they don't like it.

Tom buys mares, pays stud farms to allow him to bring them to be 'covered' by a stallion and then finds himself to be, as nature takes her due course, the proud owner of a brand-new thoroughbred foal, which he will sell as a 'weanling', a foal that has just stopped suckling. Mostly he does this on behalf of owners. The skill is to understand dam's and sire's bloodlines and form, which is to say the pedigrees and racing histories of the parent mare and stallion, well enough to create a foal that will grow into a winning racehorse. Those with a lot of money are prepared to pay huge sums for the most glamorous and dazzling bloodlines.

'They sold a mare at a local sale last week for ten million dollars,' Tom tells me.

'Ten million!'

'The Dubai and the Irish—they pay big money.

144

See, me, I'd take more pride in buying a mare for twenty thousand that gives birth to a foal worth a hundred thousand than I would in buying a mare for one million that mothered a foal worth two. One is a five-fold increase, the other only two-fold. Wanna come and see me try and sell some of my horses?'

The 'local sale' turns out to be Keeneland's November Breeding Stock Sale, the largest thoroughbred horse sale in the world. Tom has a couple of mares selling there today, so we drive over to take a look. British racing has Tattersalls, the elegant sales ring in Newmarket, Suffolk and America has Keeneland, Kentucky, equally elegant but on a much, much grander scale.

I am all for racing. It is pretty. People dress up and enjoy themselves. Yes, there is gambling, but it somehow seems a great deal less squalid than at the Trump Taj Mahal (mind you, everything on the planet is less squalid than the Trump Taj Mahal). Racing is also a sporting passion. The jockeys and horses seem happy enough and money is generated for local and national economies.

However. Wrong of me, no doubt, but none of the bloodstock equine business that takes place today interests me *anything like* as much as the sound the auctioneers make.

I am sure a true scholar of the turf would have found much more to excite his or her curiosity in the sales ring of Keeneland but—call me shallow, call me silly—for me it was all about the hypnotic, thrilling, hilarious, impressive and jaw-droppingly skilful auction chanting.

Impossible to reproduce satisfactorily on the page, American auctioneering is all about 'filler words' as Justin Holmberg, one of the Keeneland auctioneers, was kind enough to tell me. You go to auctioneer school and learn the basic art of spotting bidders and talking lots and so on, but you also learn to develop your own chanting style.

As I understand it, you state the amount that has been bid and the amount you would like to hear bid next and in between those two sums you place your filler words or phrases: 'bid me up', 'will ya give me', 'bid it up now'. Sounds simple enough, but the auctioneer's song never ends. He is talking all the time in a percussively twanging drone that is not unlike that of Native American songs blended with bluegrass banjo plucking.

'Twenty thousand bid-it-up-now thirty, twenty bid-it-up-now thirty, thirty bid-it-up-now forty, forty bid-it-up-now, bid-it-up-now fifty, forty bid-it-up-now fifty, fifty bid-it-up-now sixty' and so on.

I leave Kentucky after meeting a member of the tenth generation of van Meters, Tom's son Griff, a charming rogue of a youth, whose raffish playboy manner revealed hidden depths in his love of Kentucky and his desire to redevelop and invigorate Lexington's dilapidated downtown area. He revealed something else hidden too. A tattoo of Kentucky on his buttock. Statal love can be no greater.

'What is so great about Kentucky though?' I wanted to know.

'She's everything America should be. She's a rural farming paradise, but she has a great city in Louisville. She may be landlocked but there's twelve hundred miles of shoreline on one lake alone. She's mixed in race, but she's tolerant and neighbourly. Neither right wing nor left wing, neither Yankee nor Dixie, neither Midwest nor Eastern. Kentuckians are polite, charming and friendly but without overdoing

146

that Southern graciousness thing. Kentucky. Greatest state in the union.'

All that and unbridled spirit too . . .

TENNESSEE
KEY FACTS

Abbreviation:
TN

Nickname:
The Volunteer State

Capital:
Nashville

Flower:
Iris

Tree:
Tulip-tree

Bird:
Mockingbird

Motto:
Agriculture and Commerce

Well-known residents and natives: Andrew Jackson (7th President), Andrew Johnson (17th), Al Gore, Sam Houston, Davy Crockett, John ('Monkey Trial') Scopes, Sergeant Alvin York, Frances Hodgson Burnett, John Crowe Ranso m, James Agee, Shelby Foote, Alex Haley, Cormac McCarthy, Hermes Pan, Cybill Shepherd, Kathy Bates, Morgan Freeman, Samuel L. Jackson,

Quentin Tarantino, Brad Renfro,
Reese Witherspoon, Oprah Winfrey,
Johnny Knoxville, W.C. Handy, Bessie Smith,
Aretha Franklin, Chet Atkins, Pat Boone,
George Hamilton, Johnny Cash, the Carter Family,
Dolly Parton, Carl Perkins, Elvis Presley,
Tina Turner, Allman Brothers, Isaac Hayes,
Justin Timberlake.

TENNESSEE

'. . . *well it has to be said they really do resemble a most outrageously old-fashioned casting agency's idea of hillbillies.*'

Agriculture and Commerce? That is their motto when they can boast Johnny Cash, Tina Turner, Bessie Smith, W.C. 'the Father of the Blues' Handy, Dolly Parton, Aretha Franklin, Carl Perkins and Elvis Aaron Presley? Well, I dare say the state government up at Nashville know best . . . does seem a little weedy for a motto though.

Memphis is the biggest city in Tennessee and is of course home to Graceland, one of America's most popular tourist attractions, indeed after the White House the second most visited residence in America. The capital Nashville, with its legendary music hall the Grand Ole Opry, styles itself the Home of Country Music, but I am headed to the mountains of Tennessee to fulfil a lifelong ambition and hear another kind of

American music. I want to hear the Appalachian mountain men play.

BLUEGRASS!

My passion for bluegrass, a loose but good enough name for the style of music I am in pursuit of, began when I fell in love with Lester Flatt's and Earl Scruggs's theme tune for the American sixties sitcom *The Beverly Hillbillies*. I only dimly remember that show as a child but years later I bought an album featuring Flatt and Scruggs who had gone on to form the Foggy Mountain Boys. On that album, ace banjo-picker Scruggs performed his immortal 'Foggy Mountain Breakdown' and I was hooked for life. Some time after that I went to the cinema and saw John Boorman's *Deliverance*, one of four or five films that completely changed the way I looked at everything—at cinema, people, myself, the world. It has a great moment (no, not the 'I'm gonna make you squeal like a pig' scene—another) known as The Duelling Banjos, in which Ronny Cox (playing a guitar, as it happens) faces off against a local, rather inbred-looking youth who turns out to play the meanest, fastest banjo in the South.

I know that country men and women, real musical bluegrass players and dancers, live in the hills above Townsend, Tennessee and I have been told that some of them meet once a week in an abandoned schoolhouse they have taken over as a venue for their music-making. They don't perform to a ticket-buying crowd, just for their own pleasure, but visitors are welcome.

I arrive at the Rocky Branch Club at nine in the

evening and the place is kicking. What was once a school corridor lined with lockers and maps of 'Our State' is now filled with people who . . . well it has to be said they really do resemble a most outrageously old-fashioned casting agency's idea of hillbillies. There are men with long beards that you feel must be called Zekc (the men that is, not the beards) who dance in clogs or with heavy taps on their shoes. Swaying to the music in patched dungarees there are youths with long necks, enormous Adam's apples and splayed-out teeth and I see women with no teeth at all who look as if they had seven children before they were twenty.

From each room off the corridor, each quondam classroom, there issues a sound. And what a sound.

For an hour and a half I wander from room to room dizzy with delight. This is what I had come for, authentic hillbilly music and dancing, performed simply for the pleasure of it.

This music is made by stringed instruments only. It derives, and my word you can hear it in the five-note plaintiveness of the melodies, from Celtic folk music, the jigs and reels of Scotland and Ireland. Guitar, bass, mandolin, fiddle and banjo—there you have your basic bluegrass combo. All the percussion comes from hard-driving strums, plucks, picks, slaps and scrapes.

I find a boy called Jack whom I'd spotted hammering brilliantly at the piano on his own. Now he's playing the guitar. I marvel at the outrageous virtuosity and arrogant strut with which he plays. The moment he stops he becomes a model of southern politeness and downhome humility.

'How many instruments do you play?'

'I play the guitar, sir. I play the banjo. I play the

mandolin. I play the piano. Just not the fiddle, sir. I don't like the fiddle. Help yourself, sir.'

The 'help yourself' refers to a pot of something moist, black and rank which he has pushed under my nose.

'What the . . .?'

'That's tobaccy, sir. Don't you like it?'

'I gave up smoking, I'm afraid.'

'That ain't smoking tobaccy, sir, that's for chewing.' He pinches out a fat wad which he plugs into his cheek.

'How old are you Jack?'

'Seventeen years old, sir.'

'And how long have you been chewing tobacco?'

'Well, sir . . .' he lets a long line of drool fall into a tin, pinching off the string with a 'pwop'. 'Ever since I was four years old. My grandma taught me how.'

The crew tells me later that he was winding me up, but I'm not so sure.

In another room I find Jay, a great banjo-picker who despite looking a little less . . . well, a little less . . . *rural* than the bat-eared, crew-cut Jack, is actually a warden in the Great Smoky Mountains National Park. With him is Stephen, a fiddler who plays with a group that includes a garage mechanic and a retired professor from the University of Tennessee in Knoxville.

'I play three-finger,' says Jay. 'I can't do clawhammer.'

'Never mind,' I say, having no idea what he is talking about.

'How about we play Foggy Mountain Breakdown?'

And they do. They play without pretension or theory or any self-conscious sense of heritage, they play because they belong to the music that has grown

153

from these woods and hills and they play, like dogs who are orally intimate with their own parts, because they can.

DUCKS!

I want to go further into the woods, through the Smoky Mountains and into North Carolina which lies on the other side. But first I make a detour to Memphis. I am drawn by the lure of ducks.

No establishment in all the South is more proud of its traditions of graceful hospitality and Old World courtesy than the Peabody Hotel in Memphis, whose lobby is said to be where the Delta ends (or begins, depending on which way you are travelling).

A handful of fine ducks live on the hotel roof. Every morning they are escorted by the Duck Master (a permanent Peabody staff appointment), to the elevator. A crowd will have gathered downstairs ready for them. At exactly 11.00 a.m., as the opening bars of John Philip Sousa's 'King Cotton' roll majestically from the hotel's PA system, the elevator doors open and the ducks waddle grandly along the red carpet to the lobby's marble fountain where they will remain romping until 5.00 p.m. when a similar ceremony in reverse sees them march out to the elevator to be taken back up to their rooftop roost.

I am given the supreme honour of being officially appointed an Assistant Duck Master for today's ceremony. A certificate and silver-topped (in the shape of a duck, naturally) cane are handed to me as proof of this distinction. I join Oprah Winfrey, Kevin Bacon, Queen Noor of Jordan and a few distinguished others in being so honoured. My duties involve helping the Duck Master chivvy the ducks out of their penthouse and along the roof space towards the elevator. Fortunately there is someone else to wipe up the duck poo left in the corner of the lift.

Duck poo, unpleasant as it is, has great appeal when compared with what awaits me further north in the city of Knoxville.

CADAVERS!

Knoxville, after Memphis and Nashville the third biggest city in the state, is home to the University of Tennessee. There is an academic there that I am anxious not to meet. I am sure she is very nice but I am having second thoughts about witnessing her work.

I arrive at the campus and drive, as instructed, to a deserted parking lot. I see a grey Honda Civic in one corner. I park my taxi alongside it. A woman gets out of the Civic and comes forward to shake my hand. She leads me to a pair of razor-wired, chain-linked, padlocked gates that stand at the edge of the lot. The gates forbid entry but give no clue as to what might lie within. There is only one sign and it says 'Private'. Rebecca takes out a set of keys, opens the gates and leads me to a garden.

While Rebecca locks the gates behind her I look around, not letting my eyes settle for too long on any one feature.

I am standing in a garden. There are trees, a small hut, flowerbeds, vegetable patches and a path that leads up a hill to a copse or spinney.

'Here,' Rebecca hands me latex gloves for my hands and for my feet covers made of thick woven

155

paper. As I put them on I become aware of something unspeakable weaving its way into my body through my nose. It is a minute trace of something so evil that even a tiny quantity like this fills me with dread.

'This way,' says Rebecca.

I step forward for my tour of the Body Farm.

In 1971 Dr William M. Bass of the University of Tennessee Department of Forensic Anthropology thought that what his department needed was a way of finding out more definitively how human bodies decomposed and so he founded this facility. Donated corpses of all kinds are brought here to decompose and to have that decomposition monitored and calibrated.

Rebecca strides up to a black plastic sheet under a tree and pulls it back. 'You see the larvae and flies here?' she says enthusiastically.

'Dear God! Oh my . . . but they're . . . that's . . .' I try and stay 'professional', whatever that means when you find yourself face to rotted face with human remains that writhe, seethe and hum with tens of thousands of flying insects, bugs and maggots.

'You can pinpoint time of death with astonishing accuracy using insects,' coos Rebecca, gazing down with affection. 'Different species of fly and bug lay eggs and hatch in human cadavers at different times. You can be accurate almost to the hour.'

'Like on that TV programme *CSI?*'

'Quite. But there are other variables that police and forensic labs need. What happens when a body is left in a trashcan for instance? Come along!' Rebecca escorts me to another corner of the garden and lifts the lid off a dustbin. 'In a sealed space like this what you get is . . .'

I look down into a brown pool of sludge with a few bones sticking out.

'Liquefaction.'

Just behind the awful sight comes the awful smell in full force. It literally makes me jump backwards.

I have, in all my fifty years on this planet, never seen a dead body before. Within the space of five minutes Rebecca has shown me more than twenty, some in such appalling states of suppurating decomposition that it is all I can do not to vomit now at the memory. But it is that smell, that wrenching, clenching, suffocating stench that will never, never leave. Once inhaled never forgotten.

'There's so much we have to know,' says Rebecca. 'What happens to a corpse in cool climates in a car trunk? Or hot climates? Under a table in a house? Under this kind of soil or that kind of soil? What happens when it is burned? Or dunked in acid? We find out.'

'How do you . . . what makes someone decide to do a job like . . .?'

'Well, you mentioned the *CSI* shows? We get thousands more applicants a year on account of *CSI*. Most of them skedaddle once they discover that the work's not quite the same as on TV. But those who stay love it. We hear from the police of a murderer who's caught because of our evidence and our data. That's a moment. A real moment. And we care for these remains. I will certainly leave my body to this facility.'

'You will?'

'Oh yes. Now this cadaver is interesting. She died in a car wreck. Note the smashed right cheekbone . . .'

For all my age and experience, there had still been some sweet, small, shy flower of innocence inside me when I arrived at the Body Farm. By the time I leave it has gone forever.

I am more than ready to head for the clean air of the North Carolina mountains.

NORTH CAROLINA
KEY FACTS

Abbreviation:
NC

Nickname:
The Old North State

Capital:
Raleigh

Flower:
Dogwood

Tree:
Longleaf pine

Bird:
Cardinal

Folk Dance:
Clogging

Motto:
Esse quam videri ('To be rather than to seem')

Well-known residents and natives: James K. Polk (11th President), Edward 'Blackbeard' Teach, George Vanderbilt, Billy Graham, O. Henry, Thomas Wolfe, Edward R. Murrow, Tom Robbins, Maya Angelou, Charles Frazier, Ava Gardner, Andy Griffith, Jennifer Ehle, Michael C. Hall,

John Coltrane, Thelonius Monk, Earl Scruggs,
Ben. E. King, Nina Simone, Roberta Flack,
Loudon Wainwright III, James Taylor, Randi Travis,
Tori Amos.

NORTH CAROLINA

'Can one really just stand in a basket and be safely blown about by the wind? There is no way this will not lead to disaster.'

One of the original thirteen British colonies in North America, North Carolina's capital city Raleigh is named after Sir Walter, who famously (in popular legend and comedy at least) introduced potatoes and tobacco to the Old Country. The very first English child to be born on American land, Virginia Dare, drew her first breath a year before the Spanish Armada on what is now North Carolinian soil. The area where she was born is still called Dare County in her honour. Near to her birthplace is a town called Kitty Hawk which became very famous 316 years after her birth, when Wilbur and Orville Wright succeeded, one winter's afternoon in 1903, in making the world's first controlled, powered flight in a heavier-than-air machine. Well not the first, as it happens, but the one that everyone celebrates.

Heavier-than-air machines are all very well, but I am enthralled by the idea of lighter than air travel. I have never been up in a balloon, but just outside Asheville, NC there is a man prepared to take me up to look down on some of the astounding beauty of this part of the world.

Asheville, I am pleased to say, is one of the most agreeable towns I have yet visited.

America, as has been widely reported, is in danger of turning the parts of itself that aren't protected as wilderness or park into strip-mall hell. Hundreds and hundreds, probably thousands of miles of Comfort Inn, Days Inn, Holiday Inn, Red Lobster, Olive Garden, Denny's, KFC, Arby's, McDonald's, Burger King, Starbucks, Foot Locker, Ross ('Dress For Less'), CVC and Walgreen Pharmacies, Home Depot, Staples, Best Buy, Target, Kmart, Wal-Mart, et cetera, et cetera. All strung along the highways, all only accessible by car, all unattractive, all resolutely and horribly the same. The town centres from which these strips radiate are often dead by seven in the evening or have degenerated into ghettos of the poor, the drug-dependent and the gang-affiliated.

Asheville is different, Asheville is very much a 'why can't all towns in America be like this?' kind of a place. George Vanderbilt chose Asheville to be the seat of his enormous Biltmore mansion, the largest private house in the Western Hemisphere, which attracts an average of nearly three thousand visitors a day. Aside from the Biltmore Estate though, Asheville is a city of variety, style, vibrancy, Bohemian charm and architectural (especially art deco) beauty. I walked for miles along its streets without once seeing a Starbucks or a fast-food franchise. Asheville is said

162

to be the vegetarian capital of America, the Happiest City in America for Women—it has gathered all kinds of soubriquets and top ten listings. It has a University of North Carolina campus and other institutions of higher learning, but its charming, free and infectious liveliness cannot fully be explained by it being a college town: there are plenty of cities in America with far more campuses that have nothing like the appeal of Asheville. The New Age features that have accreted to the town in recent years I can leave alone, but batty as they may be, they are peaceful and unthreatening (except to the intellect and will of course) and perhaps contribute to the unspoiled qualities of this wonderful place.

I have arrived in North Carolina by climbing the mountain road out of Tennessee and heading for the top of the Great Smoky Mountain National Park, where the line between the two states overlooks a view of staggering drama. From the top of the Great Smokies one can look all the way across to another famous range further east, the Blue Ridge Mountains, both ranges still being part of the Appalachians.

The stunning highway down from the mountains to Asheville is called the Blue Ridge Parkway and I drive through Cherokee country to get there. The Cherokee are regarded by many as the most prosperous of the Native American peoples, the tribe that seems most successfully to have adapted to the conditions enforced upon them since the arrival of Europeans all those years ago. Its chiefs have been heads of petroleum companies and have chosen a path of greater integration than other Indian nations. Nonetheless the reservation I drive through, including the town of Cherokee itself, is not embarrassed to sell any number of 'heap big wampum' style artefacts.

163

BALLOONING

I meet Rick the balloonist in Candler, a town not far from Asheville. The weather, he tells me, favours our ascent. Two large fans direct the warm air into the envelope until it is as large as a party marquee. I walk around inside, growing in nervousness. I never had the best head for heights. Can one really just stand in a basket and be safely blown about by the wind? There is no way this will not lead to disaster. The whole science of balloon ascension suddenly appears to me to be radically flawed. Somehow I have been helped into the gondola before I can tell Rick this terrible news.

Between the fierce roaring bursts of burning, there is complete silence. We rise a mile without seeming to do anything. For the first half-mile I am terrified, vertigo turns my knees to jelly and I want to squat down in the basket. But, as in the West Virginia coalmine, I am too cowardly to admit my cowardice.

Around us there are mountain ranges and valleys of a beauty so intense and in a light so perfect that it almost makes me sad. I am overcome by a kind of astonished ache for the nobility, grandeur and scale of it all. The 'smoke' of the Smoky Mountains and the 'Blue' of the Blue Ridge are something to do with atmosphere and plant material. It is not cloud or fog per se, but a kind of hazy blue vapour that clothes these hills. Given that there has to be such a phenomenon, why should it also be so beautiful as to tear at your heart?

We descend over a wood and move along at tree height. I pluck a maple leaf from the topmost branches.

Rick is actually a futures trader. He can do all that

at home on the internet in the North Carolina countryside. In his spare time he can look down on the state that gave aviation to the world and smile with satisfaction at how much lovelier mankind's first form of flight continues to be. For all that I am glad when we set down in the driveway of someone's house. Terra firma beats terror every time.

SOUTH CAROLINA
KEY FACTS

Abbreviation:
SC

Nickname:
The Palmetto State

Capital:
Columbia

Flower:
Yellow jessamine

Tree:
Cabbage Palmetto

Bird:
Carolina Wren

Dance:
Shag

Motto:
Dum spiro spero ('While I breathe I hope')
& *Animis opibusque parati*
('Ready in soul and in works')

Well-known residents and natives: Jesse Jackson,
Jasper Johns, William Gibson,
Dizzie Gillespie, Chubby Checker, Eartha Kitt,
James Brown, Shoeless Joe Jackson, Joe Frazier,
Andie Macdowell, Mary-Louise Parker,
Chris Rock, Stephen Colbert.

SOUTH CAROLINA

'And finally I arrive at that coastline. Nothing has prepared me for the rapturous loveliness of Beaufort and the Low Country.'

And now, for the first time, I really feel I am in the South. In West Virginia, Tennessee, Kentucky and North Carolina the accents told clearly enough which side of the Mason–Dixon line I was on, but it was still a landscape dominated by the Appalachians and their daughter ranges. South Carolina is a whole other world, or a whole nother world as they would say.

The national tree is the Cabbage, or Sabal, palmetto: there are plenty on view as I travel along the highway through Low Country South Carolina, past Hilton Head and towards Beaufort (pronounced 'Bewfort', much as our Beaulieu is pronounced 'Bewley'). It is an attractive palm, native all the way from North Carolina down to the southernmost tip of the United States at the

Florida Keys. There is Virginia pine to be seen too, usually given the more undignified name of 'scrub pine'. I mention the trees because, the greater part of my time being given over to driving, they are the most noticeable feature of the roadside landscape. The bright autumnal leaves of New England were dazzling and absolutely particular, their interplay with the sun as I drove kept the long journeys interesting while I was in the North, and now the different varieties of tree down here tell me a story of the South. The palms hint at something tropical while the oaks and cypresses especially share an extraordinary Southern quality. They are all festooned with Spanish moss. This flowering plant, not actually a moss at all, drapes itself like some strange decoration over the branches of the trees, especially the great oaks. Thick beards of it hang everywhere. It lends a faintly spooky air to the landscape that combines with the sultriness and humidity of the atmosphere to give the South its characteristic air of languor and Gothic mystery.

Something else is different too: the architecture. I am not talking about great plantation houses—I have not seen any of those yet—I mean just the ordinary houses. And the shops too. They are so unusually low and squat and new and metallic and . . . then I understand. Here, close to the Atlantic shore in South Carolina we are in the heart of hurricane country. In 1989 Hugo caused billions of dollars' worth of damage and many lives were lost. Buildings have to take account of the great tropical cyclones that are generated out in the South Atlantic and scream their way towards the coastline. The lower the profile they present to the storms the better.

And finally I arrive at that coastline. Nothing has prepared me for the rapturous loveliness of Beaufort and the Low Country. Everywhere there are bodies of water and islands connected by bridges and causeways, Lemon Island, Bluff Island, Goat Island, Horse Island, Otter Island, and the very piratical Morgan Island and Port Royal.

It seems like a kind of paradise. An unspoiled historic old town set in enchanted waterways.

It is unlikely, for all its beauty, to have created that impression in the captured Africans who arrived here as slaves.

It is impossible to be in the South and not think of slavery. That is not to say the South can never 'rise again' freed of its own historic shackles, but the completeness of the slave economy and the ensuing trauma of the Civil War and its aftermath have left an indelible imprint.

THE GULLAH

I have my first meeting with Miss Anita under oaks heavy with Spanish moss. I join her on a bench and we look across the water, over the islands and towards the far Atlantic horizon. Thousands of miles ahead lie Cape Verde and Hurricane Alley where the storms are born and beyond which the Slave Coast stretches down from Nigeria to Angola.

'Now I hear you're something of a film star, Miss Anita?'

'Who told you that? Shame the devil.'

'That's what they're telling me.'

'I was in that movie *Forrest Gump*, which maybe you saw . . . we was in the choir. They shot it just over there. And *GI Jane* they shot on that island. And *The Jungle Book*.'

169

'*The Jungle Book?* But that's a cartoon, surely?'

My hand is slapped. 'Not that *Jungle Book*, th'other one.'

Miss Anita is a leading representative and historian of the Gullah people. In my shameful ignorance I knew nothing of who they were until I met her.

'We think the word comes from Gola, which also gave its name to the country of Angola. The Gullah people, we're African-Americans, but we kep' our own language and our own ways.'

'And what is that language?'

'It's what they call a Creole. African, Native American and English, all mixed up like a good salad.'

The Gullah are mostly to be found in the Low Country of South Carolina and the Sea Islands of Georgia. Anita explains the reasons for this.

'We the descendants of slaves who were set to work on the only crop that could make it here, where the land is all . . . what's the word?'

'Waterlogged?'

'That'll do. Waterlogged. The slaves brought with them—all the slave ships did—the mosquito. Now in the other parts, in the land where cotton grows, Mr Mosquito he couldn't survive, but down here in the Low Country, he loved all them marshes. And Mr Mosquito he flourish and the malaria was bad. The Africans had the resistance and fore you knew it South Carolina had a larger black population than white!' Miss Anita chuckles at this curlicue of history. 'They have a word in the cotton fields—"de-Africanise". The cotton slaves were de-Africanised good, but here in the rice paddies things it was different. Not so many whites around so the slaves weren't never so integrated into the white world.'

'So that's how your African language and music lasted longer here?'

'That's how it was.'

'But you were Christianised.'

'Praise the Lord, that we were.'

Whatever one may think of that, and whatever the oddities of celebrating the enforced religion of their slavemasters, one cannot deny that the Christianisation of the slaves gave birth to that wonder of world music, the spiritual.

'"Michael Row The Boat Ashore". You know that song?'

'Of course.'

'That was born right here. Right here in Beaufort.'

We sit and watch the sun set over the islands. I part, promising to return later in the evening to watch the rehearsal of a show she has devised.

THE SHOW

The rehearsal takes place in what we would call a village hall, the cast consisting of fifteen or so of Miss Anita's friends and family ranging from toddlers to silver-haired old ladies and gentlemen. I am prepared to be horribly embarrassed by an excruciating display of amateur dramatics.

The moment the company open their mouths to sing I find myself transported. I am listening to what used to be called in my schooldays 'negro spirituals' sung in the place where they were created by the descendants of those who created them. And sung in *that* language. This is what astonishes me. I have assumed for years now that the kind of slave talk that pronounces 'river' as 'ribber' is unacceptable Uncle

171

Remus minstrel-speak and cannot be countenanced. Here the Gullah embrace it.

The pageant Miss Anita has devised tells the story of a group of slaves who escape one Christmas on the 'underground railway', the organisation established by freed slaves and white abolitionists that sprang slaves from captivity and transported them secretly via a network of sympathisers to the North. Her dialogue is full of references to 'the Masser' and 'white folks' and the 'birthin' of babies', the sort of Mammy-talk which is straight out of Butterfly McQueen's famous lines in *Gone with the Wind* and which I had thought so politically incorrect as to be virtually illegal. It is rather liberating to know that this language has been reclaimed by its originators and to hear it spoken with such gusto and relish. The aura of taboo is lifted and one is allowed to recognise once more what a wonderful and rich kind of English it is.

Every now and again another song is sung. 'Amazing Grace', 'Nobody Knows the Trouble I See', 'Swing Low'. I am entirely captivated.

As with the bluegrass in Tennessee I am reminded once more of the extraordinary power that comes from music that is played in the place where it was born.

I decide that I like the South. Which is just as well, for there is a lot more of it to come . . .

GEORGIA
KEY FACTS

Abbreviation:
GA

Nickname:
The Peach State

Capital:
Atlanta

Flower:
Cherokee rose

Tree:
Live oak

Bird:
Brown thrasher (hurray, not a Cardinal again)

Motto:
Wisdom, Justice and Moderation

Well-known residents and natives: Jimmy Carter
(39th President), Martin Luther King Jr.,
Newt Gingrich, Joe Kennedy, Doc Holiday,
Joel Chandler Harris, Margaret Mitchell,
Carson McCullers, Alice Walker, Bill Hicks,
Oliver Hardy, DeForest Kelly, Charles Coburn,
Kim Basinger, Holly Hunter, Julia Roberts,
Laurence Fishburn, Spike Lee, Steven Soderbergh,
Dakota Fanning, Jessye Norman, Johnny Mercer,

Little Richard, Ray Charles, Otis Redding,
Gladys Knight, Michael Stipe, The B52s,
Kanye West, Bobby Jones, Sugar Ray Robinson,
Hulk Hogan.

GEORGIA

'I am a guest of a remarkable lady called Mrs Nancy Schmoe. Her family, including her sister, Aunt Snead, have gathered for Thanksgiving.'

I leave Beaufort, South Carolina and head towards the southern state line. The Savannah River forms the boundary with Georgia and gives its name to an extraordinary town.

Savannah, GA is perhaps the most perfectly preserved of all the Southern cities, certainly the most glamorous and upscale. Famed for its twenty-four residential squares, its grand antebellum townhouses, lush gardens, eccentric charm and bohemian atmosphere, the 'Hostess City of the South' leapt to popular consciousness in 1994 with the publication of John Berendt's *Midnight in the Garden of Good and Evil*, a book that went straight to the top of the *New York Times* bestseller list and stayed there for most of the year. It charted real-life steamy and deadly goings-on amongst Savannah's social elite; there was a hustler, an antiques dealer, a drag queen called the Lady Chablis and a cast of sundry other wild and exotic blooms. A few years later the book was made into a film with Kevin Spacey playing the antiques dealer and featuring Jude Law as the gay lover he apparently murders. Jim Williams, the real-life counterpart of the character Spacey played, was cleared, after an unprecedented four trials, of all murder charges but died just months after this final exoneration.

HISTORIC SAVANNAH

Jim Williams was important for reasons aside from the scandal that led to the book and film that led in turn to the great boom in Savannah's tourist industry that goes on to this day. He was more than an antique dealer, he was one of the first to embark on the project of saving, renovating and restoring the great old houses and squares of Savannah, for bringing the town to its current pitch of splendour and charm.

In all of Savannah today I do not suppose there is anyone who knows more about the houses of the historic district than Celia Dunn, the town's best-known realtor, or 'estate agent' as we would say in British English. I spend a delightful three hours in her company, unlocking the doors of grand houses for which she has the key and finding myself in closed worlds of tasteful grandeur and graceful splendour that are almost too perfect to be bearable.

Everywhere we go Celia is stopped and greeted. She is as well known a landmark in Savannah as Monterey Square and quite as grand. As we leave our last historic house, someone calls out from the street, 'Happy holiday, Celia!' and I am reminded with a shock of where we are in the calendar. Today is the third Wednesday in November, which can only mean that tomorrow is Thanksgiving Day. I have a two hundred-mile drive ahead of me, in holiday traffic too. Better hustle, Stephen.

THANKSGIVING AT BLACKWATER

I drive past the cotton fields, becoming more and more astonished by them until I just have to stop and look closer. What an insane plant. It really is just an ordinary, woody weed with no distinguishing characteristics except that it has cotton wool pads on top of it. It is not as if there are other plants that are slightly like it, or whose development tends towards suggesting that one day a cotton plant might exist. It just seems to have arrived full-born in the world with this ridiculous gift. Without it, what on earth would I be wearing? Without it, would there be such an impressive driveway as now I point the taxi down? Without it, would there be a true South?

I am a guest of a remarkable lady called Mrs Nancy Schmoe who, at the age of ninety-one, runs the Blackwater plantation house and estate in Quitman, southern Georgia, very close to the Florida border.

Her family have gathered around her for Thanksgiving. Included are her three daughters, two of her grandchildren and her older sister, ninety-eight-year-old Aunt Snead, who runs her own estate further south. As you would hope from their names, these are remarkable and captivating women.

In the kitchen of the big house I find a group of

177

three sisters, African-American, who are cooking up the great Thanksgiving Feast. It is hard not to feel slightly embarrassed talking to these loyal black servants. They have grown up and lived here all their lives, they helped bring Mrs Schmoe's children into the world and their language and loyalties seem to belong to another world. From what I can observe, unacceptably sentimental or patronising as it may appear, these women are very happy and would not want to be anywhere else. They are getting towards pensionable age but the family will not get rid of them. All very patriarchal and disgraceful no doubt, but it puts me in mind of an occasion in New York many years ago. I was having dinner with a pair of well-known novelists, one of whom was married at the time to a Southern girl who began to get rather angry at the occasional glancing references to the red-necked, right-wing South being made by the white New York literati around the table.

'Damn you!' she shouted suddenly. 'You all go on about the South and how racist we are, but how many of you have got any black friends? There are black folks in Tennessee into whose arms I run whenever I go back and we hug and kiss each other and cry for joy. We grew up together and we love each other. None of you even knows a single black person!' At which she rose and left the table, choking back tears.

The relationship began with the enforced slavery which everyone can surely agree was a wicked and monstrous institution. Today, however, there is economic segregation instead for most African-Americans, offset by a rising black middle class in areas like Atlanta and 'the New South' as they call it but, even now a few pockets exist, as here, of a strange co-dependent relationship which may look patriarchal and patronising to our eyes, but which is a real relationship nonetheless and surely beats the hell out of life in a drug-infested ghetto.

Well, I am not here to judge or to presume to understand. I am here to eat. But first, horrible to relate, the subject of riding is brought up.

A TENNESSEE BOLTING HORSE

Outside the Spanish moss profusely drips, as it should, from the live oaks and distant cypresses; all is as it ought to be at a plantation house in the Deep South. Except that I am expected to get on a horse.

Blackwater has a celebrated (apparently) stable of Tennessee Walking Horses, a breed of animal unfamiliar to me.

'Oh they are so gentle and docile and sweet!' 'Docile' rhymes with 'fossil' in American, which makes it sound even gentler. 'You will adore them!'

'Yes, but they won't adore me,' I whine.

'Nonsense! They are the kindest, calmest horses in the whole wide world. You'll see.'

We go round to the stables where a large horse called Shadow is being saddled for me.

'Look,' I try to explain, 'for some reason horses really, really don't like me. No matter how calm and friendly I am they . . .'

'Nonsense!' they giggle.

I step up from a block and just manage to get my feet in the stirrups before the sweetest, gentlest, most dossil horse in the whole wide world screams, bucks and bolts. The family are all so astonished it takes them some little while to realise what has happened. A 'some little while' that is filled by me shouting

179

'Whoa!' and pulling as hard on the reins as I dare as below me a ton of mad jumping flesh gathers its hindquarters and prepares to charge a wooden fence. A last desperate yank on the lines and the crazed beast slows down enough to give the others time to catch up and grab it.

Naturally everybody thinks this is hilarious.

'Well, he's never done that before . . .'

'I declare!'

'Who'd a thunk it?'

'I should have made it clearer,' I say. 'Every time I have ever got on a horse it has ended with the remark you have just made: "He's never done that before!" "But Snowflake is usually so calm . . ." I have heard that and remarks like it twenty times at least. There's something about me and horses. Well. Make the most of the comedy, because that is the last time I shall ever, ever be seen on the back of a horse for the rest of my natural life.'

I dismount with as much dignity as I can from my last-ever horse.

On the way back to the big house I stop off at the old kitchens, a separate dwelling now. Some family members have boiled up peanut oil in two enormous vats. I help them drop a large turkey in each one. Southern fried turkey. It is going to be an interesting Thanksgiving.

Before eating we gather on the porch where prayers are said and 'America the Beautiful' is sung. The Schmoes are a very musical family and once again my eyes are pricked by the words and music of an alien anthem.

The fried turkey is more delicious than I ever believed turkey could be. The whole dinner is wonderful. Actually it is lunch, but as with Christmas in Britain, custom allows one to call it dinner. Collard greens, sweet potatoes with marshmallows melted inside and black-eyed peas give it a Southern, soul-food quality, but the New England cranberry and the delectable pumpkin pie keep the whole meal firmly within a traditional framework that has been repeated up and down America for over two hundred years. It is to America what Passover is to the Jews. An annual ritual that retells the (largely fanciful and untrue) story of a people and their tribulations and in so doing reinforces identity and national belonging.

A fine Thanksgiving tradition is for everyone around the table to say what it is in life they have to give thanks for. When it comes to my turn I have no difficulty in being thankful for Southern hospitality, for astoundingly good food and for the privilege of being invited into the home of strangers and asked to join them in celebrating America's unique festival.

I do not add, for no one need know, that I am also profoundly thankful that my trousers have an elasticated waistband.

ALABAMA
KEY FACTS

Abbreviation:
AL

Nickname:
The Yellowhammer State, The Heart of Dixie

Capital:
Montgomery

Flower:
Camellia

Tree:
Longleaf pine

Bird:
Yellowhammer

Amphibian:
Red Hills salamander

Motto:
Audemus jura nostra defendere
('We dare to defend our rights')

Well-known residents and natives: Rosa Parks,
Condoleezza Rice, Zelda Fitzgerald, Helen Keller,
Truman Capote, Harper Lee, Walker Percy,
Jimmy 'Wikipedia' Wales, Tallulah Bankhead,
Dean Jones, John Badham, Fred Thompson,

Courteney Cox, Hank Williams, Emmylou Harris,
Tammy Wynette, Lionel Hampton, Nat King Cole,
Wilson Pickett, Lionel Richie, Bobby Goldsboro,
Dinah Washington, Jimmy Buffet, Percy Sledge,
Jesse Owens, Joe Louis, Willie Mays, Carl Lewis.

ALABAMA

'There is no "You're welcome" quite so believable as the one you get from the South.'

Alabama will probably take many, many decades to recover from the sorry reputation it earned for itself during the 1960s. Images linger of buzz-cut racists in short-sleeved white shirts screaming hatred at black children on their way into school, shouting That Word in the streets and defying the Federal government's attempts to abolish the segregation that had stained the South since the Civil War.

I have come to witness another kind of civil war.

THE IRON BOWL

If I were asked to find one example of cultural life in the United States to use as proof of how different America is from Europe, I would choose college football. Until one can unravel all the signs and meanings, tribal codes and weird social nuances behind this powerful and bewildering phenomenon I do not believe one can come close to approaching an understanding and penetration of American life. But aside from what it means, there is the simple question of scale.

Imagine Leeds University paying two million pounds a year to a manager for coaching their student soccer team. Imagine Leeds University having a stadium big enough to seat ninety thousand. Imagine Leeds University's annual match against Sheffield University drawing not just a full attendance to their ground (all their games would do that) but also hundreds and hundreds of thousands of others who would drive to the campus on the night of the match, park there and set up satellite equipment and barbecues and chairs and tents. Imagine that just about everyone in Yorkshire, for the weeks leading up the match, talked of virtually nothing else. Imagine people being unreservedly and proudly passionate in their support for Leeds or for Sheffield, despite never having gone to either university or even knowing anyone who has. It seems impossible to picture such an odd state of affairs. I suppose the closest one might have got to it in Britain would have been the Oxford and Cambridge Boat Race some time in the 1920s. In the US that is how college football is: the American variety of course, not soccer. It is not quite as mad as it sounds. There are many states where no major National Football League professional team plays. College Football is all they have and it has become, over the last century, their chief outlet for sporting loyalty and passion.

Of all the great local rivalries in America none is

fiercer or more celebrated than that between the University of Auburn (the Tigers) and the University of Alabama (the Crimson Tide). The event, which always takes place late in November, is known as the Iron Bowl and is taken very, very seriously all over the state of Alabama.

The venue alternates between the two universities: this year it is to be held in Auburn, a town some fifty miles east of the capital, Montgomery.

Six hours before the game is due to begin it takes me the best part of an hour to drive the taxi through the dense traffic in the outer parts of the campus. On either side, every spare piece of land is already occupied with trailers, pick-up trucks and cars. But this is not the car park; this is where the 'tailgaters' come to watch the match, over a mile from the stadium. It is like some vast refugee camp. A refugee camp where everyone has beer, food, television, electric light, a sound system, barbecue sauce and more beer. Down both sides of the road thousands march, chanting, cheering and waving scarves, as at Wembley. But this event is bigger than the FA Cup Final. It sounds absurd to make such a claim, but in terms of logistics, attendance, police presence and sheer hoopla it really is bigger than Britain's biggest sporting fixture. And it is between two teams of student amateurs.

We are allowed on the pitch to film the pre-game build up. Americana writ large: marching bands with those strange toy-soldier hats, cheerleaders with pompoms and hoops. As the atmosphere becomes more and more heated a man appears on the podium and leads the crowd through the chants. The University of Alabama 'Bama' fans shout 'Roll, Tide', the Auburn supporters scream 'Go Eagles!'

186

Despite being officially Tigers, Auburn are also War Eagles it seems: they have the home advantage of course and outnumber the Crimson Tide by at least ten to one.

I am recognised from film and TV roles by a group of sailors in the front row and by a dense orange bank of Auburn students. Before very long I have had my hand painted in their colours. When I walk over to the other side, where the Crimson Tide are seated, I keep that hand firmly in my pocket.

An eagle is released over the ground and circles the gridiron imperiously before returning to the arm of its trainer. An eagle. I wonder if they release anything for the Manchester and Salford University match. A ferret perhaps.

The band strikes up the American national anthem. Everyone joins in with great passion and (literal) hand-on-heart sincerity. The last line swells . . .

'The land of the free and the home of the brave.'

The 'v' of 'brave' is not off our lips when the entire fabric of our world is ripped open by three F18 fighters screaming low over our heads. The part of me that is a film and TV professional is simply flabbergasted by the accuracy of the cueing. They can't have been nearby *hovering*. How on earth did they time it so perfectly?

The teams emerge from the tunnel. At least sixty young men experience the greatest moment in their young lives. Only a very few will go on to make it in the NFL as pro footballers. This is *it* for them. The rest of their days will fizzle out into bitterness, failure and flabby alcoholism. Well, that is the film and novel cliché at least, which has always been cruel when it comes to the projected destiny of the college sporting hero. We hope for better.

187

The match is played. An enormous anticlimax. All this excitement, so superbly orchestrated, at the service of a duff game like American Football. Not a sport that I could ever find even remotely interesting. Baseball I love, basketball I can just about take (repetitive as it is), but gridiron football leaves me entirely cold, with its stop-start spasms, preposterous armour and tedious playbook tactics. This match, perhaps because of what is at stake, is more than usually uninspiring and you can feel the tension and thrill leak out of the atmosphere like widdle from a nappy.

Auburn triumphs again, achieving their winningest streak in the history of the Iron Bowl. But by the time the final whistle is blown I am safely tucked up in bed dreaming of eagles, jet fighters and pompoms.

THE BOARD OF PARDONS AND PAROLES

The judicial and penal systems of the South have always had a quality of their own. Cinema, literature, music and folklore have long revelled in the special cruelties and indignities of crime and punishment, Southern style. That mixture of vengeful Christianity, social conservatism and racial disharmony combined with a record of dreadful violent crime leaves little room, it seems, for mercy or progressive thinking.

Many years ago, Alabama's state legislature brought into being in the capital, Montgomery, an institution called the Board of Pardons and Paroles whose job it is to hear both sides of an appeal for parole petitions. By both sides I mean that both the representatives of the convicts and the representatives of their victims get the chance to speak.

I talk with the three members of the board, Robert Longshore, William Wynne and VeLinda Weatherley. They sit at their long bench, the seal of their office on the wall behind them, exuding Southern charm, courtesy and authority. I cannot believe that any equivalent British institution (were there such a thing) would ever allow a film crew to come poke around their proceedings with so little supervision or bureaucratic impediment. Mr Longshore explains to me in a drawl of stupendous charm that the pardons are the most enjoyable part of their work: as a rule these take the form of applications from criminals long since released who need a pardon in order to be able to vote or own a gun. There is rarely if ever anyone from the 'other side' to oppose their applications and it gives the Board pleasure to restore to a citizen their constitutional rights. Paroles however are an entirely different matter. This is where the pain of crime comes home; this is where the wisdom of Solomon itself cannot guarantee to bring about a happy outcome.

On either side of the back of the tribunal space, which is laid out not unlike a courtroom, there is a door. Each door leads to a waiting room, one for parole petitioners, the other for families and representatives of the victims.

After a few straightforward cases of pardoning, a parole case begins. A family shuffles through the victims' door. A late-middle-aged woman is so tearful she has to be supported. With them is a pale young white girl who works for an organisation called Victims of Crime and Leniency (VOCAL) who automatically, whatever the circumstances, always support the victims and oppose parole, whatever the case. Their default position is never to favour early

189

release. For any prisoner. Ever.

Through the other door shuffles another, equally distressed family. The young man whose case for parole they are making is not present. The prisoners themselves never are, only their families and occasionally (if they have money, which is rare) their lawyers.

A story emerges that is so sad, so squalid and so unfair that within minutes I (and many in the court, including some of the camera crew) am wiping away tears.

The prisoner is twenty-seven years old and has been in jail since he was seventeen on a charge of manslaughter. He was given a twenty-year sentence. He had been horsing around with a gun when he had shot his fifteen-year-old friend in the head. Apparently it was all part of some game that had got out of hand. No one in the original sentencing court and no one here at the Board believed that it was anything more than a terrible accident. The two boys, the two families, had been friends, but the mother of the dead boy will not hear of clemency for the imprisoned one.

She stands up now, a central casting picture of tottering maternal woe. She wails, she screams, she cannot put into words her continuing upset and has to be led from the proceedings sobbing and keening. The woman from VOCAL speaks for her. The boy in prison is still alive. He has only served half his sentence. The court wanted him in prison for twenty years; the board should respect that. He should not be allowed even to apply again for another five years, the maximum length.

The family of the imprisoned boy make their case. Their son has served exemplary time: not one punishment for infractions of prison rules. He has learned new trades and has passed examinations. He was never a criminal. What good can be done by keeping him locked up? It was an accident after all, a terrible accident.

To me it is, as they say in America, a slam dunk. Surely the boy must get his parole?

He does not. It is not the Board's duty to look into the rights or wrongs of sentencing, only to respond to the case as it is. This boy's first appeal will not be accepted, says Mr Longshore; it is too early. However, his good behaviour is noted and he is therefore given the right to appeal in four years. Another four years of hard time ahead of him.

I am astonished. Astonished that the family of the slain boy should *want* such revenge against the friend who so tragically took a game too far. Surely they should let go? It could have been *their* son who shot the other boy, had fate dealt different cards. Surely they should *embrace* the boy who killed their son, wouldn't that help them heal? I am astonished too by the callousness of the woman from VOCAL and her absolute lack of sympathy for the killer. I am no Christian, but I know that the founder of her religion would feel differently. Is it not possible to care for both victim and perpetrator?

I bid farewell to the Board and to Alabama, mixed feelings churning in my breast. Rarely have I met people more charming, more polite and more hospitable. The boy who pumps the gas in the forecourt really *does* call you 'sir', the receptionist at the hotel has a wide smile when she asks 'how y'all doing?' and the smile is warm and real. But this is not a place where I would ever want to be poor or independent-spirited, and certainly not a place where I would want to fall foul of the law.

191

FLORIDA
KEY FACTS

Abbreviation:
Fl

Nickname:
The Sunshine State

Capital:
Tallahassee

Flower:
Orange blossom

Tree:
Sabal palm

Bird:
Northern mockingbird

Pie:
Key Lime Pie

Motto:
In God We Trust

Well-known residents and natives: Janet Reno,
General Stilwell, Butterfly McQueen,
Sidney Poitier, Fay Dunaway, Burt Reynolds,
Ben Vereen, Pat Boone, Jim Morrison,
Gloria Estefan.

FLORIDA

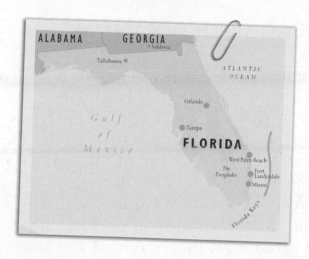

'Strange how the young of such warty and frightening creatures can be so adorable.'

The Spanish conquistador Juan Poncc de Léon landed on the shores of the tropical peninsula that forms the southernmost part of the Northern American landmass in April 1513, during the festival of Pascua Florida, or 'flowery Easter', and thus the twenty-second largest state of the union was christened.

The year-round sunshine that gives Florida the nickname that adorns its licence plates, its thousands and thousands of miles of coastline, the Disney resorts and other family-friendly attractions of Orlando, the Latin vibrancy and cosmopolitan chic of Miami and the tropical beauty of the Keys have caused Florida to be one of the most visited states in America. Certainly one of the most visited by Britons.

I participate, just like any one of those hundreds of

thousands of British tourists, in two of the most popular activities available in Florida.

SWIMMING WITH DOLPHINS

First I point the taxi's nose to the south of Miami and travel down the famous US Highway 1 which takes me to the resort of Key Largo. The Keys are long, low islands at the very south of Florida, the drops of wee that fall from the tip of this most phallic of states. The last one in the line, Key West, is only thirty or forty miles from Cuba, for this is America's Caribbean. Key Largo was made famous in the forties by John Huston's movie of the same name but is now a destination for those who want, amongst other things, to swim with dolphins.

Although the sheer pleasure of sharing the water with these amiable mammals is reason enough to do it, there has over recent years grown up the practice of Dolphin Therapy. I am due to swim with a boy, Kyle Crouch, who lives with cerebral palsy and has been coming to swim with bottle-nosed dolphins in Key Largo since he was ten years old. A young therapist called Eli has been swimming with him and supervising the sessions and it is clear that they both believe the experience has been wholly beneficial. Kyle's mother agrees.

Maybe it is the sheer exhilaration of being towed, nosed, tickled, slapped, prodded, swiped and barged by these boisterous, squeaking, clicking creatures—maybe that is therapy enough, coupled with the muscular toning resulting from active time in the seawater. I certainly feel entirely enchanted and emerge glowing with *bien-être* and a sense of one of

194

nature's highest privileges having been bestowed upon me.

I ponder man's fascination with the 'higher' mammals—great apes, whales and dolphins. When in their presence it is as if we are communing with royalty or Hollywood stars. A great grin spreads over our faces. Eye contact or attention causes our hearts to beat a little faster at the honour of having been noticed by such supreme beings. A shame that, given this, we can't seem to share the planet with them. There won't be many species of whale and gorilla left by 2020. Perhaps the dolphins are safe so long as they continue to play.

'Dolphins,' says Eli, 'they got this instinct where they only approach those in the water who are the most nervous. They always seems to pay attention to the most vulnerable and the most wounded, physically or emotionally. You'll see them gently prod these people into play.'

'But confident people?'

'Self-satisfied people, fit people, confident people they will leave alone.'

I do not know whether to be flattered or insulted by the dolphins' very clear attentions to me.

EVERGLADES AIRBOAT

The second *sine qua non* on the Miami tourist trail is the airboat trip around the Everglades. I drive back up from Key Largo towards this enormous national park, more than two thousand square miles in size, a limitless marshland of sawgrass sedge, mangrove, cypress, hammock and pine. Flat as a billiard table, the first impression as you drive through is of rich

195

fertile green fields, until you catch the dark glint of reflections where land should be and you are finally convinced that the entire landscape is under water. There is only one feasible way to move across it—by airboat.

Of all the freakish modes of transportation I have ever experienced, the airboat must be the noisiest and the most eco-dreadful. A caged aeroplane engine propeller hurtles one across the surface of the Everglades, skimming at great speed, belching exhaust fumes and snarling with a high-decibel din that one would imagine was guaranteed to send every species of animal running for cover. But animals can get used to anything, even the noxious roar of a Mad Max airboat. They appear to be the preserve of ageing hippies, like Jesse, my driver, who enjoy freaking one out with tales of alligators leaping into boats and pulling humans into the water.

Jesse has a baby alligator back at his base. He passes it over to me.

'Go on there, he won't hurt you.'

Strange how the young of such warty and frightening creatures can be so adorable.

Sometimes the cheesiest, most clichéd touristic activity can be entirely satisfactory. So it was on the Everglades.

SOUTH BEACH

The following day I spend exploring South Beach, the southern part of the finger of separated land that runs down the coast of Miami. Fifteen or so years ago the area was a desolate ruin. Chris Blackwell, founder of Island Records, undertook with others the restoration of the string of pastel-coloured deco hotels that are now the glory of this most fashionable part of the whole city. On this same frontage, Ocean Drive, stands the large square, Roman-style house Casa Casuarina, on whose steps Gianni Versace was shot and killed in 1997.

Signs of Christmas remind me that, despite all evidence to the contrary, we are in deep midwinter. I walk up towards the Lincoln Theatre, an art-deco cream and terracotta jewel of a movie house now the home of the New World Symphony Orchestra. Their Percussion Consort is practising the eccentric and exciting Ballet Mécanique, a wild futuristic, Dadaist percussion piece by George Antheil involving doorbells and aeroplane propellers not unlike those that power the airboats of the Everglades. In its first performance in Paris the propellers blew wigs and hats off the heads of audience members. I sit in on the rehearsal, pleased to think that in a metropolis whose nightclubs echo with the tedious bump of salsa, funk, mambo and soft rock there is also room for the wilder shores of experimental modernism, albeit a modernism that is now well over eighty years old.

THE SNOWBIRDS

The evening is to expose me to music again—music and so much more. For generations the warm winters of Miami have attracted temporary visitors of a certain age, especially Jewish couples from New Jersey and New York. These winter visitors are called 'snowbirds' and have made Palm Beach and the surrounding environs north of Miami almost entirely their own, creating enormous gated communities which contain their own shops, cinemas, beauty parlours, pools, synagogues and theatres. In the theatres the communities' paid Entertainment Officers arrange special dance evenings and it is to one of these that I have been invited tonight.

A gated snowbird world is like a cruise ship stuck on land. The same posted lists of Things To Do, the same excited clusters of guests checking dates, times and dress codes with the Entertainment Officers. I have come because tonight is Dance Night in one of the theatres and I am to witness snowbird world close up.

I talk to a group of professional male dancers. The youngest of them will not see fifty again, but to the more man-hungry dancing ladies of the community they are toy boys to be hooked and swung around the floor until they drop. The rapacity and dance mania of some of the women, I am told, must be seen to be believed.

'Sometimes we get home with torn jackets and pants,' says one of them, Morris.

As one who loathes dancing with a loathing so deep, so entire and so fundamental that the very prospect of swinging a shoe causes me to come out in a trembling sweat of fury, fear and distress, the prospect of being grabbed by one of these dance-mad harpies fills me with horror and I determine to hide behind our film camera for the evening.

So dotty, dreadful and glitzily, vulgarly charming is the whole evening however, that I am tempted to the floor, almost to the point of moving my body more or less to music. A little old man called Marvin is so charming, in his sparkly hat and with his delightful Walter Matthau grin, that I cannot resist chatting to him.

198

'Did you ever see such pretty ladies?' he asks excitedly. 'Pretty ladies everywhere!'

'And you've got the prettiest,' I say, gallantly bowing to the woman on his arm, who giggles and snuggles further into him.

'We been together twenty years,' Marvin tells me.

'Married?'

'No. We're a dance team. My wife passed eight years ago. Her husband passed seven years ago. They call us M and M.'

'Marvin and . . . ?'

She speaks for the first time. 'Muriel.'

'Marvin and Muriel.'

'Ain't she a princess, though?'

'Certainly. May I ask how old you are, Marvin?'

'Sure you can ask. It's a free country, despite that schmuck in the White House.'

'So, how old are you?'

'Ninety years young.'

Muriel, only a foot taller than him, nudges him and they spin off into the crowd of seven hundred other dancing couples.

It is a strange world, and one I would commit suicide to avoid being a part of, but they all seemed very happy. As soon as it is decent to do so, I tip-toe away, the triumphant snarl of 'If My Friends Could See Me Now' from Sweet Charity getting fainter and fainter until I reach the safety of the taxi.

The next morning I stand on the rocks of the beach and bid farewell to Florida. I have travelled down the east coast as far south as I can and now I must point myself west, across the gulf, to Louisiana.

THE DEEP SOUTH AND THE GREAT LAKES

LOUISIANA
KEY FACTS

Abbreviation:
LA

Nickname:
Bayou State, Pelican State, Sportsman's Paradise

Capital:
Baton Rouge

Flower:
Magnolia

Tree:
Bald cypress

Bird:
Brown pelican

Dog:
Catahoula Leopard Dog

Motto:
Union, Justice, Confidence

Well-known residents and natives: General William
T. Sherman, Huey Long, Lee Harvey Oswald,
Jimmy Swaggart, David Duke, Paul Morphy,
Lillian Hellman, Truman Capote,
John Kennedy Toole, Elmore Leonard, Anne Rice,
'King' Oliver, Louis Armstrong, Jelly Roll Morton,

Sidney Bechet, Louis Prima, Harry Connick Jr.,
Branford Marsalis, Wynton Marsalis,
Jerry Lee Lewis, Fats Domino, Lester Young,
Mahalia Jackson, Clifton Chenier, Aaron Neville,
Buckwheat Zydeco, Leadbelly, Professor Longhair,
Buddy Guy, Randy Newman, Ben Turpin,
Dorothy Lamour, Kitty Carlisle, Ellen DeGeneres,
Reese Witherspoon, Britney Spears.

LOUISIANA

'No town carnivals like New Orleans. You had better have a strong head and a forgiving liver if you mean to enjoy New Orleans at Mardi Gras.'

Beignets, lagniappes, jambalaya and gumbo. Jazz, jalousies and jelly shots. Streetcars, the levee and Tabasco. Po'boys, zydeco, voodoo and the bayou. Bienvenu à Nouveau Orléans.

Southern Louisiana is dominated by New Orleans, a city of such distinctness and quality that it has earned more nicknames than New York: The Big Easy, the Crescent City, 504, NOLA, The City That Care Forgot. I came here once before, sent by Paramount Studios in 1997 to get background for a screenplay adaptation of John Kennedy Toole's great New Orleans novel *A Confederacy of Dunces*. Since that visit one catastrophic event in late August 2005 has reshaped everything we think about this enchantingly seductive town: Hurricane Katrina. For

New Orleans, time is divided into pre-Katrina and post-Katrina.

MARDI GRAS

I arrive at the beginning of February. A good time to visit, for it is the weekend leading up to 'Fat Tuesday', the literal English translation of *Mardi Gras*. In Britain we call it 'Shrove Tuesday' and celebrate with pancakes. In more observant times this day preceding Ash Wednesday was when the faithful said their goodbye to meat, for it signalled the start of Lent and forty days of fasting and prayer. The Latin for 'goodbye meat' is *carne vale*. Hence the word 'carnival'. With the possible exceptions of Rio de Janeiro and Aberdeen, no town carnivals like New Orleans. (I was lying about Aberdeen.)

You had better have a strong head and a forgiving liver if you mean to enjoy New Orleans at Mardi Gras. Fat Tuesday is merely the culmination of Fat Saturday, Fat Sunday and Fat Monday. Each of those days sees drinking, parades, drinking, marching bands, drinking, the wearing of costumes, drinking, drinking and drinking. By Sunday the gutters in the streets of the French Quarter are already filled with hundreds of thousands of shiny green, gold and purple beads. Green for faith, gold for power and purple for justice—the official colours of the New Orleans Mardi Gras. In Bourbon Street, the scuzzy touristic heart of the Quarter, there is also human matter of a not dissimilar colour in the gutters, but let us try to concentrate on the positive. Necklaces of these coloured beads are dropped from every balcony and hurled from every parade float. It is impossible to walk ten yards without becoming festooned. With the beads comes a growing acceptance of the spirit of Mardi Gras. I soak up that spirit, and suck it down too, in the form of jelly shots, the kind of disgusting alcohol - for - people - who - don't - like - grown - up - alcoholic-drinks in which America specialises. The kind of disgusting comestible, in fact, one is secretly pleased to have an excuse guiltlessly to enjoy from time to time. In the time off between visiting Florida and coming here to Louisiana I filmed for the BBC in Brazil, where I managed to break my right arm in Amazonia, so for my journeys through the French Quarter I am escorted by members of the film crew, who protect me from being barged by those revellers too lost in drink to notice that my arm is in a sling.

At the bar of Napoleon's on Chartres Street, I fall into conversation with a group of boisterous New Orleanians and get a lesson in how to pronounce the name of the town. No two of them appears to agree, native born as they all are. N'Orlins, N'Orleeyuns, Noo Orlins, Noo Orleeeens, Noo Orleeyuns—they all seem to be acceptable. Indeed what is not acceptable in this pearl of a town? My new friends offer the opinion that New Orleans has more in common with the great ports of the world, Marseille, Rio, Amsterdam, London, Sydney, than it does with any other American cities, except perhaps San Francisco, which is also a port of course. They offer me much to eat and drink too: if nothing else, they say, I must eat a *muffuletta* sandwich (a feast of cheese and olive salad in good bread), a *beignet* (a square doughnut, dusted with icing sugar) and drink a milk punch (a kind of Brandy Alexander made with bourbon instead of cognac). I do all three gratefully and totter away into the night. All cities of consequence have their own ways of eating and drinking, and their specialities always seem to taste best in situ.

By the time Tuesday itself comes I am beginning to feel my age a little as I limp, at eight in the morning, a mile and a half to the back of the queue of carnival floats that winds all the way around the Superdome Convention Centre, that same Superdome that was a scene of such awful misery, stench and despair in the hours and days following Katrina.

I am amongst the Zulus. It is hard to explain quite who and what the Zulus are. They are a kind of club or 'krewe', made up predominantly of African-Americans and every year thousands of them pay to take part in the parade. It began in the early twentieth century as a kind of spoofing of the white Rex, the official Mardi Gras King, and has grown into a mammoth, integral and hugely popular element of the carnival. Zulus black up (despite already being that colour), put on fuzzy wigs, whiten their lips and eyes and lob thousands of painted coconuts into the crowds as they pass through the streets. This is all about mocking white America's old tradition of mammy-style minstrelsy. When I talk of walking a mile and a half I am not exaggerating. The Zulu parade is at least that long and takes many hours to pass by. Each float is pulled by a tractor and each float has its name, theme and tradition.

The rest of Fat Tuesday flies by in a whirl. What I do and where I go I shall probably never know.

OYSTERING WITH THE CROATS

I wake up in my hotel room on Ash Wednesday fully ready to do penance and be shriven for my sins.

207

Down to the very mouth of the Mississippi I go, to join the crew of an early morning oyster boat all of whom happen to be Croatian. Croats started coming to Louisiana to work on the oystermen over a century ago and they are still coming to this day. With my arm in a sling, it is my pleasure to stand back and swallow a freshly shucked bayou oyster from time to time, while they haul nets and sort the catch. The sun shines in a cloudless sky, the pelicans flap lazily above us and all is well. But there is no one you can talk to in southern Louisiana who does not have their story of Katrina. Here, huge ten-ton boats were flung around like dried leaves. John, the captain of our oysterman, tells how the levee defending the road and the neighbourhood broke. The water came up to his house to a level of seventeen feet. John is a prosperous fisherman, and he has been able to rebuild. It has been hard, but he is back at work with a new and better defended home. For others, the story has been much, much tougher . . .

THE LOWER NINTH

After saying goodbye to John and his crew, I travel to a district that has died. The Lower Ninth Ward in New Orleans was once a vibrant, humming community of African-Americans about two and a half square miles in size, lying below (hence the 'Lower' in its name) the Mississippi and the Industrial Canal that forms one side of its boundary. If any piece of land anywhere in the world is below a piece of water, whether it be the sea, a river, a canal or a lake, it is necessary to defend that land, else it will (gravity being gravity and water being water) become a piece of that sea, river, canal or lake. The Lower Ninth was defended by a levee. For those of us who, pre-Katrina, only knew the word 'levee', thanks to the song 'American Pie', as a place to take a Chevy and watch good ole boys drinking whiskey and rye, it is worth thinking of a levee as simply raised earth. A bank. A bank built between land and water to protect the former from being flooded by the latter. In the Fens of East Anglia and the polder lands of Holland they are called dykes, but the principle is the same everywhere.

On the night of 23 August 2005 came Katrina, the third-strongest hurricane ever to make landfall in the United States. Nowhere was the destruction more terrible than in the Lower Ninth. Water poured in from at least three different sources, from St Bernard Parish above and from two breaches of the Industrial Canal—one of which brought with it a huge barge which itself flattened buildings as it barrelled along in the surge. The force of the floodwaters alone was great enough to pull buildings up from their concrete foundations. I am told that 1,600 citizens of the Lower Ninth died as a result.

Today, two and a half years later, the area is a stinking, rat-infested wasteland. A terrible, desolated rectangle of waist-high weeds and rubble. What appear to be randomly placed stoups, chimney breasts, fallen roofs and mailboxes offer pathetic reminders that this was once, unbelievably, a place where thousands lived out their lives. In a state of horrified bewilderment and disbelief, I drive around in the company of Isaiah, a young man from the neighbourhood. Isaiah was on his way to Iraq, for his second tour of military duty there, when Katrina struck. A self-possessed, articulate, intelligent, handsome and charismatic young man,

Isaiah the Patriot, the marine who fought twice for his country, has found himself politicised, radicalised even, by what he and so many from the Lower Ninth see as the neglect and betrayal of his people. At a local, city, state and federal level he feels nothing has been done. 'These are wild black people, looting savages, we are well rid of them.' This is how he bitterly characterises what he interprets as the establishment's response to the devastation of the ward. More sinister theories suggest that the Lower Ninth was deliberately sacrificed, that the breaches of the levee were avoidable, may even have been purposely made to protect other, more 'valuable' parishes and districts, such as the French Quarter. I cannot judge the truth of this, but I can certainly attest to the bitterness and sense of betrayal prevalent in the blighted neighbourhood. I visit Augustine, Isaiah's grandmother and I can see the newly accreted layers of misery and anger that have grown over a woman who was otherwise born to laugh and to enjoy life. Even through the misery of her present existence she, her grandson and other friends insist on our taking a photograph on her porch.

In 1965 Hurricane Betsy flooded the Lower Ninth. President Lyndon Johnson was there immediately, Isaiah tells me, promising aid which arrived and with which the Lower Ninth was rebuilt. This time around (after an admittedly more destructive storm) it is as if, in his opinion, the entire two and a half square miles has been written off. The Lower Ninth, he reflects, was always a poor district, but was notable for containing not one single Housing Project (the equivalent of our British council houses and flats). Ninety per cent was made up of owner-occupied housing. Being poor and living on the edge, these were the kind of people who could least afford

210

insurance. As far as the most extreme white citizens are concerned, the denizens of the Lower Ninth were out with guns, looting, raping and pillaging the first night after Katrina. As far as the most extreme black citizens are concerned, their neighbours and their whole community were cold-bloodedly and deliberately murdered. Katrina left a legacy of physical destruction, but perhaps it is the destruction of faith, morale and trust which is the most terrible of all. The bright beads on the necklace of the American Dream are in the gutter.

VOODOO

That night I attend a voodoo ceremony in the Marigny district. We cross Desire Street to get there. The trolley buses that one finds all over New Orleans, known as streetcars, used to come as far out as Marigny and would bear the name of the last street at which they stopped, much as a tube train in London bears the name Cockfosters or High Barnet. Tennessee Williams, the great Southern playwright, was very taken by the common sight, back in the forties, of a streetcar which would carry the name Desire. The voodoo itself disappointingly lacks any effigy stabbing or zombie raising, but turns out to be yet another mixture of 'positive energy' and wild dancing. Not unlike Laurie Cabot and her witches in Salem, Massachusetts back at Halloween.

ANGOLA
It is time to move away from New Orleans (never an easy thing to do: she is one of those cities one never

wants to leave). We travel upstate towards Mississippi: on the way we stop off at the Louisiana State Penitentiary, Angola, once one of the most notoriously terrible and feared prisons in America.

Originally a place for 'breeding' slaves whose 'stock' came from southwest Africa, hence the name, Angola is now a prison farm. A huge parcel of land, the size of Manhattan, it is given over to cattle, crops and cultivation. The prisoners, so long as they toe the line, eschew drugs and the gang culture, can learn to work the land. We are shown round by the ebullient Warden Burl Cain (is that a name straight from southern fiction, or what?) who is particularly pleased with his dawgs. Bite dogs (one or two of whom are crossed with wolves) go for a foolish escapee's arm, Trail dogs are bloodhounds capable of tracking people across rivers and through any number of false scents, and Drug Sniffing dogs can detect a tenth of a gram of cocaine in a bag of cinnamon powder. Despite this fearsomely efficient bestiary, Warden Burl is pleased to have turned round his prison's reputation not with draconian discipline, cruelty or threats, but with a combination of motivational techniques and old-time religion. He is careful to make it plain that it is not the nature of the religion that matters, merely the sense of a future and self-respect that any religion can engender. The atheistical anti-religionist in me bridles, but results are results . . . Angola is a place for lifers and death-row convicts: certain crimes in Louisiana are punished with no option whatever for parole. What motivation to 'behave' will a prisoner have if he knows he will never see freedom, however much he toes the line? Somehow, despite this inbuilt problem, Warden Burl seems to have turned the place round. Nonetheless, I am glad to leave . . .

This slice of northern Louisiana, not far from the Mississippi state line, reminds me forcibly that we are outside the orbit of New Orleans now. Hound dogs, a dose of religion, Death Row and men called Burl. It truly is another world. I head for the state line feeling like a visitor from outer space. And loving it.

MISSISSIPPI
KEY FACTS

Abbreviation:
MS

Nickname:
The Magnolia State

Capital:
Jackson

Flower:
Magnolia

Tree:
Magnolia

Bird:
Mockingbird

Rock:
Petrified wood

Motto:
Virtute et armis ('By virtue and by arms')

Well-known residents and natives: Jefferson Davies,
Trent Lott, Medgar Evers, William Faulkner,
Eudora Welty, Tennessee Williams, Richard Ford,
Walker Percy, Shelby Foote, John Grisham,
Dana Andrews, James Earl Jones, Morgan Freeman,
Jim Henson, Diane Ladd, Oprah Winfrey,

Robert Johnson, Elvis Presley, Conway Twitty,
Muddy Waters, Sonny Boy Williamson,
Howlin' Wolf, Sam Cooke, Bo Diddley,
Willie Dixon, Bobbie Gentry, John Lee Hooker,
Bobby Rush, Otis Rush, Elmore James, Ike Turner,
B.B. King, Junior Parker, Tammy Wynette,
Lester Young, Jimmy Buffet, Leontyne Price,
Charley Pride, LeAnn Rimes, Britney Spears.

MISSISSIPPI

'. . . good Southern soul food, fried catfish, fried chicken, fried potatoes, fried coleslaw, fried salad and fried Coca-Cola . . .'

You only have to look at its list of well-known residents and natives to see that music is Mississippi's dominant product. Cotton may once have been King, but Mississippian native Elvis Presley took that title for rock and roll back in the fifties. Elvis was born here, in the town of Tupelo, but he was raised in Tennessee, just as the blues were born here and raised into more popular, commercial forms outside the state. For lovers of the true Delta blues, however, Mississippi will always be home. Look at the names: B.B. King, Howlin' Wolf, Muddy Waters, John Lee Hooker and, above all, Robert Johnson.

NATCHEZ

My first sight of what cotton gave Mississippi (or at least what it gave the white plantation owners) is given in the town of Natchez, where grand antebellum homes abound. They are fine and noble and the Mississippi river running through looks very Mark Twain, but I head for a local church to listen to some gospel singing. It has been a long drive from Louisiana and not many things could raise the spirits as high as the sound of a gospel choir. Two members of the choir, Yolanda and Celestin, very kindly invite me to dinner at their home, where I enjoy good Southern soul food, fried catfish, fried chicken, fried potatoes, fried coleslaw, fried salad and fried Coca-Cola, in the company of their children C.J. and Brandice. Yolanda and Cel are a proud and prosperous middle-class black family. Cel works as a McDonald's manager, supervising three or four restaurants around Natchez. Feeling once more warmed and physically weighed down by such generous helpings of Southern hospitality, I set off next morning for the Delta.

THE DELTA

What *is* a delta exactly? Well, it derives from the Greek letter delta, whose majuscule is shaped like an equilateral triangle. A river's delta is the area towards the mouth where sediment builds up into a triangular piece of land. It can also be called an alluvial fan. The Mississippi Delta, it is explained to me, is not a true delta at all, but a giant alluvial plain that lies between the Mississippi and Yazoo rivers. It is an enormous region, said to begin in the lobby of the Peabody Hotel up in Memphis, Tennessee (where I became an Assistant Duck Master) and to end down in Catfish Row, in Vicksburg, Mississippi. The word 'plain' should alert one to the fact that the Delta is astoundingly, remorselessly flat.

Plumb through the middle of the Delta runs Highway 61, the legendary road that, like the Mississippi River itself, flows all the way from Minnesota down to New Orleans. The section of it that passes through the state of Mississippi is also known as the Blues Highway, for where it intersects Highway 49 in the town of Clarksdale is a Holy Place for all lovers of blues music. That crossroads is where Robert Johnson, for many aficionados the greatest bluesman of them all, is said to have sold his soul to the devil in return for mastery of the guitar. The crossroads has been used in song, film and album titles ever since and the town of Clarksdale (which styles itself the Birthplace of the Blues) derives much, perhaps most, of its income from newly established Blues Trails and heritage Blues Tours that bring people here from all over the world. Bessie Smith died in Clarksdale, John Lee Hooker, Muddy Waters, Ike Turner and Sam Cooke all came from here and another local, the Oscar-winning actor Morgan Freeman, has opened a blues club called Ground Zero right by the railway tracks in the centre of the old town.

BASKETBALL

I travel late that afternoon in a classic yellow American school bus with the Clarksdale High School girls' junior basketball team. They are, in the language of showbiz magazine *Variety* 'skedded' to meet on the court of battle the girls of South Panola High in Batesville, MS.

Batesville is around forty miles from Clarksdale and I get a chance to chat with those girls that aren't plugged into their MP3 players. They will pulverise those girls of South Panola High. They have had a good season and it can only get better. Where did I get that freaky accent from?

'England. Do you know where that is?'

Two of the girls look at me with eyes clouded with contempt at the thought that I should be weird enough to expect them to know where a place so unimportant might actually be. A voice pipes up from the back.

'Sure. It's on the way to New York.'

*　　*　　*

We pull into the rival school. I am astounded by its facilities. Both South Panola and Clarksdale are publicly funded schools from the poorest state in America, predominantly attended by African-American children and yet both have indoor sports facilities infinitely more impressive than can be found in any school I've ever visited in Britain. From Eton College to the most favoured and subsidised giant comprehensive you will not see better facilities in better condition. Despite the cheerleading team's best efforts, Clarksdale High is soundly thrashed and we return in a slightly subdued mood.

ON THE SOFA

By the time I'm back in Clarksdale, Morgan

Freeman's blues club is beginning to warm up. I give myself over to fried chicken and live blues music. Ground Zero has been described as a masterpiece of 'manufactured authenticity', with its artfully burst sofas on the porch and its stylishly graffiti-ed doors and walls. Everyone inside is white: the band, the waitresses, the crowd. There is only one black man to be seen, Morgan Freeman, and he sits on the sofa next to me and talks about why he founded this club. Clarksdale, he says, is popular music's ground zero. This is where the explosion began and it is right that the community should benefit. It is a poor Southern town of some 20,000 souls. The collapse of the sub-prime property market, a series of failed harvests and a general downturn in the American economy have hit places like Clarksdale very hard indeed. 'The richest soil and the poorest people' is how Freeman puts it to me. 'It's a town that deserves to be known and deserves to prosper.' I could not agree more.

ARKANSAS
KEY FACTS
Abbreviation:
AR

Nickname:
The Natural State

Capital:
Little Rock

Flower:
Apple blossom

Tree:
Pine

Bird:
Mockingbird

Fruit:
South Arkansas Vine Ripe Pink Tomato

Motto:
Regnat populus ('Let the people rule')
Well-known residents and natives: William
Fulbright, Bill Clinton (42nd President), Mike
Huckabee, General Douglas MacArthur,
General Wesley Clark, Eldridge Cleaver,
Sam 'Wal-Mart' Walton, Maya Angelou,
Amarillo Slim, Bill Hicks, Glen Campbell,
Johnny Cash, Louis Jordan, Charlie Rich,
Sonny Liston, Dick Powell, Alan Ladd,
Mary Steenburgen, Billy Bob Thornton.

ARKANSAS

*'Considering that the Mississippi is one of the
largest and most unspoiled rivers in the world,
it is astonishing how alone we are.'*

Arkansas, rhyming with 'Darken Saw', calls its
citizens Arkansans. Bill Clinton will probably remain
the best known of these for many generations. His
blend of crinkly charm and battered disreputability
seems rather an accurate face to put on the state.

I drive through the town of Helena (weirdly known
as Helena-West Helena), another proud Historical
Blues Cultural Centre, feeling that I have stepped
back fifty years. Disused rubber warehouses and flour
mills dominate a town that looks as if it has just been
prepped for a shoot by a Hollywood production
designer. A shoot of what, though? A Depression-era
drama, or the biopic of a country-music star? Some
fantasy combination of both I should imagine.

CANOEING

On the banks of the Mississippi River I am met by John, a man who spends every hour he can boating up and down the river. He teaches young kids from disadvantaged families how to handle a canoe. There is a number of these here with him today and together they lash a comfortable wicker chair to the centre of a canoe to make me a throne. With a broken arm it would be difficult for me to sit in any other fashion, but as we set off on our Huckleberry adventure I feel a twinge of embarrassment. A large European is being paddled along a big river by black youths. It feels a little too imperial, a little too 'Sanders of the River' for comfort. The boys themselves don't seem to feel it, however, and I excoriate myself for being so gripped by self-consciousness, race-guilt, doubt and insecurity. Nonetheless, as an image . . . I shudder as I consider what my *bien pensant* friends back home will say when they see it.

Considering that the Mississippi is one of the largest and most unspoiled rivers in the world, it is astonishing how alone we are: I had expected a great deal of tourism to be on show. Once or twice a huge commercial barge comes by, but we are the only leisure craft on the water. John confirms that Americans, keen as they are to enjoy their woods and their wildernesses, hugely under-use the Mississippi, on which it is their right to sail, paddle or steam as much as they like. We make camp on a small island, that in a week or so will be gone (the melt waters that come down from the frozen north will soon be swelling the river and raising its levels), making shift with wine, beer, coffee, barbecued meat, baked potatoes, beans and cheese.

John and I discuss the mythical status that the Mississippi has in United States lore, literature and art. The river has exercised a grip on the American imagination from the earliest days of European settlement, finding its apotheosis in *Huckleberry Finn*, *Moby Dick*'s only serious contender for the title Great American Novel. Perhaps that is why Americans come to the river itself so rarely, we decide. It functions as such a potent symbol that to encounter the real mud and water might only lead to disillusionment. But a symbol of what? Well, the Mississippi divides east from west, so in the imagination it becomes the frontier that separates civilisation, law and authority from free-spirited, maverick pioneering. It is also a symbol of the American obsession with journeying, with moving on. America is a nation composed of people whose ancestors moved on, who had the restless desire to up sticks and leave their European homes. The itchy-footed need for the endless journey is in the American DNA and while it is now most often presented in its twentieth-century fictional form, the road movie, it found its first expression in Huck Finn and legends of Ole Man River. But the Mississippi also stands for a connection between north and south. With Chicago at one end and New Orleans at the other, so much of America's traffic, cultural as well as commercial, has travelled down or up.

As a matter of fact, the Mississippi is not the longest river in the United States of America. At 2,320 miles, it is some twenty or so miles shorter than its great tributary the Missouri. The short journey from jetty to small island seemed long enough. I thank John and his young crew and continue on my way.

224

DOGGING

The border of Arkansas with Tennessee is marked by the course of the Mississippi, and as I drive north I keep the river to my right. Over on the eastern bank the lights of Memphis, Tennessee are beginning to twinkle. On my side, the Arkansas side, the city is called West Memphis and it is noticeably more down at heel than its famous Tennessee brother. I am tempted by a large neon sign that reads 'Southlands'. I have been told that there is a major dog track here.

I should have passed right by. Greyhound racing was once one of the most popular sports in America but the track in West Memphis is deserted when I get there, despite a race being scheduled every half hour. So long as they are televised, who need actually attend the meetings? The bets can be laid in Sydney, Sidcup or Sidi Barrani, with betting by satellite TV and the internet it makes no difference. I talk to Paul Cohen, one of the trainers, who tells me that 'back in the day' there would be two miles of tailback traffic snaking round the interstate on race days. Today people are more drawn to the casino which has been added to the Southlands complex. Paul is keen for me to understand that the dogs are exceptionally well cared for. He loves them and it upsets him that the sport has a reputation for cruelty. I promise him that I will pass on this news (he seems to think Britain is full of people who would come to Arkansas for the racing if only they believed that the greyhounds were well treated) and bid him goodbye.

I look longingly across the river at Tennessee: I can just glimpse the top of the Peabody Hotel where my ducks will be settling in for the night. Memphis radiates prosperity and self-confidence, just as West

Memphis radiates failure and disappointment. As I prepare the taxi for the journey north to the state of Missouri I can't help feeling sorry for Arkansas. West Memphis will never be Memphis and Arkansas will never be Tennessee. But then, knowing American statal pride as I now do, I suspect most Arkansans would claim that this is exactly how they would want it to remain.

MISSOURI
KEY FACTS

Abbreviation:
MO

Nickname:
The Show Me State

Capital:
Jefferson City

Flower:
Hawthorne

Tree:
Flowering dogwood

Bird:
Bluebird

Nut:
East black walnut

Motto:
Salus populi suprema lex esto ('The well being of the people should be the supreme law')

Well-known residents and natives: Harry S. Truman (33rd President), Sen. Bill Bradley, John Ashcroft, General John Pershing, General Omar Bradley, Mark Twain, Laura Ingalls Wilder, T.S. Eliot, Marianne Moore, William Burroughs,

Langston Hughes, Tennessee Williams,
Maya Angelou, Frank and Jesse James,
Calamity Jane, Dale Carnegie, Max Factor,
Charles Lindbergh, Edwin Hubble, Joseph Pulitzer,
Adolphus 'Budweiser' Busch,
James 'McDonnell Douglas' McDonnell,
Bill 'Jct' Lear, J.C. Penney, Kenneth 'Enron' Lay,
Walter Cronkite, Rush Limbaugh, Bob Barker,
Yogi Berra, Payne Stewart, Scott Joplin,
Charlie Parker, Basil Poledouris, Chuck Berry,
Grace Bumbry, Burt Bacharach, Sheryl Crow,
Eminem, Josephine Baker, Wallace Beery,
Robert Cummings, Jean Harlow, Walt Disney,
Betty Grable, John Huston, Ginger Rogers,
Jane Wyman, William Powell, Fritz Freleng,
Vincent Price, Robert Altman, Dick van Dyke,
Dennis Weaver, John Milius, Kathleen Turner,
Geraldine Page, John Goodman, Don Johnson,
Scott Bakula, Chris Cooper, Linda Blair, Brad Pitt.

MISSOURI

'I am shown round his old haunts, desolated factories and railhead depots, where the homeless still live.'

Still following the Mississippi River, I arrive in a snowy St Louis, humming (and who doesn't arrive doing exactly the same thing?) the song 'Meet me in St Louis, Louis'. Only, as I soon discover, the town is properly pronounced not St Louie, but St Lewis. No one told Judy Garland.

Some miles to the north of the city the Missouri River, arriving from the northwest, joins the Mississippi in a great confluence.

The feeling of having left behind the Delta and the Deep South is very strong. Which part of America am I now in? Missouri is bordered by three Southern states, Arkansas, Kentucky and Tennessee, but by five true Midwestern states too: Nebraska, Iowa, Illinois, Oklahoma and Kansas. If any state could lay claim to being the middle of middle America then perhaps it is Missouri. And what a splendid mixture of distinguished natives and residents she can boast: a range of literature from Laura 'Little House on the Prairie' Wilder to T.S. Eliot and Tennessee Williams by way of Mark Twain; an impressive roster of writers plus two of America's most venerated five-star generals. Corrupt businessmen, powerful industrialists and innovators of ragtime and rock and roll: the picture is pleasingly mixed. The city of St Louis calls itself the 'Gateway to the West' and it is hard to avoid the concrete manifestation of this nickname in the shape of Finnish architect Eero Saarinen's enormous 1930s concrete construction, the 'Gateway Arch', which dominates the downtown and riverside townscape.

THE CITY MUSEUM

A pleasing sense of Missouri as an eclectic patchwork is reinforced by a morning spent in one of the most bizarre and beguiling museums I have ever visited. The City Museum, St Louis, is the brainchild of Bob Cassilly, who shows me around with the same enthusiasm and delight that is shown by the hundreds of thousands of children who come here daily to interact with his unusual creation. Museum is perhaps not quite the right word for so interactive and compelling a public amenity. A vast converted space, once the world's biggest shoe factory, this dreamlike fantasy describes itself as 'an eclectic mixture of children's playground, funhouse, surrealistic pavilion, and architectural marvel'. I would be happy playing all day but I have a lunch appointment with someone who plans to show me another side of the city.

HOMELESS IN ST LOUIS

McMurphy's Grill in North Street is a pleasant and well-run restaurant offering the best kind of mid-range American menu, somewhere between fast and fancy food. I am especially taken by the toasted ravioli, a St Louis speciality, but I have come more for the company than for the food and for once in my greedy life the person beside me absorbs more of my attention than the plate in front of me. McMurphy's is a restaurant run by recovered alcoholics and drug addicts, by those who have slipped from the lowest rung of the ladder and are being given a lift back up. Owned by the city's St Patrick Project, the idea (familiar to those of us who watched Jamie Oliver create his Fifteen restaurant in London) is to help the homeless and the addicted by giving them a skill in which they can take pride. It is not very easy to give up drink or drugs when there is nothing awaiting you the other side of addiction: the restaurant and catering trades seem to offer just the right blend of attainable skills, social interactions and high professional standards. Pride in self, my lunch companion William tells me, is the hardest thing to find when you wake up from the nightmare of addiction and start trying to live a new life. William should know. For a quarter of a century he survived on little more than alcohol and crack cocaine. St Patrick's brought him in from the cold, literally. He worked the kitchen and the front of house here at McMurphy's and he attends 12 Step programmes in the rooms above the restaurant. Giving up is only the beginning, he says: once you are free of your drugs and drink you then have to face the person, the real you, who's been hiding under them all that while.

William has been stuffing me with toasted ravioli for a good reason. He wants me to see the streets and doss-houses that were his home for so long and at this time of year, with snow on the streets and a bitter wind howling, internal fuel is important. In a derelict area behind a disused power station I am shown round his old haunts, desolated factories and railhead depots, where the homeless still live. Mark and Lauren and Harry, three guests of the 'Riverfront Hilton', a ruined old warehouse, invite me to warm my hands round their fire. It is bitterly, bitterly cold and I stamp my feet hoping that I will soon be able to leave for the warmth of my cab. I find it impossible to imagine that this could be my home, my life. Harry and Mark take turns to show me piles of receipts they keep in their wallets, receipts which prove how much money they make selling old scrap.

'See, three hundred bucks a day . . . I can make more than that some days.'

Despite their abject poverty, homelessness and alcoholism they think of themselves as successful people. The receipts are so old as to be illegible. This pride and self-delusion is touching and bewildering.

We say goodbye and William takes me back to McMurphy's where a poetry evening is promised.

People (even Americans) often find it difficult to talk about themselves. Poetry gives them a kind of verbal costume in which they can express themselves with more dignity and confidence than the common dress of everyday speech will allow. I stand to talk to William's fellow addicts and poets, but I offer no poetry of my own. My own experiences seem so exotic, so well-fed and yet so ordinary next to theirs.

I drive north to Iowa alternately hugging myself and excoriating myself for my good fortune.

KENTUCKY
'To be honest, by the time
I've inhaled all those
fumes from the vats and
tasted the liquor in its
various stages of ageing
nothing much sinks in.'

WEST VIRGINIA
I am reminded that the
ceiling could collapse at
any point.

'Welcome to
Rocky
Branch, son.'

TENNESSEE
Sharing a humerus moment with Rebecca.

NORTH CAROLINA
With Rick the balloonist, taking off
over the North Carolina countryside.
Vertigo is replaced by astonishment.

SOUTH CAROLINA
Miss Anita explains the history
of the Gullah.

GEORGIA
I am a guest of a remarkable lady called Mrs Nancy
Schmoe. Her family, including her sister, Aunt Snead, have
gathered for Thanksgiving.

ALABAMA
There is no 'You're welcome' quite so believable as
the one you get from the South.

FLORIDA
Sometimes the cheesiest, most clichéd touristic activity can be entirely satisfactory.

Marvin, the happiest ninety-year-old
I ever met.

Zulus on parade.

LOUISIANA
Isaiah and Augustine of
the Lower Ninth.

MISSISSIPPI
Talking the blues with Morgan Freeman.

ARKANSAS
A little too 'Sanders of the River' for comfort . . .

MICHIGAN
A replica of Ford's original Detroit factory.

MISSOURI
Sharing warmth with
the homeless.

INDIANA
'So . . . you didn't want
to stay and help put
out the fire?'

IOWA
I am in a
thoroughly
bad mood
by this time.

ILLINOIS
Chicago: beauty and greatness.

WISCONSIN
'But will the sucker go on
the tit?'

MINNESOTA
Hard to tell which is bigger, the pike or my mighty sun fish.

IOWA
KEY FACTS

Abbreviation:
IA

Nickname:
The Hawkeye State, the Tall Corn State

Capital:
Des Moines

Flower:
Wild Rose

Tree:
Oak

Bird:
Eastern Goldfinch

Rock:
Geode

Motto:
Our liberties we prize and our rights
we will maintain

Well-known residents and natives:
Herbert Hoover (31st President),
Mamie Eisenhower, 'Buffalo' Bill Cody,
Grant 'American Gothic' Wood,
Meredith 'Music Man' Wilson, Bix Beiderbecke,

Bill Bryson, Johnny Carson,
George 'Superman' Reeves, Donna Reed,
John Wayne, Kate Mulgrew, Tom Arnold,
Michelle Monaghan, Ashton Kutcher,
Brandon 'Superman' Routh, Elijah Wood.

IOWA

'I am in a thoroughly bad mood by this time.'

Iowa's best-known fictional native is probably James Tiberius Kirk of the Starship Enterprise. In several *Star Trek* episodes he is called, or calls himself, an Iowa farmboy. Indeed, most Iowan natives will be called that or something similar when they leave the state to start at university or a new career. There is corn in the state seal and there is corn in the state's image and reputation. The seal also shows a riverboat, although in truth Iowa is wedged between the Mississippi and the Missouri, those rivers making up the border with Illinois and Wisconsin to the east and with Nebraska and South Dakota to the west. Iowa is known for illimitably huge flat cornfields, for Midwestern dullness: it is a place to escape from, as did Marion Morrison—wisely changing his name to John Wayne—and the two Supermen, George Reeves and Brandon Routh. The state's reputation for

243

sameness and tedium makes me determined to like it. Circumstances do not lend a hand in this well-meaning enterprise.

We have come to Fairfield, the county seat and principal town of Jefferson County, which lies somewhere between Iowa City and the Missouri state line. There is nothing much to mark it out from other small prairie towns in this part of the Midwestern United States: a square, a convention centre, a fine red-brick courthouse that looks like a mini St Pancras Station, a centre for the performing arts (notable for being the first named in honour of the composer Stephen Sondheim), remnants of the old railway lines that used to connect Fairfield to the greater world—all the amenities and municipal edifices you would expect in any medium-sized county seat.

Just north of the town there had flourished in obscurity for a hundred years an educational establishment called Parsons College, which enjoyed a brief bout of notoriety in the late sixties as a haven for Vietnam draft dodgers and academic last chancers. 'Flunk Out U', as it was known, eventually had its accreditation removed and was closed in 1973.

Whip-pan to a flashback of the Beatles arriving at Rishikesh, India to study Transcendental Meditation with the Maharishi Mahesh Yogi. TM becomes all the rage and adherents from around the world flock to courses and schools, nowhere more so than in the United States of America. With the business acumen that seems always to characterise self-styled spiritual people, the Yogi's team happen on that recently closed Parsons College in Jefferson County, Iowa, which they buy for an undisclosed sum.

M.U.M.

Since 1974 the Maharishi University of Management (formerly Maharishi International University) has opened its doors to students from around the world. I have come to have a look round both at its campus and a new township that has been built just outside, Maharishi Vedic City.

I look in on the office of one Dr Fred Travis, who has got his daughter Dariana wired up with dozens of electrodes to a computer. He is monitoring her EEG activity as she goes in and out of TM states. He explains to me what these data on screen reveal, but I am ashamed to say the theory has all gone out of my head. I seem to recall being surprised that the claim for TM is not that the brain relaxes but that it becomes more active. I may have got that wrong. I have never met any regular TM practitioner who has struck me as having a mind of any especial speed, dynamism or creative energy, but I have no doubt the practice gives pleasure and rewards to many. When the electrodes are implanted in my brain I cannot tell what it is that is different about the readings, but Dr Travis, whose qualifications are real enough, assures me that these experiments prove something. He is less comfortable when I ask him about yogic flying and other aspects of Vedic 'science'. Ah well.

Next I wander around the campus, noting the Maharishi Tower of Invincibility. There are almost no signs of the original Parsons College. Despite most of that campus being on the National Register of Historical Places, nearly all of it was bulldozed to make way for new buildings that accorded with the Maharishi Sthapatya Veda, which is a kind of Vedic Feng Shui. A few years before he died the Maharishi informed the world that it was vital for the whole planet to live and work in buildings constructed according to Sthapatya. It seems to come down to everything facing east and looking like a ghastly impersonal hotel.

I am in a thoroughly bad mood by this time. I wouldn't mind all this nonsense if it didn't arrogate half-understood principles of Western science, attempting to marry its 'philosophy' with the ideas behind quantum mechanics, probability, chaos theory and other essentially mathematical and empirically derived concepts. You cannot simultaneously insult Western thinking and use its precepts to 'prove' your moronic theories: not without losing my respect at least.

I go to the dining hall and eat with some of the students. The food at least is excellent, all organic, all fresh, none processed or frozen. I sit with some students, mostly Muslims, who come to the university to study computer science, which seems to be far and away the most popular course. They all appear to put up with the strictures of the university (lights out by 10.00 p.m., enforced physical exercise and TM) as a price they are willing to pay for an American education. I ask them if they will continue to adhere to the Maharishi's teachings and to TM after they leave. They all laugh. Of course not.

A painful night follows. I am staying in a hotel in Vedic City, which turns out to be a collection of houses off the main road with no focal centre and no sense at all of being a city or a community. The hotel does not serve alcohol. No winding down glass of wine or warming tumbler of whiskey for Stephen. I go to bed in a very bad mood indeed.

Early the next morning I watch the rush of

246

studentry to the main dome. They have to get there by eight o'clock to swipe their cards through a machine, pad into the hall and meditate for twenty minutes, which gives them course credits. If they miss more than a few of these daily rituals, they will be fined and docked their credits. I find this all very creepy. The film crew say that they think the students look too pale, too thin and too unhealthy. Where is the laughter, the fun, the boisterousness? Cynical about this weird place as I am, I point out that it is after all five minutes to eight in the morning. To find a student awake at that hour is miracle enough—to expect boisterousness would surely be asking too much.

I am pleased to put Maharishi University of Management and its Vedic City behind me, pleased to see the Tower of Invincibility diminishing in the rear-view mirror as I join the Mississippi once more and prepare to head back east and towards the Great Lakes.

OHIO
KEY FACTS

Abbreviation:
OH

Nickname:
The Buckeye State, The Heart of It All

Capital:
Columbus

Flower:
Scarlet Carnation

Tree:
Buckeye

Bird:
Cardinal

Beverage:
Tomato Juice

Motto:
With God, all things are possible

Well-known residents and natives:
Ulysses S. Grant (18th President),
Rutherford B. Hayes (19th President),
James Garfield (20th President),
Benjamin Harrison (23rd President),
William Howard Taft (27th President),

Warren Harding (29th President),
General George Armstrong Custer,
General William Tecumseh Sherman,
Clarence Darrow, John D. Rockefeller, Jack Warner,
Lew Wasserman, Ted Turner, Larry Flynt,
Annie Oakley, Gloria Steinem, John Glenn,
Neil Armstrong, Jim Lovell, Thomas Edison,
Orville and Wilbur Wright, Harvey Firestone,
Harriet Beecher Stowe, Sherwood Anderson,
James Thurber, Zane Grey, Toni Morrison,
James Levine, Steven Spielberg, Jim Jarmusch,
Chris Columbus, Theda Bara, Lillian Gish,
Dorothy Dandridge, Roy Rogers, Clark Gable,
Tyrone Power, Bob Hope, Doris Day, Dean Martin,
Phyllis Diller, George Chakiris, Paul Newman,
Hal Holbrook, Joel Grey, Martin Sheen,
John Lithgow, Rob Lowe, Tom Cruise,
Woody Harrelson, Halle Berry, Beverly D'Angelo,
Alison 'CJ' Janney, Sarah Jessica Parker,
Drew Carey, Nancy 'Bart Simpson' Cartwright,
Carmen Electra, Chrissie Hynde, Marilyn Manson.

OHIO

'I wish I could tell you of great adventures enjoyed in Ohio. I am photographed at the state line and . . . well, that is it.'

Yes, Ohio's State Beverage really is tomato juice. Not a word of a lie. I have not included the other states' choice of beverage because all but five choose milk (mostly because they are states that have cattle in them) and the lists would become repetitive. Only Ohio goes for tomato juice. Maine has Moxie listed, a weird fizzy potion composed of gentian root and other bitter herbs. It claims to be America's first soda pop. Alabama is the only state to elect an ardent spirit, Conecuh Ridge Whiskey. California has wine, predictably enough, while Florida and Massachusetts each opt for their native orange and cranberry juices. Indiana, pathetically, chooses water. Twenty-three states do not have a State Beverage at all. What spoilsports. Boo to them.

In a moving ceremony on 6 October 1965 the following was enacted into the State Legislature:

5.08 Official state beverage.
Text of Statute
The canned, processed juice and pulp of the fruit of the herb Lycopersicon esculentum, commonly known as tomato juice, is hereby adopted as the official beverage of the state.

It's up there with Magna Carta and the Bill of Rights.

NEIL YOUNG

I wish I could tell you of great adventures enjoyed in Ohio and great sights seen. I fear I have really done the state no favours at all. I can't even claim to have driven through it. I paralleled its border when I was in Kentucky all those weeks ago and I parallel its border now on the way to Indiana. I am photographed at the state line, I record a small piece to camera about Neil Young's song 'Ohio'. And . . . well, that is it. Farewell, Buckeye State, land of contrasts. We will carry you in our hearts for ever. And sorry.

Entirely not Ohio's fault. It was a matter of logistics. Although maybe Ohio is to blame for bordering so many states in such a contradictory fashion. That is why it calls itself 'The Heart Of It All', I suppose. It isn't a state so much as a connective tissue, joining the east, north, south and Midwest. It is technically designated an East North Central state, which tells you just how confused it is. It touches Canada to the north, Kentucky to the south and Pennsylvania to the East. There are big towns,

Cincinnati, Cleveland, Columbus (so much begins with C . . . even its state bird and flower) and there are Akron and Dayton, all big enough to make the state the seventh most populous in the union.

Neil Young's 'Ohio', incidentally, is all about the shootings by Ohio National Guardsmen, in May 1970, of thirteen unarmed student protesters on the campus at Kent State University, Ohio. Four were killed, one paralysed for life and another eight seriously injured. Perhaps the most shameful and shocking example to date of ruthless state power perpetrated in America against its own citizens, the massacre mobilised yet more people against Richard Nixon and the Vietnam War.

The students at Kent had been protesting the American involvement in Cambodia, although some of those shot were merely passers-by. The aftershock of the event was enormous, school and university strikes and shutdowns, and a 100,000-strong demonstration in Washington. One of the best-known images of the entire era is that of a female student screaming in pain and disbelief over the body of Jeffrey Miller, one of the students killed by the guardsmen. It was carried instantly around the world and played its part too in inflaming international opinion against the war.

If you don't know the Neil Young song, listen to it. It's really pretty good.

MICHIGAN
KEY FACTS

Abbreviation:
MI

Nickname:
The Wolverine State, the Great Lakes State,
the Automotive State, Water-Winter Wonderland,
the Mitten State

Capital:
Lansing

Flower:
Apple Blossom

Tree:
White Pine

Bird:
American Robin

Reptile:
Painted turtle

Motto:
Si quaeris peninsulam amoenam circumspice
('If it's a pleasant peninsula you're after, then look
around you')

Well-known residents and natives:
Pontiac (American Indian leader), Thomas Dewey,

Charles Lindbergh, Betty Ford,
Elijah 'the real' McCoy, Jimmy Hoffa,
Aileen Wuornos, Ivan Boesky, Edna Ferber,
Elmore Leonard, Joyce Carol Oates, Neil LaBute,
Ring Lardner, Richard Ellmann, Theodore Roethke,
Jim Bakker, Malcolm X, James (Barnum and
Bailey) Bailey, W. K. Kellogg, C.W. 'Grape Nuts'
Post, Henry Ford, Horace and John Dodge,
David Buick, John De Lorean, William Boeing,
Larry 'Google' Page, William 'Packard' Hewlett,
Steve 'Microsoft' Ballmer, Edgar Bergen,
Sandra Bernhard, Casey Kasem, James 'Inside The
Actors' Studio' Lipton, Jerry Bruckheimer,
Francis Ford Coppola, John Hughes,
Michael Moore, Sam Raimi, Paul Schrader,
George C. Scott, Tom Selleck, Steven Seagal,
Lily Tomlin, Robert Wagner, Elaine Stritch,
Lee Majors, Dick 'Rowan &' Martin,
George Peppard, Gilda Radner, Jason Robards,
Betty Hutton, James Earl Jones, Ellen Burstyn,
Tim Allen, Smokey Robinson, Diana Ross, Eminem,
Madonna.

MICHIGAN

'Despite my passion for driving I am relegated to the passenger seat.'

Google, breakfast cereals, the motor car, Diana Ross, Madonna, Eminem—Michigan seems to have done a great deal to help create the twentieth century. Its rather schizophrenic plenitude of nicknames hints at a state that cannot quite decide upon a stable identity. Cold in winter and blessed with an abundance of lakes ('Water Winter Wonderland'), the home of the Big Three car manufacturers ('The Automotive State') and—as a sop to nature perhaps—a place where you might, if you weren't busy, seek and find wolverines. Also, nature has decreed that the main peninsula is in the shape of a mitten, hence the final nickname. Like Chicago, which lies just over the water to the west of the state, Michigan is one of those places whose French presence in its history is betrayed by the soft 'ch' sound in its name. It would have been spelled Mishigan if the British had got there first, just as the city would have been Shicago, for they are both approximations of Native American names that were never written down. To a Frenchman, the Ojibwe Indian 'mishigami', meaning 'big water', was most naturally spelled michigami, which in its turn became Michigan.

The longest freshwater shoreline in the world of which Michiganders (for so they style themselves) are justly proud, is often frozen. When I arrive at the hotel in Dearborn, a town some eight miles west of Detroit, there is snow on the ground and a crisp snap in the air that tells me I had better dress up good and warm for the next day's open-topped motoring.

FORD'S GREENFIELD

Dearborn is Michigan's most popular tourist destination. An unprepossessing city of some 100,000 souls, it has no shoreline amenities, no fishing, hunting or kayaking on offer, but only the fruits of one man's vision. And what a man: one of the most intensely unlikeable figures of the twentieth century, fanatical anti-Semite, enemy of labour unions and proud recipient of medals from Nazi Germany, where Hitler held him in veneration, Henry Ford was also an employer who paid his workers more than his competitors, an innovator who pioneered the assembly line and a visionary whose part in the creation of the twentieth century was so great that Aldous Huxley, in his *Brave New World*, prefigured a society whose calendar was divided into BF and AF—Before Ford and After Ford: citizens in the book exclaim 'My Ford!' instead of 'My Lord!', say 'Ford's in his flivver, and all's well with the world' and make the sign of the T instead of the sign of the cross, in honour of Henry's most famous creation, the Model T.

Early in the cold, cold morning, I am all wrapped up and sitting in the passenger seat of a mint condition Model T, whose engine starts first time and continues to tick sweetly all day like a sewing machine. Despite my passion for driving I am relegated to the passenger seat because it is deemed unlikely that in my wounded state (the broken arm is still mending) I will be able to control this ancient conveyance safely around the icy streets of Greenfield Village, its hand-operated throttle and idiosyncratic transmission being notoriously difficult for the modern driver to master. Reluctantly I am brought to believe that the decision is the right one: here is a car where the right pedal operates the brake, the middle pedal engages reverse gear and the left pedal does something outré involving high gear and neutral. A weird set-up to us, but in the 1920s, most American drivers had learned to drive on one of these. Known affectionately as the Flivver or the Tin Lizzie, the Model T was the most successful motor car of its time, and perhaps remains to this day the most successful production model ever. Cheap and reliable, Ford's brilliant breakthrough was to create a car that his own workers could afford. Indeed, it was only four-months' salary to one of his workers. Contrary to widespread belief, for most of its nineteen-year run it was perfectly possible to buy one in a range of colours aside from the famous black.

This example, expertly driven by Kathy Cichon, is black as it happens and manages admirably the streets, which are as glass and cannot be walked on without slipping.

Ford had worked early in his career as an engineer with Thomas Alva Edison and admired the great inventor all his life. Indeed he is said to have captured the dying Edison's last breath in a glass vessel which can be inspected to this day in the Henry Ford Museum. It is certainly true that he transported the whole of Menlo Park, Edison's factory/research facility, all the way from New Jersey to Greenfield, Dearborn.

For Greenfield Village is Ford's mixture of a Disneyland re-creation of a folksy middle-American small town and a 'living' museum of American achievement. It contains not just Menlo Park, but also the North Carolina bicycle shop where Orville and Wilbur Wright first built a powered heavier than air flying machine. Not a replica of the bicycle shop, the actual bicycle shop itself, transported brick by brick, pane by pane. Thus within one small area one can commune with the birthplace of recorded sound, the light bulb, the aeroplane and the motor car. There is more besides: there are small dry-goods stores, Robert Frost's house, Rosa Park's bus, the theatre seat and limousine in which Lincoln and JFK were shot, models of aeroplane and motor car and home interiors from the ages.

The museum, known as The Henry Ford, is fantastically popular and successful: it is hard not to note the melancholy contrast between it and its founding corporation. Where once nine out of every ten cars owned in America were Fords, the Ford Motor Company is now struggling desperately, posting a recent loss that ran into the billions.

GM

Not so General Motors, the company that overtook

Ford in the thirties and has been the largest motor-car manufacturer in the world ever since. It is just managing to hold off Toyota, but its brands— Cadillac, Chevrolet, Buick and Pontiac (not to mention Saab, Opel and Vauxhall)—consistently outsell those of Ford and of the other member of the Detroit gang of three, Chrysler.

I go to GM's design and technical centre in Warren, a fabby creation by rationalist architect Eero Saarinen, whose concrete arch in St Louis, Missouri we have already met. I meet up with John Manoogian, designer of the latest Cadillac and am taken for a ride all round the campus. Inside, I am allowed a glimpse under the sheet at their new concept eco-car, the Volt, so long as our cameras are strictly turned off. The paranoia of automakers knows no bounds.

One thing is certain as I drive around industrial Detroit, allowing our cameraman views of the Ford Rouge Works (once the largest industrial centre in the world) and other smoky landscapes: they have never seen a car like my cab in Motor Town. At every traffic light in this car-conscious town I am stopped and quizzed about my black beauty. Some (insultingly) seem to believe that it is German, others wonder if it is a new Detroit concept car that I am street-testing.

Detroit can lay claim to being an urban vision of all America, characterised as it is by cars, crime and popular music. But across the water lies an altogether more beguiling and appealing city. Chicago.

But between Detroit and Chicago lies the northern part of the state of Indiana. First things first.

INDIANA
KEY FACTS

Abbreviation:
IN

Nickname:
The Hoosier State

Capital:
Indianapolis

Flower:
Peony

Tree:
Tulip Tree

Bird:
Cardinal

River:
Wabash

Motto:
The Crossroads of America

Well-known residents and natives:
William Henry Harrison (9th President),
Lew 'Ben Hur' Wallace, Wendell Wilkie,
Dan Quayle, Will 'Commission' Hays,
Orville 'Popcorn' Redenbacher, Colonel Sanders,
Halston, Bill Blass, Amelia Earhart, Gus Grissom,

Alfred Kinsey, John Dillinger, Jimmy Hoffa,
Eli Lilly, Jared Carter, Theodore Dreiser,
Lloyd C. Douglas, Gene Stratton Porter,
Booth Tarkington, Kurt Vonnegut, Irene Dunne,
Anne Baxter, Clifton Webb, Carole Lombard,
James Dean, Karl Malden, Steve McQueen,
Sydney Pollack, David Letterman, Shelley Long,
Greg Kinnear, Brendan Fraser,
Forrest Tucker, Hoagy Carmichael, Cole Porter,
John Mellencamp, Michael Jackson, Janet Jackson,
Axl Rose, Crystal Gale.

INDIANA

'I already look like ten types of twat, but worse is to come.'

Hoosier? Hoosier? What the *hell* is a Hoosier, you are entitled to ask. I don't know. Nobody seems to know. It is one of the best-known state nicknames in America. But it also seems to be a state secret. Citizens here are called Hoosiers more often than Indianans; every bar, realtor, lawyer's office and insurance company contrives to work the word into its name or its advertising. The 1954 Indiana State Champion basketball team had a film made about them called *Hoosiers*, starring Gene Hackman, Barbara Hershey and Dennis Hopper. It was nominated for two Oscars.

And yet *no one knows what the word means or where it comes from*. I mean, how careless is that? The state is less than two hundred years old. How could they have forgotten something as elementary as the origin of its nickname? The 's' in Hoosier, by the way, is often (but not always) pronounced 'zh', as in 'leisure' or 'measure'.

Here are just some of the explanations I have gleaned from various sources including native Indianans themselves.

Version 1
It's a corruption either of 'Who's yer' as in 'Who's yer friend?' or 'Who's here?' Both are said to be anxious equivalents of the kind of 'Who goes there? Friend or foe?' cry that is familiar in other cultures. **Verdict?** You don't need to tell me how utterly feeble and unconvincing this is as an explanation. Poppycock.

Version 2
Ear-biting was so common in brawls that 'Whose ear?' was a common cry as various body parts were picked off the saloon-bar floor. **Verdict?** Even more pathetic a theory than Version 1.

Version 3
There was once a businessman called Hoosier whose employees were known as 'Hoosier's men'. Well, if that's true it surely clears the whole issue up. Except that there is no record of such a man, or such a name, anywhere either in Indiana or anywhere else. **Verdict?** Drivel.

Version 4
To win a fight is to *hush* your opponent, so the brawny brawlers of Indiana became known as *hushers* which corrupted to Hoosiers. **Verdict?** In a pig's arse.

Version 5

A man called Colonel Lehmanowsky came to Indiana in the 1830s and lectured on the Napoleonic wars, taking especial care to praise the Hussars. Which Hussars? The French, the British? The Polish? The story doesn't say but goes on to suggest that young Indianan men listening to the lectures were so impressed that they went around the place putting on the airs of Hussars, which they had misheard as 'Hoosiers'. **Verdict?** Arse gravy of the worst possible kind. For a start Indianans were already called Hoosiers by the time this dubious-sounding Colonel came to Indiana.

Version 6

Hoosa is an Indian word for corn. Oh yeah? Research has not found a single one of the hundreds of Native American languages or dialects in which there is such a word for corn. It may be that the word was once in one of the many languages that has become extinct since the 1830s, but it's all a bit suspicious. **Verdict?** Highly doubtful.

Version 7

Hoose is an old English word for a disease suffered by cattle, which gives them a wild look consonant with the Indianan self-image. **Verdict?** Hmmmm . . . it is true that there is a parasitic bronchitis in cattle called hoose, but . . . it sounds suspiciously like someone hunted through the dictionary for words beginning with 'hoo' and tacked on an explanation afterwards.

Version 8

A *hoo* is an ancient English word for a rise in the

land, a promontory or cliff, as in Sutton Hoo and Luton Hoo. Maybe the word is from Hoo Shire, a place of rising land, so Hoosiers are basically hillbillies. **Verdict?** No, no, no. You're just thrashing about now.

Version 9
A Cumbrian word *hoozer* has been noted, meaning something uncommonly large. Same derivation as 'huge', I suppose. **Verdict?** Feeble. What's so huge about Indiana or the people of it? I'm getting bored with this now.

Version 10
It derives from a Hindustani word *huzur*, a term of address to anyone of rank or superiority. **Verdict?** Pure bottywash from start to finish. Hindustanis influencing Indiana in the 1830s? About as likely as a Bulgarian word for 'lawnmower' deriving from the Welsh for 'fondle'. Get a grip.

Version 11
From husker, as in corn *husker*. **Verdict?** Mm. Yes, all very well, but they are pronounced so differently: words don't take that kind of a pronunciation journey in so short a time. Nebraska is called the Corn Husker State after all, not the Corn Hoosier State.

So. There you have it. A complete mystery.

ELKHART

Indiana's biggest city is the capital, Indianapolis. The second-largest, Gary, like much of the northern part of Indiana, is overshadowed by the vastness of the Chicago metropolitan area. My destination is a smaller town still, which lies just about halfway between Detroit, MI and Chicago, IL.

Elkhart's greatest distinction is that it is the RV Capital of the World. RV stands for Recreational Vehicle—in other words the mobile homes (MH) that Americans are besotted with, expensively fitted with jacuzzis, microwaves and satellite TV. More than caravans, these customised behemoths are the ultimate expression of America's love affair with the road trip. Film stars use them as dressing rooms and places in which to hang out off-set, where they are known as trailers or Winnebagos, but for the America that is hooked on the 'RV lifestyle' they are motor homes and campers. All around the Elkhart area there are RV companies and the subsidiary industries that support them. And, this being America, you can of course visit the town's unique RV/MH Hall of Fame and Museum.

Elkhart strikes me as being just about a perfect example of the American small town. Large enough to offer ice rinks, colleges, a performing arts centre and its own newspaper, *The Truth* (I wonder if they know that's the same as the Soviet *Pravda*?), it is not so big as to be strip-malled into bland anonymity.

My appointment is with the fire chief, Mike, a ripely mustachioed figure who combines natural leadership with a wry sense of humour. He lets me ride up front in his huge truck. I feel like a little boy whose Christmases have all come at once. He even lets me sound the siren.

Dressed in the fire-fighting kit of a brown heat-resistant suit and a helmet, I already look like ten types of twat, but worse is to come.

266

Mike decides I am ready to try a real exercise in the crew's training tower where a fire has been started. The enemy, of course, is smoke more than flame and breathing apparatus is laid on my back and goggles and a mask attached to my face to make me look even more ridiculous. But appearance is of little significance when you are forced into a room where the smoke and gas is so noxious that you could lose consciousness in a minute.

Into such a room I go, with nothing but a thermal camera and a walkie-talkie to protect me.

Up the stairs to where the fire is raging. Hell's teeth. I cannot see a thing. I bump into crew members who move me gently aside, like grooms patiently pushing a horse away. Instinctively I crouch and begin to crawl along the floor. I know that the breathing apparatus will help me, but I cannot help coming close to hyperventilation: this world is so hellish and so impossible to interpret that panic seems like the best option. I feel a great source of heat and point the thermal camera in the direction of its source. The screen whites out.

Voices say things into the walkie-talkie that I cannot understand. People clap me on the shoulder and make elaborate gestures with their arms. I nod vigorously as if to show that I understand and to communicate that they are not to worry about me.

Slowly, I back out towards the stairs, turn and tumble down. Once outside it takes me five minutes of fumbling panic to get the goggles and mask off.

I made it! I survived the hell of a fire.

Ten minutes later the rest of the crew come down, laughing and chatting.

'So,' says Mike, a little puzzled, 'you didn't want to stay and help put out the fire?'

Ah. Yes. The triumph of my staying in the inferno for three minutes without screaming or knocking over any firemen is suddenly diminished. In all the excitement I have forgotten that I was there to help do some real fire-fighting. That was, after all, the point. The idea of being in that hell and working, thinking, cooperating and communicating . . . incredible.

At this moment I decide that a) firemen are remarkable and b) I will never ask to accompany them on their work again.

We return to the fire-station and Mike tells me about 9/11. He saw, like the rest of us, the planes hit the towers and the towers collapse. That evening he and half his crew were in their trucks on their way to New York City. They hadn't been sent for; they just knew that they were wanted. He stayed there, at Ground Zero, for over a month. God knows what kind of horrors he witnessed. I did not feel I could press him.

He points out with a mirthless grin that another disaster, Hurricane Katrina, whose ravages I saw back in Louisiana, did nothing but good for Elkhart. All that rehousing created an unprecedentedly huge and urgent demand for RVs.

I allow him to sit in the taxi, which is a treat begged for by many dignified and superficially cool and hard to impress Americans, before waving him goodbye.

ILLINOIS
KEY FACTS

Abbreviation:
IL

Nickname:
Land of Lincoln, The Prairie State

Capital:
Springfield

Flower:
Illinois Native Violet

Tree:
White Oak

Bird:
Cardinal

Snack food:
Popcorn

Motto:
State sovereignty, national union

Well-known residents and natives:
Abraham Lincoln (16th President), Ulysses S. Grant (18th President), Ronald Reagan (40th President), Richard J. Daley, Adlai Stevenson, Louis Farrakhan, Jesse Jackson, Richard M. Daley, Hillary Clinton, Barack Obama, Al Capone, Frank Nitti, Eliot Ness,

269

Enrico Fermi, Ernest Hemingway, James T. Farrell,
David Foster Wallace, John Deere, Marshall Field,
Montgomery Ward, Richard Sears,
Frank Lloyd Wright, Buckminster Fuller,
Mies van de Rohe, Walt Disney, Gregg Toland,
Michael Mann, Roger Ebert, Gene Siskel,
Jack Benny, Burl Ives, Rock Hudson,
Dick van Dyke, Gene Hackman, Richard Pryor,
George Wendt, Vince Vaughn, Miles Davis,
Muddy Waters, Buddy Guy, Bo Diddley,
Herbie Hancock, Alison Krauss, Kanye West,
Michael Jordan, Oprah Winfrey, Hugh Hefner,
Cindy Crawford.

ILLINOIS

'I am assured that here I will find the most glamorous objects in Chicago, perhaps, in the whole wide world.'

North Lynch Avenue in Chicago's dowdy and unremarkable Jefferson Park is far from glamorous and yet I am assured that here I will find the most glamorous objects in Chicago. In all America. The most glamorous objects, perhaps, in the whole wide world.

OSCAR

On a bitterly cold morning I find this neighbourhood entirely without appeal and begin to wish I had not bothered to come. I am standing outside the door of a low, aesthetically null building, the wind and snow whipping my face with cruel, icy flails. After a

271

muffled knock that is the most my bemittened hands can manage, the door opens. A wave of warm air wafts about me, bearing the alluring scents of kielbasa sausage, stove enamel, glue and swarf: a seductive aroma that says 'workshop', 'precision', 'skilled routine', 'cosy warmth' and 'breakfast' in equal and beguiling helpings.

I am here to help make an Oscar. A genuine Academy Award. For I have entered the factory of R.S. Owens, where the most famous statuette in the world has been made for the last quarter-century.

I am given an apron and gloves while the various stages are demonstrated before I am allowed to take a turn on my own. The basis of the Oscar is Britannia Metal, or Britannium, a Sheffield pewter alloy compounded of tin, copper and antimony. Antimony is highly toxic, of course. So Oscars are poisonous. A splendid murder mystery suggests itself—The Actress who Shaved off Parts of her Oscar and Fed Them to her Agent . . .

The rough figure, once it has emerged from its mould, is buffed on a buffing wheel (my hand keeps slipping) and then taken through to be dipped in copper and nickel. Within a surprisingly short time I do the final dunk, into a tank of pure gold, and there it is. My own Oscar. At this moment I am as close to an official Academy Award as I am ever likely to be.

Of course Owens makes hundreds and hundreds of other awards too, acrylic, perspex, plastic, copper, silver and bejewelled, but the Oscar is the one that everybody knows.

I wonder where mine is now. On a Coen brother mantelpiece, in Javier Bardem's lavatory, on a shelf in Daniel Day Lewis's bathroom? I shall probably never know.

Just so long as they don't lick it . . .

BUDDY GUY

There is time to stop for a genuine Chicago hot-dog at the Wiener Circle, one of the most appealingly impolite fooderies I have ever visited. Their Vienna beef franks are served up with heaping handfuls of onions, gherkins and rudeness, or 'sass' as the local listings paper calls it. This kind of food is worth living in Chicago for. I dare say the dogs are made of the worst kind of meat ('eyelids and assholes' a fellow diner suggests, chomping happily) but they work.

I am on my way to visit Buddy Guy, one of the last of the great bluesmen. He has his own club, Legends, where I will hang out this evening, but first he takes me on a tour of the South Side, the tough, mostly African-American neighbourhood where this native Louisianan made his bones as a young guitarist and singer of the blues.

Over the past weeks I have travelled up the Mississippi—through the Delta and up here to the Lakes. This is how Buddy travelled, when he was a boy, how Louis Armstrong travelled and it is how jazz and the blues themselves travelled.

Buddy is relaxed in the back of the cab as he shows me the haunts of his youth, and he is relaxed on stage as he sips from a brandy glass and jokes with his fans. In his seventies, he dresses as snappily as ever and flirts charmingly with girls young enough to be his granddaughters.

SKYSCRAPERS

Music is not the only cultural product that Chicago has exported around the world: I will come to that dread bitch, comedy, in a moment, but first it is worth remarking on Chicago's pre-eminence as a centre of great architecture. Most people who have visited both would agree that the quality of Chicago's skyscrapers is every bit as good, if not better, than New York City's. Mies van de Rohe, Frank Lloyd Wright and Buckminster Fuller are just the best-known architects to have lived and worked in Illinois; they and their reputations attracted hundreds of others. From its completion in 1973 until the erection of the Petronas Towers in Kuala Lumpur, the tallest building in the world was the Sears Tower in Chicago's Loop, the historic heart of downtown. The view from the Sears Tower Sky Deck at night shows that Chicago is still a heartstoppingly beautiful city, one of the greatest in the world.

THAT BITCH, COMEDY

Mike Nichols, Elaine May, Ed Asner, Paul Mazursky, Alan Arkin, Joan Rivers, Peter Boyle, Harold Ramis, John Belushi, John Candy, Bill Murray, George Wendt, Shelley Long, Jim Belushi, Dan Castellaneta, Mike Myers, Chris Farley, Steve Carell, Stephen Colbert, Kevin Dorff, Tina Fey . . . the list of Chicago Second City alumni is extraordinarily impressive. It is here in Chicago that the traditions of improvisational sketch comedy have reached their pitch of refinement and influence. TV comedies like *Saturday Night Live* and Hollywood have all consistently been fed by those who have trained here.

Absolutely not my thing. I may have started my life in comedy, but this kind of improvising is as alien and embarrassing to me as the prospect of ballet or powerlifting in public. It brings me out in hives just to think about it. And so what happens when I go and pay the Chicago Second City a visit? They, charming, fluffy, gleaming-toothed and sweet-natured every last one of them, insist on my joining in as they rehearse. Worse than that, I am slated to participate this evening on stage. In front of an audience.

Hell's teeth, arse and damnation. Never again. Not if my best friend's life depended on it. I can remember almost nothing of the deep torment of the performance, which passed in an agony of embarrassment and horror. Audience members shouted things out and we had to respond to them. The troupe was all very kind afterwards and claimed that the show had gone well, but frankly I have never dived into a vodka and tonic with such reckless abandon in all my life. I thought I would never emerge.

What a way to say goodbye to one of my favourite places in the world, Chicago, IL.

WISCONSIN
KEY FACTS

Abbreviation:
WI

Nickname:
Badger State, America's Dairyland

Capital:
Madison

Flower:
Wood Violet

Tree:
Sugar Maple

Bird:
Robin

Dance:
Polka

Motto:
Forward

Well-known residents and natives:
Golda Meir, Joseph McCarthy, William Rehnquist,
King Gillette, George 'Pen' Parker, Edna Ferber,
Georgia O'Keefe, Ella Wheeler Wilcox,
Thornton Wilder, Jim Lovell, Harry Houdini,
Frank Lloyd Wright, Alfred Lunt, Fredric March,

Don Ameche, Pat O'Brien, Orson Welles,
Spencer Tracy, Carole Landis, Joseph Losey,
Nicholas Ray, Jim Abrahams, David Zucker,
Jerry Zucker, Gene Wilder, Willem Dafoe,
Gena Rowlands, Mark Ruffalo, Jackie Mason,
Chris Farley, Tyne Daly, Tony 'Mr Monk'
Shalhoub, Eric 'CSI' Szmanda.

WISCONSIN

'But will the sucker go on the tit?'

What a lot of top-class comedy seems to have come out of Wisconsin. Jackie Mason, Gene Wilder and Abrahams, Zucker and Zucker, who gave us the *Airplane!* and *Naked Gun* movies. Maybe it's the weather.

I wake up in my bed-and-breakfast hotel room in Westby and despite the comfort of the bedclothes something in me just knows that it is shatteringly cold outside. And it is. A thermometer tacked onto a post of the porch reads -25°. Bear in mind that America talks Fahrenheit, where freezing is +32°. So we are 57° below freezing, or -31°C. Cold enough, frankly. They have had 88 inches of snow already this winter in Westby and there is more on the way.

When I get outside my body is so shocked I can only laugh. Or I think I am laughing. Actually, I realise, it is my lungs choking on the freezing water

278

vapour that I am inhaling. They have never ingested anything so cold in all their fifty years on the planet. It is so cold that the snow is freezing. So cold and so dry that if you throw a cup of scaldingly hot water into the air, the water will not freeze, it will actually disappear, be sucked instantly into the vapour-starved atmosphere.

Westby is in the centre of Vernon County, Wisconsin, a place of rolling hills and rich farmland worked by scattered Amish communities and the descendants of the large numbers of Norwegians who settled here in the nineteenth century. Viking paraphernalia and Scandinavian names are in evidence everywhere. Only hardy Norsemen can survive these dreadful temperatures.

One of Wisconsin's major products is cheese. You will notice that as well as calling itself The Badger State, Wisconsin considers herself 'America's Dairyland'.

You should trust by now that I love, respect, venerate and adore most things American. The people, the places, the institutions and the landscapes. So much here is of abiding value, charm, beauty and quality.

But not the cheese.

America doesn't get cheese.

They put up with the most hideous orange melted gunk, weird vestigial descendants of Munster and Cheddar, and with a processed liquid substance which is closer to a polymer than a foodstuff and which you can squirt from a bottle and, I promise you I'm not making this up, spray from a can. Cheese, in the real sense of the word, along with proper bread, can only be found in special places in America, usually cities with a student and artist population.

279

In Wisconsin they gather their cheese into a ball, cover it in breadcrumbs and deep-fry it. That is how little they regard their premier export.

There are however, tiny pockets of cheese literacy and cheese standards where 'artisanal' *affineurs* are producing cheese that one would use for more than the grouting of bathroom tiles. If my taxi will start and once started, will negotiate the icy, snow-packed roads, I shall visit one such farm.

Mirabile dictu, the taxi does start, at the merest twitch of the key she springs into life. Her suspension and steering are not set up for ice, however, and I have to be immensely careful as we climb the hills to my destination. It is an unimaginably beautiful drive, nonetheless: on a crystal-clear day, along snow-sculpted lanes, passing trees so overladen with snow that I am fearful the vibrations from my taxi will cause them to dump their loads on me as I pass.

I arrive at last at the most perfect farm I have ever visited. From the main barn I hear the sound of a thousand newborn lambs bleating for milk.

Brenda Jensen, who runs this farm with her husband Dean, puts me to work straight away. Attaching electric suckers to the teats of ewes is not as easy as you might think. It would be easier to pierce Mike Tyson's nipples against his will. The ewes are *desperate* to be milked and their full thick-veined udders swing in front of me as they line up in the milking shed. I am distressed at their distress.

But will the sucker go on the tit? I do my best and manage to hook up about six sheep, but at the rate I'm going it will be time for evening milking before I've drained the last bag. It is the animals' own blasted fault. It seems that every day a ewe must, like some *rive gauche* existentialist, reinvent herself daily and

280

consequently she will have no idea what she did yesterday. She is frantic to be milked but cannot recall that the metal suction cups, far from being her enemy, are her friend and will bring her and her swollen udder nothing but relief. Such are the trials of being a Left Bank intellectual. Either that or she is very, very, very stupid.

As a reward for my efforts, Brenda takes me to the outbuildings where the cheese-making takes place. Stirring the cream and adding the animal rennet that kickstarts the fermentation, that I can manage. I am even allowed a taste of their excellent cheese.

Brenda's farm does not use tractors or much modern machinery. She prefers carthorses and sledges to motorised transport and there is much to be said for it. I notice a pair of donkeys in the field.

'They work too?' I ask.

'Oh yes,' says Brenda. 'Security.'

It seems that donkeys will scare off coyotes, wolves, humans—anything or anyone who comes close to the farm at night. Rather than patrols, electric fences, TV cameras or dogs, all a farm needs to keep its livestock safe is a pair of guard donkeys.

I ride by horsedrawn sled to the neighbouring Amish farm, where there is some extra milk to be picked up. Two Amish men help me load churns onto the back of the sled.

You are probably wondering why there are no photographs here of the Amish men. The Amish, members of a strict religious grouping descended from German and Swiss Mennonites, forbid electricity, telephones and—explicitly—photography. I found them charming, friendly, funny and kind, much more lively and high-spirited than I had expected of a people who live so old-fashioned a life: a life without formal

281

education, television, radio, internet and cars. They speak a variation of German, the men grow beards without moustaches (an oddity they share with some fundamentalist Muslims) and their clothes are home made, as are their houses and barns. Their village was astoundingly beautiful and hauntingly quiet.

Brenda and Dean tell me they are the perfect neighbours, kindly, helpful and strong, but also discreet, modest and completely unpushy.

This part of Wisconsin is one of the few places I have visited in America where life feels simpler and more traditional than in even the remotest areas of Europe. And it is the first place in America I have visited where they *get* cheese. For that reason and that reason alone it will have a secure and permanent place in my heart.

MINNESOTA
KEY FACTS

Abbreviation:
MN

Nickname:
North Star State, Land of 10,000 Lakes,
The Gopher State

Capital:
St Paul

Flower:
Pink and White Lady Slipper

Tree:
Red Pine

State muffin:
Blueberry

Bird:
Common Loon

Motto:
L'Etoile Du Nord ('The Star of the North')

Well-known residents and natives:
Hubert Humphrey, Eugene McCarthy,
Walter Mondale, Frank Kellogg, Charles 'Clinic'
Mayo, John S. 'Doughboy' Pillsbury,
Charles Lindbergh, Kofi Annan, J. Paul Getty,

Billy Graham, Robert Mondavi, F. Scott Fitzgerald, Sinclair Lewis, Robert 'Zen' Pirsig, Robert Bly, Anne Tyler, August Wilson, Charles 'Peanuts' Schulz, Garrison Keillor, Terry Gilliam, Mike Todd, William Demarest, Gig Young, Jane Russell, Tippi Hedren, Richard Widmark, E.G. Marshall, James 'Gunsmoke' Arness, Gale Sondergaard, George Roy Hill, Peter 'Mission Impossible' Graves, Mike 'BJ in MASH' Farrell, Jessica Lange, the Coen Brothers, Winona Ryder, Josh Hartnett, Vince Vaughn, The Andrews Sisters, Tiny Tim, Bob Dylan, Prince.

MINNESOTA

'I catch a fish. And what a whopper. A sun fish that must have been nearly four whole inches. Possibly even four and a half.'

In terms of temperature, Wisconsin, it turns out, was a mere John the Baptist to Minnesota's Shivering Messiah of Cold.

I arrive at the Twin Cities of St Paul and Minneapolis and have pointed out to me the enclosed pedestrian bridges above us. They link buildings across the streets at first- or second-storey level and there seem to be scores of them. They are called skyways and exist for one reason only. It is so unbearably freezing in winter that no one, no one, no matter how well wrapped up, wants to venture out onto the streets. The skyways allow the citizens to travel the city centre, shop, eat and work, without once exposing themselves to the arctic temperatures without. The car is in a heated garage at home, they drive to an underground car park (heated) and ascend by elevator to the office where they work or to the shopping centre they have come to visit. It means that in the coldest city in America most of the citizens go out in temperatures of -40 without gloves or a hat. The smart ones keep something in the trunk/boot, however. Just in case.

Incidentally, you may be asking yourselves whether I mean Fahrenheit or Centigrade when I write -40°. Let me cause a frown of puzzlement to crease your pure and noble brow. It makes no difference. None whatever.

Huh?

Well, it just so happens that -40° is the temperature at which Celsius and Fahrenheit exactly meet. It's one of those things.

THE ICE HOLE: AUGURS AND SONAR

Anyhoo, as they say up here in that Scandinavian–American accent made popular by Minnesotan natives Joel and Ethan Coen in their film *Fargo*. I am here to make the best of the cold weather. Those urbanite Minnesotans who avoid it in the Twin Cities have counterparts who embrace it.

One of the most popular activities in the state is ice-fishing. In a 'land of 10,000 lakes', as Minnesota proudly calls itself, with winters in which the temperature often stays below freezing for months, you can devote almost half the year to an ice culture. Camper vans, tented villages, whole encampments grow up on the bodies of water that surround Minneapolis and St Paul. You can drive ten-ton trucks onto the ice, so thickly frozen it is.

Viewed from the air (and I am lucky enough to get a plane ride over the city) these encampments can be seen to number in the hundreds. Mostly men. All devoted to fishing. And here we come close to the heart of the American character and its self-contradictory mosaic of oddities.

Ice-fishing, as imagined by you and me, is a traditional sport, passed down from the Eskimos and Indians (we eschew the incorrect political correctness that would have us say 'Inuit' and 'Native American'—they don't say it themselves and they think we're silly for trying). A traditional sport, but a simple one. A small hole is made in the ice. A little rod and line with a baited hook at the end is dangled in and we wait for our quarry to bite . . .

Such a proceeding, ancient, primal and atavistic, is surely to be desiderated in a modern America of shopping malls and leaf-blowers? Time to wind down. To commune with a chilly but benign nature. To be at one with the wind and the snow and the frozen waters. A farewell to machinery and noise. Simplicity.

If you think that, as I confess to having done, then it shows you still have much to learn about America. Principally about the American male, who is closer to Homer Simpson than ought to be allowed.

Tools. Gear. Power machinery. Big trucks. Gadgets. Noise.

I meet Tim at the bait and tackle shop where I buy my fishing licence. We drive in his enormous pick-up truck to the shores of Lake Minnetonka. The Minne element derives from a Lakota word meaning 'water'. Minnesota means 'clouded water'. If like me, as a child you were made to learn parts of Longfellow's 'Song of Hiawatha' (which is all set in Minnesota) you will remember the lines about Hiawatha's lover: 'Minnehaha, Laughing Water, / Handsomest of all the women'. Actually Minnehaha doesn't mean laughing water, it means 'curling water', or waterfall, but I prefer Longfellow's interpretation. Minnetonka, means 'big water' and driving around it to find Tim's preferred fishing site, I could see that it was well named. It is nothing to Lakes Michigan or Superior, but its 140 miles of shoreline rather put Derwentwater and Windermere to shame.

Tim turns off the road and suddenly we are on the lake. We drive towards a huddle of tents and other trucks where Tim's fishing cronies have already set up. I close my eyes and gulp a little. Of course Tim knows what he is doing. It is February and the ice is thick. It will not crack or melt. But that same part of me that cannot help thinking when the helicopter takes off or the plane bumps against the wind— 'Today is the day it all goes wrong. Today is the day I die'—that part of me is fully active. I can almost hear the ice creak beneath our preposterously huge tyres. 'We are the straw that is breaking this mighty camel's back,' I whisper to myself. 'It's all over. Goodbye, cold world.' The fact that I am writing this now shows how futile were my fears. Had I known what a battering the ice was yet to take I should have been even more timorous, however.

While the fishing apparatus is taken down from the back of the truck I go for a ride on a Ski-doo. Strange machines and a little bumpier than my healing humerus would have preferred, but a style of travel that can certainly be described as fun. When I return, pink and frozen-cheeked, the equipment is ready to be put into operation.

First there is the Icemaster King Power Auger. A

pull on the start-rope and the sound of fifty chain saws rends the air. Tim grins widely. An American in heaven. He is a noble pioneer pitting his wits against nature and he has the plaid and the power tool to prove it.

Within about forty seconds a perfect round hole has been made in the ice. Tim complains about the pile of slush that has to be kicked down into the hole before one can see it in all its perfection. It is natural that as the auger revolves and descends, slushy ice is sent up to the surface, like wood shavings or masonry powder when you drill. But there is a new piece of kit recently launched, which Tim will be buying next week—the Slusher. This attaches to a power drill and allows you to kiss goodbye to the misery of that pesky pile of slush. Instead of kicking it back down the hole (the work of a minute) you can now power it back down the hole. Bliss.

So now we have a hole. But technology has more to offer. Down the hole is lowered a long tube at the end of which is sonar equipment. Yes. Sonar. The same sonar that was developed by the Royal Navy in the war to defend shipping against the U-Boat wolf packs.

At the surface a screen reveals the results of the sonar's soundings in green shapes that represent fish.

Now Tim lowers a camera. A colour video camera.

Finally I am handed a little rod which is weighted, baited and lowered.

Ice-fishing is now a question of watching the sonar, which shows fish from some distance, and—as they approach the hook—turning your attention to the television monitor. When a fish swims into view you can twitch your rod a little to interest the fish in it and then—evil cackle—they are yours. Mwah-haha.

Poor creatures. They really don't stand much of a

chance do they?

Not much time passes, then, before I catch a fish. The first I ever caught in all my life. And what a whopper. A sun fish that must have been nearly four inches from head to tail. Four whole inches. Possibly even four and a half.

Tim's friends at some neighbouring hole catch a pike that may be technically a little larger than my sun fish, but it is a lot less appealing. They return it to the frozen deeps, whilst I keep my sun fish. Naturally Tim has full cooking equipment: gas, pans, flatware and so forth. It is the work of a moment to sauté my fish in butter and share it around. Exquisitely delicious. The best fish I have ever had.

What the huntsmen say is true: it tastes better if you have caught it, trapped it, shot it, netted it, harpooned it yourself.

After all that excitement in the wilds of the lake, with nothing but engines, motors, heaters, snow machines, generators, computers, cooking equipment and trucks between us and raw, savage nature, it is time to return to the comforts of civilisation.

AMONG THE HMONG

The next morning, before saying farewell to Minnesota I go to the Hmong market, to breakfast and to shop with State Senator Mee Moua, America's first and only Hmong legislator.

The Hmong, pronounced and sometimes spelled Mong, are a people who originated in China, but lived for many years in exile in Laos. They supported the US during the Vietnam War and many of them were settled in America during the 1970s, principally in

Fresno and the Twin Cities of Minnesota.

They thrived very quickly and their skills in agriculture and hunting were so impressive that they caused some resentment amongst established Minnesotans, who claimed they must be cheating and not obeying licensing and close season regulations. Despite not using two-stroke ice augers, wi-fi crossbows, motorised hunting knives, electric buttock-warmers and heat-seeking harpoons, the Hmong hunters seem constantly to outperform their European neighbours.

This discomfort aside, the Hmong have integrated over the last generation or so to the extent that there is now some concern among their elders who are worried that the ancient language and traditions may be lost as Hmongs enter the army, serve abroad and generally enter mainstream life, indistinguishable from any other Chinese-Americans. Thus the cycle of insecurity and tension that has always characterised immigrant populations that join the great melting pot.

My next state has faced fewer of these tensions than most. I am headed for Montana and the buffalo.

THE ROCKIES, THE GREAT PLAINS AND TEXAS

MONTANA
KEY FACTS

Abbreviation:
MT

Nickname:
Treasure State, Big Sky Country,
Land of Shining Mountains,
The Last Best Place,
The Bonanza State, the Stub Toe State

Capital:
Helena

Flower:
Bitterroot

Tree:
Ponderosa Pine

Bird:
Western Meadowlark

Grass:
Bluebunch wheatgrass

Motto:
Oro y plata ('Gold and silver')

Well-known residents and natives:
Theodore 'Unabomber' Kaczynski, Norman
Maclean, Richard Brautigan, Evil Knievel,

Gary Cooper, Myrna Loy, George Montgomery, Sam Peckinpah, Peter Fonda, Carol O'Connor, David Lynch, Patrick Duffy, Dirk 'A-Team' Benedict, Dana Carvey, Charlie Pride.

MONTANA

'There is a lot of space here. A lot of space.'

Not the most effulgent list of prominent citizenry, but while only Alaska, Texas and California may be larger in size than Montana, it is also true that only Alaska, Delaware and the Dakotas have lower populations. There is a lot of space here. A lot of space. And there is a line . . . a very famous line:

> I see a long, straight line athwart a continent. No chain of forts, or deep flowing river, or mountain range, but a line drawn by men upon a map, nearly a century ago, accepted with a handshake, and kept ever since. A boundary which divides two nations, yet marks their friendly meeting ground. The 49th parallel: the only undefended frontier in the world.
>
> *From the prologue to the film* 49th Parallel

The phrase '49th Parallel' is often used to describe the entire border between the US and Canada. Perhaps the title of that Powell and Pressburger film, starring Eric Portman and Laurence Olivier (wearing a moustache and one of his most absurd accents, that of a French Canadian trapper), contributed to this fallacy, for it is chiefly in the west that the frontier actually follows that line of latitude. Further east, cities like Toronto and Montreal are actually quite a long way south, on the 44th and 46th parallels. But here in Montana, all 550 miles of northern border are shared with Canada and follow—so much as the mapping technology of the nineteenth century allowed—the 49th line of latitude.

As for the film's claim that it is 'the only undefended frontier in the world' . . . well, poor dear Canada may not have a reputation as a hotbed of insurgency and terrorism or arms, people and drug smuggling, but all American frontiers in the post-9/11 era are now guarded with a new and implacable urgency, so undefended it is not. Since 2002 the US Customs and Border Protection Service has been part of an overarching government body, the fearsome Department of Homeland Security. This status is reflected in new uniforms, a bigger budget and an even higher sense of patriotism and moral purpose.

THE BORDER

I visit the border with patrolmen John and Alex, driving up from Shelby through the delightfully named one-truck towns of Sunburst and Sweetgrass.

And there she lies: the 49th Parallel. A fence. Not a formidable barrier, but a fence all the same. I watch

297

with envy birds flying over without documentation or security checks of any kind. It is cold, very cold facing Canada in the northernmost part of Montana. It therefore comes as a shock when John tells me, with the smug air of one who knows that he is delivering a knockout blow, that here on the 49th we are on the same line of latitude as France. The line goes through Paris, for heaven's sake.

'So how come P-p-paris doesn't get this c-c-c-cold?' I ask, through chattering teeth. John has no answer for that. I have no doubt it has something to do with the Arctic (which is no nearer to us than it is to Paris, but no matter) and with mountains and winds and gulf streams. All the same.

There is no action on the border. No would-be immigrants pressing their faces up against the wire.

The following morning, when I fly over in a European AS350 A-Star helicopter (we are shown a grounded Black Hawk, but the rest were all in service, I am told) the same atmosphere of muffled winter hush pervades. This would be no time to attempt an illegal border crossing. Any human would be visible for miles. And there would be footprints that even I could track.

Not for the first time I am forced to contemplate the melancholy truth that, in one significant way at least, Al Qaeda has won. Its victory in the interior of the United States may not be complete, but it is enough. Through one outrageous and atrocious act and the credible threat of more, they have ensured that America's freedoms and conveniences have been unprecedentedly curtailed. Queuing up for security checks in every international and domestic airport, having one's sun-cream, nail scissors and mineral water binned and one's patience worn down, these are minor but palpable victories. No one dares say it in the queues as they build and build, it would be considered unpatriotic. That fact, that the truth itself is now unpatriotic, that too is a victory. Al Qaeda have cost the US and its citizens untold billions in time and manpower, in inconvenience and stress. And along the thousands and thousands of miles of international borders, they are costing American tax-payers billions more. New helicopters, thousands of new recruits. The bill is incalculable.

TURNER BISON SYSTEM

The ugliness of man seems a long way from the glaciers and mountains below, which create a landscape as monumentally beautiful as any I have ever seen. I drive the taxi from Helena, the state's capital through the Gallatin Forest, skirting entrances to Yellowstone Park which is, frustratingly, closed to visitors between November and mid-April. But the Gallatin National Forest is beautiful enough, and takes me closer to my destination, Bozeman and the Flying D Ranch.

Who is the biggest landowner in Britain? Most Britons would suggest the Crown. Followed by the Church. Followed by Trinity College, Cambridge and the Duke of Westminster. Or something similar. And they would have been able to proffer the same names for hundreds of years. But who is the biggest landowner in America, not counting the Federal Government? It is an individual who began buying tracts in a serious way only twenty years or so ago. He is now far and away the possessor of the most private land in all of the United States of America, owning

299

ranches in South Dakota, Kansas, Oklahoma, Nebraska, New Mexico and—which is why I'm here—Montana. In all he owns around 3,000 square miles of land. The land is used to graze bison. He has the largest herd in the world.

Bison (often called buffalo) once roamed the Great Plains of North America (the vast swathe of steppe east of the Rocky Mountains) in unimaginable numbers, sustaining tens of thousands of Plains Indians who were nourished by their flesh and warmed by their hides. Then the Europeans arrived with their horses, their rifles and their scientific ways of killing. There were 'bags' of between 2,000 and 100,000 bison *a day* during the height of the slaughter. Within twenty years the numbers had been so drastically reduced that the entire species was under threat. Even William Cody, Buffalo Bill himself, pleaded for legislation to protect the herds. President Ulysses S. Grant and others deliberately squashed any bills for the bison's protection, however, for they knew that if the bison went extinct then the lives of those pesky Plains Indians would be made immeasurably more difficult. Not America's finest hour. So-called civilised men colluding to perpetrate both genocide and the extermination of an entire animal species in one fell swoop. Fortunately for the bison, one or two enlightened ranchers maintained small private herds and kept them alive. Since then they have bounced back impressively. It is estimated that there are now 500,000 bison in total, of which approximately 300,000 are in the United States and 50,000 belong to the Mouth of the South himself, Mr Ted Turner.

Turner is best known in Britain for marrying Jane Fonda and founding CNN, but in America the Turner

Broadcasting System also provides the popular channels TBS, TNT and TCM. An extraordinarily generous and, some would say, eccentric philanthropist, he has famously donated one billion dollars to the United Nations. As much, one cannot help feeling, to annoy the American Right who abominate that institution as for any other reason. I have no doubt that is unfair, but he does seem to enjoy his maverick status as one of the richest liberals in the world, taking time to insult equally the Iraq war, religion and the gun lobby. He also promotes environmentally sensitive land ownership and the protection of native flora and fauna.

The ranch he spends the most time in is the Flying D, outside Bozeman, Montana. I drive through the gates and urge the reluctant taxi along mile after mile after mile after mile after mile of road until we arrive at the ranch house. He has consented to have breakfast with me and show me around the 'spread'.

A trim, silver-haired, sexily moustached sixty-nine-year-old, he stands and greets me in the log-beamed dining room in jeans and cowboy boots, every inch the rancher, affectionate dogs frisking at his heels and every inch the billionaire, attentive people lurking within earshot in case he should need anything.

While he is pleased to own these bison, he tells me, sitting down in front of a bowl of granola and bidding me do the same, the purpose is to demonstrate to the world that you do not need to keep them for charitable and environmental reasons alone. Unstoppable entrepreneur that he is, he has made a true-blue, hard-headed business out of the animals: Ted's Montana Grill, of which there are now sixty branches nationwide, and which all bear the slogan 'Eat Great. Do Good'. The bison steaks and burgers they serve are, claims Ted, higher in protein and lower in fat and cholesterol than any comparable meat. Nothing is frozen or microwaved and everything is as eco-friendly as he can make it. The take-away cups in the restaurants are made of corn-starch, the menus are printed on recycled paper, the soaps in the restrooms are biodegradable and the drinking straws are made of paper, not plastic. He is clearly most proud of this and is happy to dedicate the latter part of his life to promoting healthy and environmentally aware eating the American way: no arty-farty salady nonsenses, nothing but good red meat western style.

Ted Turner has that characteristic I have always found in hugely successful entrepreneurs: a disposition to talk uninterruptedly without listening to anyone else who might be in the room. Years of power, of being proved strategically and tactically right in almost everything he has done and of being surrounded by sycophantic adherents have led to this trait no doubt, though to be fair it is also true that his hearing is not what it was and it is also true that he has no reason to suppose that I, or anyone else, can tell him anything he doesn't know or anything even remotely interesting. I have no problem with his loquacity: I am here, after all, to record an interview with him and the more he talks the better, especially as his people have told me that I have only an hour and half before he needs to fly off to Atlanta.

Again with the confidence and arbitrary certainty of the super-rich, he suddenly rises as if bored with my conversation (which he might well be since I haven't had the chance to say anything more than 'yes' for the last ten minutes) and says, 'Let's go find some bison.'

He has tens of thousands of them on this ranch, but that doesn't make them easy to track down, for the

Flying D is an enormous piece of land in which ten of thousands of brontosaurus could happily lose themselves without fear of discovery.

After a consultation with a ranch hand, we drive off and—near a house belonging to one of Ted's sons— we spot them. Shaggy-coated, goatee bearded and hump-backed, there is something primally satisfying about the shape of these vast creatures. Ted tells me that they are in fact, technically at least, *dwarf* bison, the really huge species having died out as recently as 10,000 years ago, along with American mammoths and elephants.

Nonetheless, dwarf or not, these are far from friendly beasts and we dismount from the truck and approach with caution. Ted tells me that he is keen for his land to sustain, not just bison, but all kinds of native species. Prairie dogs, for example, which are gopher-like burrowing creatures regarded as a 'keystone' species whose presence will encourage all kinds of eagles, hawks, foxes, ferrets and badgers to flourish.

We film away as close to the herd as possible and then Ted looks at his watch.

'Okay,' he says, 'I have to go now. Stay as long as you like.'

And he is gone. A likeable, stylish individual who seems to have got more pleasure from his money and done more with it than most.

We finish up our filming without him and, after skirting the herd like hunters, we get our footage and leave the ranch. Ten bouncy miles later we are back on the public highway and heading for Idaho. But first we stop off for ten minutes to admire some wolves and bears in a small sanctuary on the way. Bison, wolves, billionaires and grizzlies all on the same day—I couldn't be happier.

303

IDAHO
KEY FACTS

Abbreviation:
ID

Nickname:
The Gem State, The Spud State

Capital:
Boise

Flower:
Syringa

Tree:
Western White Pine

Bird:
Mountain bluebird

Slogan:
'Great potatoes. Tasty destinations.'

Motto:
Esto perpetua ('Let it be forever')

Well-known residents and natives:
Chief Joseph, Ezra Pound, Edgar Rice 'Tarzan'
Burroughs, Ernest Hemingway, Lana Turner.

IDAHO

'I pour water on the Idaho side and it will make its way to the Pacific . . . I pour it a tad on the Montana side, and it will flow to the Mississippi.'

Oh dear. I feel immeasurably guilty about my time in Idaho. It was just one of those things, one of those unfortunate logistical necessities. A glance at the map will show you how our journey down the Great Plains, from Montana to Texas, including Wyoming, the Dakotas, Nebraska, Kansas, Colorado and Oklahoma, is higgledy-piggledy enough without including Idaho on the itinerary. But include it I had to, for it would not fit into the next journey up from New Mexico to Washington State either.

En route from Montana to Wyoming, therefore, I stop off at the state line that Montana shares with Idaho. I choose that particular section of the state line that is also the Continental Divide, for I have a piece to camera to do explaining this geographical phenomenon.

No matter how hard I try and grasp the nature of landscape and terrain, it still astonishes me how much it is all a question of gravity. That there are floodplains, valleys, estuaries and deltas is all down to one ineluctable fact. Water will flow downwards. And if there is no downwards—i.e. if it is in a piece of flat land—it will not flow at all.

The entire continental United States is divided in two, for fluvial or river-ish purposes. Water will either flow into the Atlantic or into the Pacific. If it flows south into the Gulf of Mexico, that counts as the Atlantic of course.

Right. I get that. I may have given up geography at school very early and still be unsure of what a rift valley or a terminal moraine is, but I can get the fact that any water that falls from the sky or tumbles from the melting snow of the mountains must end up somewhere. Given that America is not, despite appearances, a flat bowl in the middle, the water follows gravity and makes it to the sea. The sea is at a lower level than the land and therefore all water must inevitably end up there.

The Great Divide, the name given to the continental divide in the United States, is surprisingly far west. Part of it runs down between Idaho and Montana before it makes its way a little further eastwards and down through Wyoming, Colorado and New Mexico.

I stand on the divide itself and demonstrate to camera, with the aid of a bottle of mineral water, the significance of this line. I pour water on the Idaho side and it will make its way to the Pacific . . . I pour it a tad to the east, on the Montana side, and it will flow to the Mississippi and out into the Gulf.

Do I find time to tell the BBC audience that Idaho is best known for being the potato capital of

America—hence its secondary nickname, The Spud State? One in every three potatoes bought in America is grown here. Do I explain that it was to this state that Ernest Hemingway came to live for a few years, before ending his life with a shotgun blast to the head in 1961? Do I mention that the very name of the state, Idaho, was apparently made up by an eccentric called Willings in the 1860s, claiming without foundation that it was based on a Shoshone Indian phrase meaning 'gem of the mountains'—the so called Idahoax?

I am ashamed to say I do none of these things. Of all the states I have visited, Idaho gets the shortest shrift. A glass of water and no more. I feel terrible about this and have promised that I will make up for it with a private visit just as soon as I am able.

Heigh ho. Farewell, Idaho.

WYOMING
KEY FACTS

Abbreviation:
WY

Nickname:
Equality State, Cowboy State

Capital:
Cheyenne

Flower:
Wyoming Indian Paintbrush

Tree:
Plains Cottonwood

Bird:
Western Meadowlark

Fish:
Cutthroat trout

Motto:
Equal rights

Well-known residents and natives:
Dick Cheney, William 'Buffalo Bill' Cody,
Jackson Pollock, E. Annie Proulx, Harrison Ford.

WYOMING

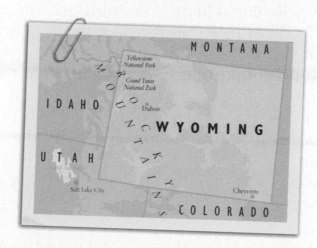

*'It was the French who discovered the Grand Tetons
. . . they gave them the name that the French just
would: The Three Tits. Les Trois Tétons.'*

Why oh why, oh ming? Land of Laramie and
Cheyenne, true cowboy country at last. I remember
as a boy watching westerns and being confused by
the fact that, while they were usually shot in deserts
dotted with scrub and cactuses and bleached cattle
skulls, the cowboys were often shown riding through
ice and snow too. It seemed contradictory to me that
a country could be both burning hot and freezing
cold. Like picturing snow in the Sahara or palm trees
in Antarctica. But that is the true west for you. A land
of extremes.

Wyoming has it all: the Rocky Mountains, the
Range and those High Plains where Clint Eastwood so
famously drifted. It is the least populous state in
America, containing less than half a million citizens,

each having, on average, more than five square miles to play in all by themselves. Wyoming shares with its neighbour Colorado the distinction of being one of only two states which are entirely rectangular. Looking at them in an atlas you can picture bearded nineteenth-century politicians and surveyors in Washington leaning over a map of the United States with a ruler and a set square in their hands.

But for all its wilderness and maverick spirit, Wyoming is becoming an increasingly popular destination for the well-heeled. Jackson Hole in the Grand Teton National Park is one of the swankiest skiing resorts in the world, up there with Gstaad and Aspen.

I am embarrassed to say that I had never heard of the Grand Tetons before. Part of the Rockies, they abut Yellowstone and are as majestic and beautiful a mountain range as any I have seen. Were they in Europe they would vie with some of the Alps for supremacy. But like so much that is tucked away in the vastness of America, they are there to be discovered. It was the French in fact who discovered them for Europe and it was the French who gave them the name that . . . well they gave them the name that the French just would: The Three Tits. *Les Trois Tétons*. This is not to be confused with the 'Teton' that is another word for the Sioux nation of American Indians. That Teton derives from the Lakotan language and means . . . well, nobody knows quite what it means, but you can be fairly certain that it doesn't mean tit.

ELKS

I head round the Grand Tetons, my destination an elk

310

park. The elk, a massive ungulate not dissimilar to our own European red deer, is in trouble here. Misnamed by European settlers who thought it looked like a moose, it is listed as having a conservation status 'of least concern'. That may be true worldwide, but in North America there has been a growing problem with their population for some time. For that reason the National Elk Refuge in Wyoming was founded in 1912 to protect the habitat and encourage healthy stocks. I drive out across miles of spongy terrain with the wardens. We are following a feeding vehicle that spits out from its rear a long trail of green alfalfa pellets. The elk come shyly down to nibble them. Their habitat is shrinking and recently one of their natural predators was reintroduced into the Wyoming wilderness. I now wind my way back around the Tetons towards the town of Dubois to find out more about this controversial reintroduction.

THE PREDATOR

John and Debbie Robinet are ranchers. Not on the scale of Ted Turner perhaps, but the 70,000 acres that they manage and graze cattle over is impressive enough. It takes an age to drive from the roadside to the ranch house itself, a delicate and perilous business in the snow. I am keen for the taxi not to break down or get stuck in a drift. There is no mobile-phone signal here, it would take hours to walk to the ranch house and maybe . . . just maybe those predators are about.

I arrive at the ranch house without being rent from limb to limb. John and Debbie welcome us into the suffocating warmth of the interior and tell us their story. Six of their pet dogs have been lost to the Predator. A foal too, and plenty of cattle. The issue divides them, for John approves of the Predator's reintroduction, despite the harm it does to his own animals. Debbie is all for getting out her gun and 'letting the darned critters have it'.

The Predator in question is, in case you hadn't guessed, *canis lupus*, the Gray or Timber Wolf. The question this part of America faces is yet to be settled: can man and wolf coexist? John believes that despite everything they can and must. But with food prices rising and the tolerance of most ranchers worn thin, Debbie believes that the wolf's days are numbered. They were reintroduced to Yellowstone National Park in 1995 and have thrived ever since, ranging all round the Rockies in Montana, Idaho and Wyoming and doing what wolves do best—killing livestock. Debbie thinks it is time to take them off the endangered species list, which would allow ranchers to shoot them. John shakes his head sadly.

'Dear John,' says Debbie. 'Like all men he's a sentimental romantic. It takes us hard-headed businesswomen to see the truth.'

I am all for wolves too. In theory. Would I be quite so generous if I had children, pets and a herd of cattle to protect? I am not so sure.

As it happens, Debbie got her way. Exactly two weeks after I left their ranch (the taxi getting stuck in the snow and ice on the way out, necessitating a dig out and rescue) the United States Fish & Wildlife Service removed the western gray wolf from the federal endangered species list. At least ten wolves were immediately shot and killed in Wyoming, including one large male who had become something of a star with the public in Yellowstone. Whether Debbie was responsible I don't know, but I can picture her mouth setting in a grim line as she sights along the rifle and squeezes the trigger with a breathed 'Goodbye critter . . .'

'A coalition of environmental groups' is apparently now planning to sue the federal government in order to force them to categorise the gray wolf as endangered once more and therefore bring an end to the legalised killings. John and Debbie's household, it turned out, was representative of America: a house divided on the issue of these beautiful but dangerous beasts.

MUSH, MUSH!

There is one descendant of the wolf that does have a secure place here: the husky. It has long been an ambition of mine to be pulled in a dog sled and today I am about to have that ambition realised. The crew (and I too, in my heart of hearts) are a little worried that the bone in my arm hasn't knitted well enough to take the bumps and bounces that accompany a sledge ride, but I am determined.

Ten miles or so from Jackson Hole, along the switchback roads, lives Stacey and her pack of dogs. She has picked out a fabulously, absurdly old-fashioned sled for me to be conveyed in. All I have to do is help her attach the dogs (a complicated business involving leashes and reins looped in improbable ways) and then lie down and enjoy the ride. Which I do. The snow is falling thickly in the woods, the huskies are as yelpingly, sparklingly happy as any animals I have ever seen, and the rapid sliding motion

313

is surprisingly bumpless.

Not for the first time on this epic journey do I realise how insanely lucky I am.

NORTH DAKOTA
KEY FACTS

Abbreviation:
ND

Nickname:
Peace Garden State, Roughrider State,
Flickertail State, Norse Dakota

Capital:
Bismarck

Flower:
Wild prairie rose

Tree:
American elm

Bird:
Western meadowlark

Fruit:
Chokecherry

Motto:
Liberty and union, now and forever, one and
inseparable, or Strength from the soil

Well-known residents and natives:
Warren Christopher, Angie Dickinson,
Ann Sothern, Lawrence Welk, Peggy Lee,
Bobby Vee, Roger Maris.

NORTH DAKOTA

'The waitresses are all over sixty and frighteningly Germanic.'

The highest and lowest temperatures ever recorded in North Dakota are 121° and -60° F (49° and -51° C) respectively. I don't know if anywhere else in America can match that for extremes—in fact I can't think of many places on earth that can. And yet the primary occupation of your North Dakotan is farming. Good luck, dear.

They call it 'Norse' Dakota (ho, ho) on account of the large number of Scandiwegians in the state, but in fact it is those of German ancestry who make up most of the population. Two and half per cent of all North Dakotans speak German at home. I am to discover more about this when I visit the capital, Bismarck, where more than half the citizens are of German stock, but first I need to understand the bigger picture. Since I crossed over from Minnesota to Montana I have been wondering at the large number of roads, schools and commercial establishments named after two men called Lewis and Clark. I think I need to give myself a small history lesson, for what they did means a great deal hereabouts.

I was always a little hazy about the Louisiana Purchase, mistakenly believing that it involved America buying the state of Louisiana. In fact it was the sale, in 1803, by France of its entire *Louisiane* territory, a massive swathe of mid-western America, including Arkansas, Missouri, Iowa, Oklahoma, Kansas, Nebraska, Minnesota and the Dakotas, not to mention a healthy chunk of New Mexico, Texas, Montana, Wyoming, Colorado and Louisiana. It cost the United States about twenty-three million dollars which added up in the end to about three cents an acre. Something of a bargain for doubling the size of the country. This was land occupied by American Indians. Naturally they were not informed about the sale.

The President at the time, the nation's third, was Thomas Jefferson, the author of the Declaration of Independence and perhaps the most revered of all the founding fathers. He determined that more ought to be discovered concerning this enormous tract of land, since neither the French who sold it nor the Americans who bought it really knew much about it. Jefferson was a great believer in what was already known as the 'manifest destiny'—America's right to expand westwards to the Pacific, and to hell with the Indians or anyone else.

A very short time after the purchase had been concluded, therefore, President Jefferson appointed a man called Captain Meriwether Lewis to undertake an expedition which would obtain more knowledge about the new territory, principally its rivers, for this was an age in which the only way commerce and traffic could be managed in such terrain was by water. The idea was to track the Missouri River to its source. The aim was specifically, and in Jefferson's own words, to explore 'for the purposes of commerce'.

Lewis and his fellow expedition leader Clark with their 'Corps of Discovery' travelled thousands of miles to the Pacific Ocean and back, reporting to Jefferson some three years after setting out. Now written indelibly into American history and legend, the expedition mapped most of the new territory with surprising accuracy and contributed to the making of the modern United States. Only when you have travelled in some of the lands they covered can you appreciate what a gigantic achievement it was. I have a London taxi, modern highways, air conditioning, heating and all the conveniences of the twenty-first century and I still feel like a hero when I've completed a four-hundred-mile leg of my journey. Lewis and Clark had canoes and horses and no idea into what hostile Indian lands or impenetrable ravines their journey would take them.

In Montana, Wyoming, Idaho and here in the Dakotas many diners, streets, hotels, dry goods stores and lakes are named after Lewis and Clark. Their camp sites are national shrines and their navigational routes, or parts thereof, annually reproduced by hardy canoeists and kayakers in all the states of the Midwest.

The Missouri River, which was their principal point of interest, snakes right through the centre of North Dakota before turning west and disappearing into Montana. The Red River (sadly not the one immortalised by Howard Hawks in his western masterpiece, *Red River*) forms the state line with

Minnesota to the east, and it is here that the major towns of Grand Forks and Fargo lie.

But my destination is the capital, named Bismarck in 1873 after the great European statesman who had just succeeded in forging a dozen disparate states and kingdoms into the new nation of Germany. Incidentally, the town of Bismarck didn't give itself that name because it was full of patriotic Germans who loved their Chancellor, but rather because it wanted to attract Germans over to the Dakotas. The total population of the entire state back then was around 3,000. The renaming ploy worked: Bismarck was soon flooded with hard-working, God-fearing Teutonic farmers who put up with temperatures that they could never have experienced back home. I cannot but wonder how the Dakota Territory as it was known back then (it wasn't divided into North and South until 1889) was sold to those Germans? Was there a brochure promising lush, fertile countryside and balmy weather? And were the Germans who arrived *bitterly* disappointed? For North Dakota, although by no means unpleasant, is neither notably lush nor even slightly balmy. Scraggy scrub and featureless plateaus characterise much of the state.

Whatever their feelings, they came and they stayed, those Germans. And they brought with them their food. I have always believed that the best way to understand any culture is through its cuisine and so as soon as I arrive in Bismarck I head straight for Kroll's Diner on Main, a legendary German restaurant.

The moment I enter what appears to be a traditional fifties-style diner, I know I have come to the right place. The waitresses are all over sixty and frighteningly Germanic.

'Sit down unt eat!' I am commanded. I discover that

319

this is their motto. Were the 'girls' who work here not famous enough with the regular lunchers, they have become state-wide celebrities through their TV commercials, which I would urge you to watch. They are collected together on the Kroll's website, www.sitdownandeat.com. They demonstrate better than I can the bizarre postmenopausal atmosphere that pervades here.

Many Bismarckians are descended from people who lived in ethnic German enclaves in Russia. The food therefore is as much Russian as German. The signature dishes of the house are *Knoephla* (a chicken, potato and dumpling soup), *Fleischkuechle* (a hamburger wrapped in pastry and deep fried) and the classically elegant and sophisticated 'Fried Dough'.

Needless to say, I tried them all. I am a hearty eater, rarely defeated by anything, but it was all I could do to rise from the table and totter to the car park without falling over on my back and waving my legs in the air like a capsized beetle.

A massive ingestion of calorific fat, starch and protein will at least, I rationalise to myself as I ease my stomach under the steering wheel and point the taxi south, prepare me for the rigours of life on the next leg of my journey—three days and nights on an Indian reservation.

SOUTH DAKOTA
KEY FACTS

Abbreviation:
SD

Nickname:
The Mount Rushmore State

Capital:
Pierre

Flower:
American Pasque flower

Tree:
Black Hills spruce

Bird:
Ring-neck pheasant

Soil:
Houdek loam

Motto:
Under God the people rule

Well-known residents and natives:
Sitting Bull, Hubert Humphrey,
George McGovern, L Frank 'Wizard of Oz' Baum,
Seth Bullock, Wild Bill Hickok, Crazy Horse,
Mamie van Doren, Russell Means, Calamity Jane,
Pat O'Brien, Tom Brokaw, David Soul,
Cheryl Ladd.

SOUTH DAKOTA

'Mind you, Mount Rushmore itself isn't exactly the Parthenon or the Sistine Chapel either.'

Merely to list the legendary landmarks of South Dakota gives me a kind of thrill. A thrill in which hero-worship and dread are painfully mixed. The wide skies of Texas and New Mexico, the cactus deserts of Arizona and the High Plains to the north—these have light and space and optimism built in. But the very names of South Dakota's Badlands and Black Hills and Deadwood and Wounded Knee carry within them heavy hints of the tragic, the cruel, the bloody and the lost.

At Wounded Knee, the US 7th Cavalry disgraced itself and its name eternally with the cruel and savage massacre of three hundred men, women and children of the Sioux Nation. In Deadwood Wild Bill Hickok was slain at the poker table by that no-good cowardly skunk Jack McCall. To this day the two pairs Wild

Bill had been dealt seconds before his death, aces and eights, are called the Dead Man's Hand. Men and women like Wild Bill and Calamity Jane had come to the Black Hills in the 1870s, (sacred to the Sioux and granted to them in perpetuity only a few years earlier by treaty) in search of gold. The boom soon fizzled out, forcing those who remained to scratch out their existences in unforgiving dirt farms. The Lakota Sioux tribes were enclosed within reservations where, denied their traditional hunting grounds and historically nomadic way of life, their morale and social structure disintegrated: disease, poverty, unemployment and alcoholism stalk these reservations to this very day.

Well, that is to put the most negative construction possible on South Dakota. The state itself would tell you that its National Parks and tourist attractions make it one of the most amiable and desirable destinations in all of America.

Certainly Mount Rushmore attracts an average of nearly six thousand people a day and I have every intention of being one of those six thousand but first, in deference to the Lakota people, I am on my way to another monument: the largest sculpture in the world, a South Dakotan attraction quite as preposterous as Mount Rushmore but a little less well known.

CRAZY HORSE

Lakota is the word I will use from now on to describe the major Plains Indian tribe of South Dakota, often also referred to as the Sioux. They are divided into seven 'council fires', such as Oglala, Hunkpapa and Miniconjou, but unless it is necessary I will say

323

Lakota. Lakota also refers to their language, which is not to be confused with Dakota or Nakota . . . but that is another story.

In 1868 the Lakota were granted by the Treaty of Laramie all rights of possession over the Black Hills, which they held sacred. In fact some scholars, including some Indian historians, are a little cynical about this as there is evidence that the Lakota had driven out by force other Indian tribes from the hills less than a hundred years earlier. In any event, it was the Lakota's arch nemesis, General Custer, who returned from the Black Hills in 1874 bearing talk of gold which resulted in an instant betrayal of the treaty. The Lakota got their final revenge on 'Yellowhair' at the Battle of Little Big Horn two years later, a victory that soon turned into defeat as the US Army exacted its own revenge the following year, capturing and killing Chief Crazy Horse.

It is to the Crazy Horse Monument that I have come. The vision of a sculptor called Korczak Ziolkowski who had himself worked on Mount Rushmore, this giant and unfinished enterprise carved out of the rock of Thunderhead Mountain features Crazy Horse astride his stallion, pointing out over the land below.

Ziolkowski embarked on the project in 1948 after receiving a letter from Chief Henry Standing Bear in 1939 which said, in reference to work Ziolkowski was doing on Rushmore, 'My fellow chiefs and I would like the white man to know that the red man has great heroes, too.'

I am driven up the hill to the site in an ancient, stickshift vehicle by Ziolkowski's son, Kaz. The old man himself died in 1982, leaving his widow and children to complete the work. We inspect the 87-

foot-high head of Crazy Horse (the heads on Mount Rushmore are 'only' 60 foot high), which was completed and dedicated in 1998, fifty years after the project began. The face looks good in profile, to my eye, but a little less dramatic full on. The scale of the enterprise is astounding, daunting, mind-boggling. It seems to me that Kaz's grandson is unlikely to be alive by the time it is finished, if it ever is.

The monument is also controversial. Some would dismiss it on the grounds of taste alone, for it must be admitted it does resemble—the horse especially—those tacky designs in rock crystal advertised every week in the Sunday supplements and celebrity gossip magazines; a more serious criticism is levelled by some Lakota Indians who believe that the very idea of carving a human sculpture into a mountain is degrading and insulting. They call attention to the fact that in his lifetime, Crazy Horse refused to be photographed. It is all very difficult. For my part, I applaud the idea behind memorialising a romantic warrior chief like Crazy Horse, whose tragic and noble life should be remembered by all, on the other I do wish something less distressingly kitsch could have been managed . . .

RUSHMORE

Mind you, Mount Rushmore itself isn't exactly the Parthenon or the Sistine Chapel either. After the naïve daftness of the Crazy Horse monument, I find the pompous idiocy of those four presidents somehow more risible still. Wishing to show respect or feel a vicarious thrill of admiration and pride, I can only giggle. For which I am very sorry. Any loyal

American reading this who feels outraged and insulted is free to explode with derisive snorts of laughter at any British equivalent.

RESERVATION

On my way to Pine Ridge, the second-largest Indian reservation in America, I drive through the South Dakota Badlands. The landscape here is like no other. Beautiful but strange, contorted and dreamlike. The highway winds on for miles and miles, past weird rock formations, parched gullies and grey, windswept plains until I turn off the blacktop road and head for my destination. The settlement of Porcupine is reached by a brown dusty track called Indian Service Road 27; in a desperate attempt to make it sound more touristically attractive someone has given it the pointless soubriquet 'The Bigfoot Trail'.

I have come to talk to Russell Means, a celebrated and controversial American Indian writer, activist and, latterly, film actor. I have been reading his autobiography, *Where White Men Fear To Tread* and am anxious to meet him.

Means comes across gloriously like the noble and romantic Indian chief of one's imagination: a mahogany face, hawk nose, hair braided into long plaits and a voice that summons drums in the mind. He is angry, however, and as he tells his life story, his rage at what the white man has done to the Indian surfaces. He tells of his early days, drifting around America at the whim of the Bureau of Indian Affairs, his political enlightenment and recruitment into AIM, the American Indian Movement which paralleled for the Indians what the Black Panthers were doing for the African-Americans. All this led to the sit-in of Mount Rushmore (on which he famously relieved himself) and the occupation of Wounded Knee, a 71-day siege that captured the attention of the whole world in 1973.

Means's rhetorical gifts, his genuine fury and his unquenchable energy make him a splendid subject for interview. He has some views which are unsustainable in fact and unorthodox to the point of lunacy: there are no Lakotan words for 'war' or 'weapon', he tells me firmly at one stage, adding that the whole idea of warlike Indians was invented by the Europeans. He overplays the spiritual 'earth father' card in that tiresome way that suggests all Europeans are emotionally constipated, materialist, bellicose, territorial and entirely without spirituality in their history or culture. Such exaggerations, distortions and wishful thinking do little to add credibility to his cause, which has now become the secession from America of the entire Lakotan people, whom he has declared a sovereign nation with rights over the Dakotas and large parts of the neighbouring Great Plains states, withdrawing his new nation from all existing treaties with the United States. He claims that some UN countries are interested in recognising this new state and he is dismissive of the majority of the Lakota people who have not followed him and whom he does not, in any political sense, represent, comparing them to the French under Vichy rule. For all his faults, vanities and bombastic overstatements, I admire Russell Means enormously. He has behaved with extraordinary courage throughout his life and been a passionate, eloquent and determined advocate for his people.

WOUNDED KNEE

The next morning I stop off at Wounded Knee. I try to imagine being born an American Indian in today's United States. Who am I? What are my prospects? A life of alcohol and sugar-rich junk food which my system has not evolved to process without the risk of alcoholism, obesity and diabetes and the grim spectre of almost permanent unemployment. I would have nothing to look back on but an outrageous history of cruelty, betrayal and neglect by the White Man, the heritage of such monstrous crimes as the Wounded Knee massacre and a sentimentalised view of the previous unsullied holy perfection of my own people. How terrible for my pride to know that much of my income comes from my mother and sisters making dream-catchers and beaded knick-knacks for white tourists on the very site of that massacre and that my best hope of prosperity is to leave the lands my ancestors fought so hard to retain and to try and make it as an integrated, miscegenated American in the big city. Why would I not feel victimised and oppressed, why would I not become bitter and angry?

Mel, a Lakota deputy sheriff I meet, tells me that such negative thinking must stop. 'It is time,' he says, 'for young Indians to shake off their sense of being victims and to take responsibility for who they are *now*. We can go on howling about the past or we can embrace the future.' Mel is married to a white woman, Lisa, who happens to be the local tribal court judge. She lets me sit on a sad case of 'elder abuse'.

That evening I watch the children at Pine Ridge High playing 'the hand game', a traditional Lakotan betting game, I listen to the boys drumming and chanting and I sit in on a class in which traditional decorative beading is being taught. In another one-to-one class, a young boy called Jesse is being taught the Lakota language by his grandfather.

Somewhere between Deputy Sheriff Mel's insistence that his people must forget the past and the sight of young Lakotans enthusiastically connecting with their ancestral traditions must lie a future in which these proud and abused people can lead fulfilled modern lives without turning their back on their history or losing their unique identity.

To be honest I had been dreading three nights on a reservation. In the end I enjoyed myself here as much as I have anywhere.

NEBRASKA
KEY FACTS

Abbreviation:
NE

Nickname:
Cornhusker State

Capital:
Lincoln

Flower:
Goldenrod

Tree:
Cottonwood

Bird:
Western meadowlark

State dance:
Square dance

Motto:
Equality before the law

Well-known residents and natives:
Gerald Ford (38th President), Crazy Horse,
William Jennings Bryan, Dick Cheney,
Malcolm X, Gutzon 'Mount Rushmore' Borglum,
L. Ron 'Ludicrous Fraudster' Hubbard,
Warren Buffet, Harold Lloyd, Fred Astaire,

Darryl F. Zanuck, Gordon MacRae, Henry Fonda,
Robert Taylor, Marlon Brando, Dorothy McGuire,
Montgomery Clift, Sandy Dennis, Ward Bond,
James Coburn, David Janssen, Nick Nolte,
Hilary Swank, Dick Cavett, Johnny Carson,
Ruth Etting, Max Baer, Andy Roddick.

NEBRASKA

'I finally succumb and buy a hat, the kind of western cowboy hat that no Briton can wear without looking like ten types of dick.'

Mile after mile after mile of grassy plain lies between Nebraska's border with South Dakota and my destination, the town of Grand Island. They call this country the sandhills, where the plains undulate gently and the grey-green grass heaves and swells like the sea.

Nebraska is a farming state: it was born of the great land grabs of the mid-nineteenth century when the federal government offered free land to whomever could scramble to it and claim it for their own. These homesteaders grew corn and raised cattle and lived a Great Plains life. Then came the Union Pacific railroad, which passed right through Grand Island, giving it quite a reputation as a place of high living and loose morals. The great days of the railroad are over of course, but Grand Island has since benefited, if that is the word, from having one of the great Interstate Highways run plumb spang through it.

HIGHWAYS AND BYWAYS

It has taken me some time to get my head around the way the American road system works. There are words that anyone who has watched as much American cinema and television as I have is *bound* to be familiar with: interstate, highway, turnpike, parkway and so on, but what do all the numbers mean and how does it all connect up? Allow me to quote more or less directly from the US Department of Transportation's Federal Highway Administration website.

America's National Highway System consists of 160,000 miles of road. Within that there are the following subsystems:

Principal Arterials: these are highways in rural and urban areas which provide access between an arterial and a major port, airport, public transportation facility, or other intermodal transportation facility.

The Strategic Highway Network (the Orwellian sounding STRAHNET): a network of highways important to the United States' strategic defence policy providing defence access, continuity and emergency capabilities for defence purposes.

Major Strategic Highway Network Connectors: highways which provide access between major military installations and highways which are part of the Strategic Highway Network.

Intermodal Connectors: these highways provide access between major intermodal facilities and the other four subsystems making up the National Highway System.

The Eisenhower Interstate System. I have no idea what the foregoing means either. I wouldn't know an 'intermodal facility' from a lettuce leaf. The important fact for our purposes is that there is a whole separate network within the main Highway System, the *Eisenhower Interstate System*—the equivalent of our motorway network but more, so much more.

THE EISENHOWER INTERSTATE SYSTEM

You might blanch at the prospect of me enlarging any further on this subject, but—as they say in call centres—bear with me, it really is jolly interesting. It concerns, after all, the greatest public-works project in the history of our species.

In the 1950s, President Dwight D. Eisenhower and his administration released the budget and set in motion the creation of an enormous network of major roads, connecting all the great metropolitan areas of America. Those who fought in Europe had been mightily impressed by the German autobahn system and the American automobile industry, amongst other pressure groups, was desperate for the United States to have something similar. In today's money the whole project can be estimated as having cost something in the region of half a trillion dollars: $500 billion. A bargain. America could never work the way it does without these roads: 46,000 miles of high-quality, federally funded roadway connecting east to west, north to south in a vast network. As one who has travelled along what seems all of it, I can testify to the astounding quality; there are amazingly few cones, construction sites and contra-flows and while much of it passes through thoroughly boring, samey and uninspiring countryside, there are interstate sections as beautiful as any railway line in Europe, traversing mountains and forests and lakes and gorges and valleys of heart-stopping beauty. Sometimes an interstate is a two-lane road, sometimes three or, in cities, as many as four, five or six lanes wide. Sometimes the speed limit is 55 mph, sometimes 75. It will depend on the state.

The numbering system is simple once you get the hang of it: east–west roads have *even* numbers designated to them and north–south get the *odd* numbers. Hence the monumental I-95, the east coast interstate from Maine to Florida or the I-70 from Utah to Maryland, which was the first interstate to be built in America.

Which brings us back to Nebraska. The railroad which once dominated the economy of Grand Island has been replaced by the I-80, one of the great transcontinental roads, second only in length to the I-90 (Boston to Seattle).

Interstate 80 begins life in downtown San Francisco and ends in the New York suburb of Teaneck, New Jersey. Or should that be it starts in Teaneck and ends in San Francisco? Who is to say?

In the West and Midwest it passes through Oakland, Berkley, Sacramento, Reno, Salt Lake City, Cheyenne, Lincoln, Omaha, Des Moines, Chicago, South Bend and Cleveland before heading off through Pennsylvania and New Jersey, crossing between those two states on the beautiful Delaware Water Gap.

The I-80 also passes through Grand Island, Nebraska.

All along such a great road, it goes without saying, there will be filling stations, eateries and motels, services encapsulated in the common sign 'Gas Food Lodging'. For me in my taxi these are the scourge of my waistline. A three-hundred-mile journey along an interstate is only made tolerable by regular stops for diesel, beef jerky, Rees's Peanut Butter Cups, trail mix, fizzy drinks and bottles of weird energy drinks that keep one awake at the price of tremblings and shakings and manic screechings at the wheel.

But there are other road users for whom my piffling journeys are as nothing. I am talking about the long-haul truckers.

For this legendary figure there has grown up an institution called the truck stop. Rarely glimpsed by the non-professional road user, I am to be given an insight today . . . if I can reach Grand Island in time, that is. My route south from the Dakotas is via slow state highways through the towns of Valentine and Broken Bow and I am anxious to arrive at the truck stop before sundown.

Some truck stops are little more than diners with big enough forecourts for lorries to park in—not much different from our own transport cafés, but the Boss Truck Stop, is on a bigger scale entirely. There are shops, showers, truck-washing facilities, a variety of food outlets and a massive area for parking the rigs in herring-bone formations in designated bays. Motel rooms are on offer, but most truckers prefer to sleep in their cabins. There are also rumours of that legendary creature, the Lot Lizard, a prostitute who specialises in truckers. Naturally her existence is denied by all.

My first stop is the main store, which sells everything: silver trucking mascots, dentist-style mirrors for checking under your vehicle, more of those judder-inducing energy drinks, all kinds of clothes. Having promised myself I wouldn't be such an ass, I finally succumb and buy a hat. Not a ten-gallon Stetson, but unmistakably the kind of western cowboy hat that no Briton can wear without looking like ten types of dick. Oh well. I also manage to add to my collection of American state fridge magnets. By the end of my journey I should have them all. Time to go outside and pick up a trucker.

The European juggernaut has nothing on the great American trucking rig. The pride in the paintwork, the vertical chimney-style exhaust, the sheer scale is of another order entirely. I stand around hoping to fall into conversation with one of the drivers. It is close to sunset now and lorries are turning in from the highway at a rate of ten a minute.

Finally I meet Bruce as he clambers down from his huge magenta cabin. He agrees to take me out on the road the following morning. He is headed for Pennsylvania.

'Eight o'clock sharp,' he says on his way to the main complex.

'On the dot,' I assure him.

Someone in our crew oversleeps. We arrive at 8.20 a.m., Bruce's engine is running and he is all ready to go. He is too American and therefore too polite to bawl us out but I can tell he thinks little of the professionalism of a film crew that can't honour an agreed rendezvous time.

We drive east along I-80, into the rising winter sun.

Bruce is the perfectly imperfect interviewee—laconic and unsentimental. He comes from North

Carolina and went into trucking because he likes to be his own boss and because, quite simply, he enjoys driving. I ask questions about the maverick status of the trucker, his ideals, his world view, his sense of himself and the great Open Road of America. Bruce vouchsafes little more than a grunt or an 'I don't know' to what now sound like, in my ears, absurdly pretentious and irrelevant questions.

He is a trucker. He drives a truck. He does this in America, so the distances are sometimes great. He likes to be punctual. He enjoys his work. He is a trucker, not a philosopher or a poet or a songwriter. He drives trucks. End of story.

I respect that.

KANSAS
KEY FACTS

Abbreviation:
KS

Nickname:
The Sunflower State

Capital:
Topeka

Flower:
Sunflower

Tree:
Cottonwood

Bird:
Western meadowlark

Song:
Home on the Range

Motto:
Ad astra per aspera
('To the stars through hardships')

Well-known residents and natives:
Dwight D. Eisenhower (34th President),
Bob Dole, Marlin Fitzwater, Gary Hart,
John 'body lies a-mouldering' Brown,
Amelia Earhart, Clyde 'Pluto' Tombaugh,

Carrie Nation, Erin Brockovich, Walter Chrysler, Clyde Cessna, Damon Runyon, William Inge, William Burroughs, Langston Hughes, Gordon Parks, Fatty Arbuckle, Buster Keaton, Louise Brooks, Hattie McDaniel, Ed Asner, Dennis Hopper, Don Johnson, Annette Bening, Kirstie Alley, Charlie Parker, Coleman Hawkins, Wendell Hall, Samuel Ramey, Melissa Etheridge.

KANSAS

'Somewhere in the wilds of Shawnee County, past battered, storm-shattered shacks, I find Subterra Castle.'

Is there a state in the Midwest that does *not* have the western meadowlark as its official bird? Montana, Nebraska, North Dakota, Oregon and Wyoming have all chosen it. There are sandhill cranes which fly in stunning formations over the waving grasslands of Nebraska, why should the western meadowlark be so special? And now Kansas too has joined the unimaginative majority of Great Plains states in electing this bird, which is after all no more than a blackbird in fancy dress, to stand as avian ambassador for their state.

If you were asked to look at a map of America and stab your finger down in the middle, the chances are it would land in Kansas. Authoratitive sources tell me however that 'the geographical centre' of the United

States is in fact seventeen miles to the west of the town of Castle Rock in Butte County, South Dakota. To my eye that just looks wrong. Too far north, surely? You have a look at the map and see if I'm right.

The *geodetic* centre of America, whatever that might be, is in Osborne County, Kansas—or at least was until 1983. It is all very odd. I am beginning to think geographers and cartographers are unseemly weirdos in need of a good slap.

What comes to mind when we say 'Kansas'? Tornadoes of course, thanks to Dorothy and *The Wizard of Oz*. Kansans suffer on average more than fifty serious episodes a year. Sunflowers—Kansas is America's leading producer. 'I'm as corny as Kansas in August,' Nellie sings in *South Pacific*, revealing that corn too is a major crop, although in fact Kansas grows more wheat than maize. The state, like Noël Coward's Norfolk, is very flat. Perfect for planting cereal crops no one can deny, but perhaps not the most geographically dramatic or aesthetically enticing experience that America has to offer.

Glen Campbell's lineman came from Wichita, which is in Kansas of course, as is Smallville, Clark Kent's beloved home town. I guess Siegel and Shuster chose Kansas for the Man of Steel because it is precisely the state most Americans think of when they picture the Midwest. In other words, whether it is geographically and geodetically central or not, Kansas is in many respects the emotional and cultural heart of the Midwest, which is itself often referred to as America's Heartland. All the downhome virtues and none of the metropolitan vices—that is the image.

And where shall my journey to the heart of the Heartland take me?

Why, underground. Deep underground. And back in time to the height of the Cold War.

A CASTLE IN KANSAS

Somewhere in the wilds of Shawnee County, twenty-five miles or so from the state capital Topeka, past battered, storm-shattered shacks that look as though Dorothy and Toto might still be living in them, I find Subterra Castle, the home of Ed and Dianna Peden. They look like what they are, gentle ageing hippies who could do with a good steak and kidney pie and a pint of ale inside them. How strange then that they should choose to live in a place that was designed to be able to deal out remote megadeaths at the push of a button.

The Pedens were the first people to buy and convert an American underground missile launch complex into a home. The *first?* You mean others followed? You bet. A missile bunker, you would imagine, is a cold, concrete place, inimical to cosy domesticity and vibrant hippie values and yet somehow this remarkable and kookily likeable couple have created as comfortable and desirable a pad as you can imagine.

The American military built the complex in the early sixties at a cost of around $4 million—a vast sum in those days. The Pedens bought it for $40,000 twenty years later in 1982. It was constructed originally to house a 78-foot-long Atlas missile—essentially a long rocket with an A-bomb built in. Everything about this place is massive. The main door weighs 47 tons and the walls are 18 feet thick—all designed to withstand a nuclear blast.

The rocket would lie on its side and be 'erected'—Ed enjoys the innuendo of this and repeats it in various forms many times until I take pity on him and laugh—into an upright position, so the chamber, as you might imagine, is more than double height. Below is a deep pit, designed to take the heat and flames from the thrusters on take-off. There was something similar on Tracy Island for the Thunderbird rockets, I seem to remember.

The control room and its panel of instrumentation is still there, together with the tunnels and signage and other evidence of the complex's first use. But Ed and Dianna have managed to lay over it a rich fog of patchouli, hippie ornament and happy vibe. Ed's plan was always to counter the 'heavy negative energy' of the place with his and Dianna's 'positive energy'. They are unreconstructed and proud peaceniks and it is hard not to agree with them: their possession and conversion of this sinister place is a kind of victory over war and militarism. I cannot imagine what the buzz-cut military figures who first occupied this place would think if they knew it would one day resound to the etiolated guitar strums, bongos and flutes of New Age music. How would they react if the space–time continuum somehow got confused and they were to walk round a corner and encounter a nude Ed and Dianna, smoking weed and humming mantras?

There may be little natural light down there in Subterra, but these places are warm in winter and cool in summer. They are, Ed maintains, the modern equivalent of castles, secure, dramatic, prestigious and desirable. Remote cameras, operated by joystick allow them to see who their visitors are and to sit out the blizzards, supercell storms and tornadoes that rage impotently overhead.

For all their blithering about energy and their sweet natures, Ed and Dianna are true Americans and therefore equipped with the focused minds of hard-headed entrepreneurs. They now run a business that advises those who want to live a similar life. No one will ever get such a bargain again, of course, but many are prepared to pay fabulous money for a decommissioned Cold War complex. Americans. Even within the fluffiest hippie there will beat the cold heart of an unsentimental businessman.

GHOST TOWN

The next place I visit could do with an even bigger makeover yet. White Cloud is in Doniphan County, in the top right-hand corner of the state, right on the Missouri River. It is now a ghost town and I walk through with Wolf River Bob (aka Bob Breeze) the local historian and a White Cloud citizen who can remember the glory days.

Where once there was a prosperous river port, churches, saloons and a thriving community now there is next to nothing. No shops are open, despite signs inviting me in for ice creams and sodas. Another sign points to a lookout on the hill from where, on a clear day, four states can be seen: Kansas, Nebraska, Missouri and Iowa.

In a land so huge not every town can be connected to mainstream America. It seems that a river port like White Cloud is too far from the interstate and the railway to stay prosperous in the modern world. It has no USP, as they say in business these days, no unique selling point which can bring business or tourism flocking to it. White Cloud is just another town and despite Bob's efforts, it looks as though its decline is permanent. Maybe that is where its future lies. A little more dilapidation, some artful sagebrush and tumbleweed and he could have a heritage ghost town on his hands . . .

The day is ending: I drive to my Topeka hotel and collapse on a hammock. Tissues must be restored and energies recharged for the long journey south into neighbouring Oklahoma.

OKLAHOMA
KEY FACTS

Abbreviation:
OK

Nickname:
The Sooner State

Capital:
Oklahoma City

Flower:
Oklahoma rose

Tree:
Eastern redbud

Bird:
Scissortail flycatcher

Waltz:
Oklahoma Wind

Motto:
Labor omnia vincit ('Work conquers all')

Well-known residents and natives:
Geronimo, Daniel Patrick Moynihan, Wiley Post,
Belle Starr, Pretty Boy Floyd, T. Boone Pickens,
Sam 'Walmart' Walton, Lynn Riggs, Ralph Ellison,
John Berryman, Gene Autry, Lon Chaney Jr.,
Will Rogers, Joan Crawford, Van Heflin,

Vera Miles, Dale Robertson, Walter Cronkite,
Dan 'Laugh-In' Rowan, Blake Edwards,
Jennifer Jones, Tony Randall, James Garner,
Chuck Norris, Gary Busey, Jeanne Tripplehorn,
Ron Howard, Brad Pitt, Woody Guthrie,
Chet Baker, J.J. Cale, Eddie Cochran,
Roger Miller, Tom Paxton, Garth Brooks.

OKLAHOMA

*'When they start the rodeo itself, it is all I can do
not to cry out in joy and wonder.'*

Only New Mexico and Arizona of the forty-eight
connected or 'contiguous' states, were admitted to
the union after Oklahoma. Gore Vidal's grandfather,
the blind Thomas Pryor Gore, was a founding senator
when it finally achieved statehood in 1907. Before
that time it had been a territory for the displaced
American Indians who had been booted out of their
ancestral lands in the southern states. Their enforced
journey is known in Indian lore as the Trail of Tears.
As agricultural real estate became more valuable in
the latter part of the nineteenth century, however, the
tribes were ejected yet again when white settlers
came over for the famous Land Run, a first-come
first-served scramble for farmland. Those who broke
the rules and grabbed their land before the official
time were known as 'sooners', which gave the state

349

its nickname. Out went the Indians, in came the homesteaders and statehood for *okla humma*, which means, with cruel irony, 'land of the red man'.

Nature exacted a harsh revenge on those white homesteaders in the early 1930s when drought, high winds and poor agronomy came together to curse the land and create the notorious dustbowl. Thousands and thousands of poor farmers upped sticks and headed for California. John Steinbeck's character Tom Joad in *The Grapes of Wrath* came to stand for this kind of downtrodden Okie. Henry Fonda in the John Ford film adaptation of the novel made famous a speech of Joad's which has since become a kind of fanfare for the common man:

> I'll be all around in the dark—I'll be everywhere. Wherever you can look—wherever there's a fight, so hungry people can eat, I'll be there. Wherever there's a cop beatin' up a guy, I'll be there. I'll be in the way guys yell when they're mad. I'll be in the way kids laugh when they're hungry and they know supper's ready, and when the people are eatin' the stuff they raise and livin' in the houses they build—I'll be there, too.

It is no coincidence that around the time of the dustbowl, Lynn Riggs wrote the play *Green Grow the Lilacs*, which looks back to a time when the Oklahoma Territory, just before statehood in 1906, seemed like a kind of agricultural paradise. In 1943 Rodgers and Hammerstein turned the play into the hit Broadway musical *Oklahoma!* Coming only three years after the John Ford film, Oklahoma must have felt like the most examined state in the union around this time.

But it wasn't all dustbowl, depression and doom for the Okie. Oil made Tulsa one of the richest cities in the country from the 1920s onwards and today the state is amongst the most prosperous in America.

SALVATION

Which is not to say that there are no poor. I am in a Salvation Army hall in downtown Oklahoma City this afternoon. Every week they feed the homeless with meals cooked up by the cheerfullest and sweetest-natured kitchen staff you could ever hope to meet. Today, which is Good Friday, sees an especially big crowd lining up outside.

I talk to Captain Vance Murphy, an officer of the Salvation Army. They really do mimic the military with their ranks and hierarchies. Maroon epaulettes on his clean white shirt bespeak his rank as clearly as a silver gorget on a Lifeguard. As one who abominates religion and most religious organisations, I have always had a soft spot for the Salvation Army. They are so resolutely unsexy, so affably unhectoring, so charmingly unconditional in their kindnesses. They just get on with feeding and clothing the poor while expecting nothing in return. The only hint of preaching is confined to a rather hopeless but good-natured moment of biblical exegesis which is delivered by one of the officers as the 'clients' eat. Nobody appears to be paying much heed, a few of the homeless women nod their heads encouragingly enough for the officer to pick up a guitar and sing. A ghastly rendition of 'Amazing Grace', predictably enough, but a small price to pay for what looks like truly excellent hot food on a cold March day.

I speak to Terry, one of the homeless, and to a companion of his whose name I never quite catch. They like this place. They respect the lack of interference and religiosity. Terry's companion finishes his meal and gets up from the table to help the Salvation Army kitchen staff stack chairs. It is his way of saying thank you.

The spokesperson for the Salvation Army (old-fashioned as they are, they have succumbed to the twenty-first century mania for PR people) who is there to facilitate our filming is a sparky, pretty and amusing young blonde called Heidi. She reveals, as if it is the most natural thing in the world, that she is a belly-dancer. There is not a hint of eastern blood in her—but every week she belly dances professionally in restaurants and nightclubs around Oklahoma City. None of us in the film crew is prepared to let it go at that. We make an appointment to come and film her that evening. But first, one of the great American institutions awaits us: the rodeo.

RODEO

The Central Oklahoma Junior Rodeo Association, COJRA, holds its meetings several times a season in the Tyler Blount Memorial Arena in Guthrie, OK. It is possible that this is the juiciest slice of American pie that I have yet tasted. The sight of young children wandering around in cowboy hats and boots is endearing enough, but when they start the rodeo itself, it is all I can do not to cry out in joy and wonder.

The event is open to any single boy or girl who has never been married and is 18 years old or younger.

There are five divisions, according to age: 14–18, 10–13, 7–9, 6 and Under and 4 and Under. When you have seen a three-year-old child in a Stetson trying to rope a steer or ride a sheep, you have seen it all.

The rodeo begins (and I have been in America now long enough not to be surprised by this) with the National Anthem. Hats are doffed and placed over hearts as a young man rides round the arena bearing the 'Star-Spangled Banner'. I am, much to my own annoyance, deeply and inexcusably moved. I console myself with the thought that I would be just as emotionally stirred by the Bulgarian National Anthem being played at an archetypally Bulgarian event. I am of course fooling no one but myself by imagining this.

We kick off with 'Goat Undecorating on Foot for 4s and Under'. How do you undecorate a goat? Well, first a supervising adult has to decorate one, in other words they have to attach a ribbon to it. At the sound of the bell the child then runs up, holds the goat between its legs, detaches the ribbon and runs back. Quickest time wins. A wealth of comedy is concealed in that simple phrase 'holds the goat between its legs', for while each child may be clear about the rules of the game, the goat is not and there is much chasing and falling over to be gone through before it will consent to be undecorated. As it is the same goat in each instance, the proceeding becomes more and more fraught each time as the goat grows increasingly impatient at the whole proceeding and begins violently to wish itself elsewhere.

For 6 and under there is an added wrinkle: 'Goat Undecorating on Horse', which is essentially the same but mounted. This is no trivial addition, for goats and horses do not get on well. It all adds to the broad comedy, however, and by now I am red, watery-eyed and wheezy from laughter.

Mutton Bustin', Goat Tying and Steer Riding all follow. Mutton Bustin' isn't quite as alarming as it sounds. The wild horse and the bronco are considered too much for toddlers to cope with, even here in *laissez faire*, libertarian, devil-may-care cowboy country, and so the youngest age categories are given sheep to ride. The longer they can stay on without being thrown the better. They may be dressed in protective clothing, but for all that these are brave little cowboys and cowgirls. Their determination and seriousness is marvellous to behold.

The sun sets, the moon rises and the older children show off their skills, which are much greater but so much less appealing.

You cannot attend such an event without reflecting on the contingencies of life, birth and destiny.

America has its millions of urban children, ghetto children, born to gangs and drugs and guns and violence and abuse. And it has these children, raised in the countryside, born to goat undecorating, mutton bustin', lassoing and riding. The two kinds of child will probably never meet in all their lives. Will they ever respect each other, learn about each other or even consider each other? Probably not. There were children eating in the Salvation Army hall this afternoon who may well never see a horse, unless it is a police horse, in all their lives.

BELLY

Whether children from either side of the tracks will ever see belly dancing is another question altogether.

From Guthrie to a kind of rodeo of human flesh in the Shishkabob Restaurant, Oklahoma City. Our old friend Heidi is dancing with a girl who is by day a staff sergeant in the United States Air Force. I tuck a dollar bill into an area that I can look at without blushing and head for bed.

COLORADO

KEY FACTS

Abbreviation:
CO

Nickname:
The Centennial State

Capital:
Denver

Flower:
Rocky Mountain columbine

Tree:
Colorado blue spruce

Bird:
Lark bunting

Mineral:
Rhodochrosite

Motto:
Nil Sine Numine ('Nothing Without Providence')

Well-known residents and natives:
John Kerry, Horace 'Go West Young Man' Greeley,
James Michener, Allen Ginsberg,
Clive Cussler, Antoinette 'Tony Award' Perry,
Ken Kesey, Douglas Fairbanks, Lon Chaney,
Bill Murray, Roseanne Barr, Tim Allen,
Don Cheadle, Trey Parker, Matt Stone,
Paul Whiteman, Glenn Miller, John Denver.

COLORADO

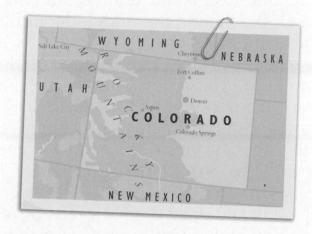

'Someone suggests a slug of Tabasco hot pepper sauce as a specific against altitude sickness. I fall for what is a crude, cruel and childish practical joke.'

A vast rectangular slab, the boundaries of Colorado were determined not by its rivers, valleys, mountains or other natural features, but by mankind's arbitrary lines of latitude and longitude. For all that, one cannot but think of natural features when contemplating this grand and beautiful state. Here the Rocky Mountains climax into their highest peaks, indeed Colorado is everywhere above 1,000 feet, the capital Denver being at an elevation of precisely 5,280 feet, thereby accurately earning its nickname of the 'Mile High City'.

357

POWWOW

It is to the capital I come first, to witness one of Denver's regular events, the annual March Powwow (that's March the month, not march the military strut or political demonstration). A powwow is a Native American gathering, any kind of intra-tribal or inter-tribal conference. These days, large-scale powwows like Denver's are opportunities to celebrate American Indian music, costume, history and culture. From all over North America the tribes people come: Black Foot, Crow, Cree, Apache, Comanche, Cherokee, Choctaw, Ojibwa, Lakota, Navajo, Hopi, Passamaquoddy and dozens and dozens of others.

Denver's downtown Coliseum Convention Center is enormous and at the climax of the powwow its main arena is entirely filled with thousands of men, women and children in their traditional buckskins, beads and feathers. The whooping and stamping are precisely like the 'war path' scenes of cowboy movies. Hollywood used 'real live Indians' in its movies of course, so there is no reason for the authentic dances and moves to be any different from what I've seen in westerns, but nonetheless it gives me a shock.

The colours, the gorgeous costumes and the spirit of celebration completely overwhelm me. For all the negatives that I encountered on the Pine Ridge reservation in South Dakota, for all the righteous fury of Russell Means and others, it is clear to see that for many American Indians what comes first is pride.

THE SLAUGHTERHOUSE WOMAN

The next day is Easter Sunday, which I spend in Fort

358

The front porch of the Flying D.

It was the French who discovered the Grand Tetons . . . they gave them the name that the French just would: The Three Tits. Les Trois Tétons.

MONTANA
With Ted Turner, unwisely turning our backs on the bison.

WYOMING
Another ambition realised: hauled by Stacey's huskies.

Russell Means:
Indian activist,
writer and film
actor.

NORTH DAKOTA
'Sit down und eat.'

SOUTH DAKOTA
'Mind you, Mount Rushmore itself isn't exactly the
Parthenon or the Sistine Chapel.'

OKLAHOMA
Mutton bustin'.

NEBRASKA
Bruce's rig at the Boss Grand
Island Truck stop, Nebraska.

KANSAS
Battered,
storm-shattered
shacks that
look as though
Dorothy and
Toto might still
be living in
them.

UTAH
Monumental.

TEXAS
Disgusting stuff . . . And my dear, the smell . . .

Powwow
celebrant,
Denver.

Colorado
Stephens don't ski.

ARIZONA
Ready to take a
sentimental journey.

Waiting to board the
trolley car in San
Francisco.

NEVADA
Where are the representations of
casinos, lowlifes, strippers, losers,
Elvis impersonators and hookers?

CALIFORNIA
With Art and Judd Finkelstein at Judd's Hill.

OREGON
Black water rafting on the
Rogue River.

WASHINGTON
Here in Seattle, the city of
Boeing, Microsoft, Starbucks
and grunge, I will bid
farewell to the taxi.

Lee, me and an Irish Lord.

ALASKA
Henry the whaling captain: 'a warm, friendly and very proud Inupiat'.

On the lava fields, bidding farewell to an America that is making new pieces of itself behind me.

HAWAII
'I swam with sharks!'

Collins, an attractive college town sixty miles or so due north of Denver. Our sound recordist, Adam, is so entranced by the atmosphere and charm of the place that he tells us all he is determined one day to come back and live here. Not since Ashville, North Carolina have we been in a town so refreshingly devoid of big-name chain restaurants and corporate franchise businesses and hotels. Adam is not alone in his delight. Fort Collins was voted Best Place To Live by *Money* magazine in 2006. Perhaps the presence of Colorado State University helps: certainly the profusion of pleasant, cheap restaurants and coffee shops bespeaks the student town.

It is to the campus I come on Monday, to see Professor Temple Grandin, a person fully as remarkable as her name. My Easter Sunday day off has given me time to read her book *Animals in Translation*.

Temple Grandin was born with autism. During her childhood the only diagnosis for this condition was 'severe brain damage'. Possessed of a formidable will, a fine brain and an instinctive love of and connection with animals she grew up determined to use all those qualities. She has found the perfect job. She is—wait for it—America's leading designer of humane slaughterhouses.

Temple can 'think like an animal'—that is to say she notices all the things that stress a stockyard animal during handling and transportation. When her work began she actually used to go on the walkways, crawl along the chutes and personally reproduce the journeys animals took from field to truck, from truck to yard, from yard to slaughterhouse. All rather grim. But she noticed *everything*. She noticed when rusty signs creaked, she noticed bright colours and

367

reflections, she noticed blind turns, forbidding corners and spooky shadows. She instinctively understood the little things that freak animals out, little things that a 'normal' human would never pick up on. All these go together to create doubt, fear and stress, causing the animals to brace their legs and refuse to be budged, which congests the stock handling systems which in turn creates more congestion and more stress farther back down the line. Out come the electric cattle prods, the cattlemen zap and yell, further increasing the stress and further slowing down the system. Everyone's day becomes increasingly hard and slow and strained, the profits go down (stress hormones prior to slaughter markedly reduce the quality of the meat) and no one is happy.

It used to be that people believed all this bother was inevitable. According to conventional wisdom, animals are ornery and dumb, they are hard to shift and hard to push round the stockyards and they always will be. Temple visited dozens and then hundreds of farms, ranches and slaughterhouses and was able to redesign systems and teach basic interpretative skills to the ranch hands and workers. The results were remarkable and Grandin is now Numero Uno in all of America when it comes to designing slaughterhouses, chutes, pens, walkways and the like. She also lectures regularly to veterinary students at Colorado State University. Quite an achievement for one labelled as 'retarded', 'brain damaged' and 'unable to function in the world'.

You may think that a person who loves animals would want nothing to do with systems designed for slaughtering them, but Temple is far from fluffy-bunny in her attitude to animals. Indeed, the whole point of her approach is to recognise how unlike us animals are. Their ideas of discomfort, unease and discontent are very different from ours. It is clear that her apprehension of what spooks, stresses and alarms an animal is extremely accurate: I wonder however if someone will come close one day to understanding what thrills, delights and pleases an animal? Do they respond to beauty in nature, for example? Can they detect, appreciate and value the difference between a dull urban sprawl and a mighty mountain landscape?

ASPEN

I defy any human not to be astounded and enchanted by a drive like the one I now take, from Fort Collins to Aspen. As we climb the switchbacks that girdle the Rockies it is easy to see why this region has become so desirable a winter destination and why resorts like Vail, Beaver Creek and Aspen have become so exclusive and so shatteringly expensive.

Aspen, the best-known town in this string of chi-chi ski resorts is about 7,890 feet above sea level, almost exactly a mile and a half: high enough for me to huff, puff and gasp and be glad that I gave up smoking a year ago.

Michael Douglas and Catherine Zeta-Jones, David and Victoria Beckham, Antonio Banderas and Melanie Griffith, William H. Macy and Felicity Huffman . . . Mariah Carey, Don Johnson, Jack Nicholson . . . Aspen is the Dubai of the North when it comes to glitzy residents, for many of whom Aspen will be the seat of their third or fourth residence, a little eight- or nine-million-dollar chalet—nothing fancy.

They tell me the skiing is first rate, absolutely first

rate. Stephens don't ski, however, so this news is of little more than passing interest to me. I do like alpine resorts though; I enjoy the fresh air, the dazzling whiteness and the rumbustious rosy-cheeked cheerfulness of the adults and children. I have been on several skiing holidays where I have been content to get myself a ski-pass and be transported every morning to the highest café where I will sit writing letters, reading and sipping hot chocolate with rum in it while my friends fizz down the slopes. We meet for lunch and the whole thing is repeated in the afternoon.

This morning in Aspen, I ascend the mountain, which adds another 3,000 feet or so to the elevation and also increases my breathless dizziness. Someone suggests a slug of Tabasco hot pepper sauce as a specific against altitude sickness. I fall for what is in my opinion a crude, cruel and childish practical joke.

At the very top of the mountain I find a place which serves hot chocolate with a tot of rum, just the way I like it: the Aspen Mountain Club, annual subscription fees $175,000. Yes *I* know alcohol is the last thing one should have two miles above sea level, but fortunately my body doesn't. I sip gently, taking away the taste of Tabasco and building up the strength to venture out onto the slopes. I am to join the resort's Ski Patrol as they go about their duties and their training.

The members of the patrol are what passes for Cool Dudes today—in other words they are skinny and sexless and skimpily bearded. They are entirely charming, however, and with great patience they drag me over the snow, pulling me on a sled until we reach an area where they are to set off a bomb. The idea is to prevent avalanches by starting small controlled ones. A klaxon sounds and we watch, from a safe distance, as a puff of snow blossoms out from the

370

mountainside and, five seconds later, the sound of the explosion reaches our ears. No actual avalanche is precipitated by this detonation, which is apparently a good thing. I am most disappointed, however. I wanted a real show.

The next thing to do is to find some children to bury. This is easily done. A bunch of pert, intelligent and fabulously self-confident children bump into us and enquire about the cameras and sound equipment and, hey, wasn't I in that film *V for Vendetta?*

'I was, as it happens, yes,' I tell them. 'Perhaps you would like to be in *this* film?'

'Sure. What's the fee?' Their father is a show-business agent in New York City.

Once the negotiations have been agreed—which is to say once I have appealed to the children's better natures and persuaded them to perform for free—two of the boys are taken off to be buried in the snow while I distract a sheepdog. The idea is that the dog will sniff around the snow, find out where the kids are buried and alert the patrol with a peal of frenzied barking. It would be cheating if the dog actually saw them getting into their hiding place, so I do my best to take its mind off the task ahead with cheerful prattle about sheepdogs I have known in Scotland.

When all is ready, the dog is released and finds the children in their secret cache instantly, barking with joy at its own cleverness. Personally, I suspect it of peeping out of the corner of its eye while we were talking. We dig the children out and move on to the next job: piste maintenance. Aspen's famous slopes are kept in their perfect condition by a fleet of specialised vehicles which comb, roll, tease, smooth and generally perfect the surface of the snow. Every night for hours and hours and hours the drivers of these snow cats groom the mountainside so that the rich and their children might slide happily down the mountainsides the following day. I try one of the vehicles out and, fun though it was, I decide not for the first time that work of this kind is best left to others. I return to the hotel and fall in with a couple of rich women who suggest I accompany them to a nightclub.

I am faced then with two options: a) a nightclub filled with the rich, beautiful and famous or b) an early night alone in bed with a book. Never has any decision been easier.

The book was gripping. I hope the girls had a nice time in their club.

TEXAS
KEY FACTS

Abbreviation:
TX

Nickname:
The Lone Star State

Capital:
Austin

Flower:
Bluebonnet

Tree:
Pecan

Bird:
Mockingbird

Cooking implement:
Dutch oven

Motto:
Friendship Before Statehood

Well-known residents and natives:
Lyndon B. Johnson (36th President),
George H.W. Bush (41st President),
George W. Bush (43rd President), Stephen Austin,
Sam Houston, Jim Bowie, Davy Crockett,
Admiral Nimitz, Audie Murphy, Lady Bird Johnson,

Sandra Day O'Connor, Jeb Bush, Ann Richards,
John Wesley Hardin, Clyde Barrow, Bonnie Parker,
David Koresh, Katherine Anne Porter, Rex Reed,
Patricia Highsmith, Horton Foot, Larry McMurtry,
Kinky Friedman, Howard Hughes, Red Adair,
Ross Perot, Michael Dell, Robert Rauschenberg,
Julian Schnabel, Tex Avery, Joan Crawford,
Greer Garson, Cyd Charisse, Debbie Reynolds,
Dooley 'Play It Again Sam' Wilson, Sharon Tate,
Larry Hagman, Dabney Coleman, Rip Torn,
Farrah Fawcett, Gene Roddenberry, Shelley Duvall,
F. Murray Abraham, Morgan Fairchild,
Powers Boothe, Wes Anderson, Patrick Swayze,
Sissy Spacek, Terrence Malick, Tommy Lee Jones,
Gary Busey, Kate Capshaw, Woody Harrelson,
Dennis Quaid, Ethan Hawke, Forest Whitaker,
Jerry Hall, Anna Nicole Smith, Robin Wright Penn,
Jennifer Garner, Renée Zellweger,
Jennifer Love Hewitt, Owen Wilson, Luke Wilson,
Carol Burnett, Steve Martin, Bill Hicks.

TEXAS

'I cannot guess how many gallons of blonde colorant have been poured onto the assembled heads.'

This entry is big, for Texas is big. Texas is very big. Everyone knows that. Nonetheless the Lone Star State likes to remind itself of this at all times. Commercials on TV and advertising hoardings talk of 'Texan-size servings of beef', 'Enough space in the trunk of this car even for a Texan', 'Only one toilet paper is big enough for Texans . . .' and so on. If ever a place mythologises itself that place is Texas.

With its size, that tendency to self-mythologise, its iconography, its accent, its props, its cuisine and its history, Texas is able (and willing) to think of itself as a land apart more than any other state in the union ('It's a whole other country' is the current state slogan). The Republic of Texas was a sovereign nation for the best part of ten years in the nineteenth century—its embassy in London was in St James's and it remains memorialised to this day by a 'cantina' restaurant just off Trafalgar Square called The Texas Embassy.

When Mexico won its independence from Spain in 1821 it immediately claimed those lands we know today as Texas. Over the succeeding years European settlers and landowners, led by Steve Austin and Sam Houston (whose names live on in Texas's capital and largest city respectively), prepared to secede from Mexico and claim independence. One day in 1835 Will Travis, Davy Crockett, Jim Bowie (of knife fame) and over a hundred other volunteers and regular soldiers came to defend the Alamo Mission in San Antonio from Mexico's Generalissimo Santa Anna. A massacre and a defeat for the defenders, this action led to the Battle of San Jacinto in which the Mexicans were soundly beaten and Santa Anna was captured. The independent Republic of Texas was declared. By 1845 her experiment with nationhood was over and she joined the Union as the twenty-eighth state.

The official slogan may be 'Friendship before statehood', yet one cannot but feel that for every true-born Texan the real state motto would be the words with which Sam Houston's men went into battle at San Jacinto: 'Remember the Alamo'. Statal pride is bigger here too.

A cowboy state and an oil state: this image of Texas has continued right through history and through the thirteen-year run of the TV series *Dallas*. Oil is still important to the state, and in ways of which many Americans are not aware.

STRATEGIC RESERVES

Today I am visiting the federal government's Strategic Petroleum Reserves in Freeport, TX, just sixty-five miles south of Houston, right on the Gulf of Mexico.

In the mid-seventies America and the rest of the world got one hell of a shock when the oil-producing OPEC countries not only began to push up the price of oil but also to embargo those nations that had traded with Israel. Rationing, mini-riots, hyper-inflation— the cost was disastrous and the United States government vowed that such a calamity would never happen again. And so they planned for the construction of vast sites where oil could be stored against any future shortage that might imperil the good order of the Republic.

This being America and not Britain, all the data on the Strategic Petroleum Reserve is instantly available. A quick glance at the Department of Energy's dedicated site www.spr.doe.gov tells me that the reserve currently stands at 703.4 million barrels of oil, divided into 280.7 million of sweet crude and 422.7 million of sour. That is somewhere in the region of £90 billion dollars worth (though as I write the price of oil is rising daily). The full capacity is 727 million barrels, but this is deliberately being run down in order to help increase the amount of oil out in the market and therefore to reduce the price.

There are four SPR sites: all of them are sited along the Gulf of Mexico and all of them employ the same technique for storing the oil. Essentially the oil is pumped into huge salt domes, natural phenomena that have formed over millions of years. The oil replaces the natural brine within and can remain in its salty caverns in tip-top condition, theoretically for eternity. Freeport is the largest of the US government's facilities, capable of holding over a quarter of a billion barrels at any one time.

I am allowed into Freeport's heart after a fretful hour and a half's wait in the most tigerishly fierce security area I have yet to visit in America. It took ten minutes to get on board the USS *Springfield* nuclear submarine in Groton, Connecticut, but here they really mean business. For some reason our director's name and passport number had not been sent ahead and, despite the security guards believing in our bona fides, and the Freeport SPR press people being present to welcome us, we could not enter until the mystery of the director's clearance was solved. He, poor man, got on the phone to Washington, in order to try and speak to the Department of Homeland Security PR person who had his official security clearance details and by a freak of good fortune he was wrongly put through to Alex, the very Border Patrol fellow who had escorted us to the Canadian border back in Montana, weeks ago. Words were spoken, faxes and e-mails sent and before another half hour had passed we pierced the perimeter.

Jorge, the officer who was escorting us around the premises, explained to me the difference between sour crude oil and sweet. Sweet has fewer impurities and can be converted into gasoline cheaply, whereas sour needs to undergo extra refinement processes. Jorge even poured a flask of crude for me to inspect. Disgusting stuff: the smallest splash of it ruins clothes forever. What it does to the feathers of a seabird we know all too well from news footage of spills. And my dear, the smell . . . It is for this noxious, evil-textured stuff that wars are fought and fortunes made. It is somehow fitting that the black gold that fuels our entire civilisation is almost more disgusting than faeces.

DOING DONUTS

After an exhaustive and exhausting tour, my taxi and I feel like expending some of that vile substance in the most childish and politically unacceptable manner imaginable. Freeport, I have discovered, is only a few miles from Quintana Beach, one of only two in all America on which one is allowed to drive a private road vehicle without restrictions. The taxi and I spend a happy half-hour carving huge donuts on the sand. At one point I get a little overexcited and plough right into the surf—huge quantities of salt water invade the bonnet. I only hope there won't be Consequences. Some of you reading this are doubtless thinking that they would be fully deserved. All I can say in my defence is . . . er . . . carbon offset. I promise. Honest.

Anyway. Moving on.

THE GALLERIA

It would be madness to cover the United States without having investigated a little more deeply than one usually does the phenomenon of the Shopping Mall. In Europe we are used enough to these monstrous entities by now, but to visit one of the first and largest is nonetheless instructive.

The Houston Galleria calls itself a city within a city: it has an ice-rink, car parking for 14,000, 400 shops, 11 beauty salons and two hotels. Over 24 million people a year come here. It is the fourth-largest mall in America and proudly caters for the high-end shopper with outlets including Neiman Marcus, Cartier, Gucci, Macy's, Tiffany & Co., Saks Fifth Avenue, Louis Vuitton, Dior, Bvlgari and Nordstrom. And, to make me happy, an Apple Store. I wander about under the enormous glass roofs in a delirious daze. Two Texans in cowboy hats tell me that they and many friends come here just as you might to an art gallery. To look and to wonder.

A proportion of the richer people who come regularly to the Galleria would count as members of Houston's 'social register'. For all its 'good ole boy' image, Texas like much of America has its class system, its roster of the rich, ritzy and respectable. To be fair to this elite, they almost only ever assemble en masse for the sake of charity.

GALA

I have been invited this evening to a gala (pronounced the same way Durham miners do: 'gayla') in aid of the Houston Society for the Performing Arts. I arrive at the reception and am immediately served a tumbler of enough whiskey to knock out a bison. The theme of the evening is the great American musical and the women here have gone to great lengths to look sensational and glamorous in the American mode, a mode which involves a great deal of facial make-up and careful attention to hair. I cannot guess how many gallons of blonde colorant have been poured onto the assembled heads. Perhaps there is a Strategic Clairol Reserve in

Houston. It has always struck me as bizarre that when in Europe American women should be so loud in their praise of the elegance and beauty of Parisians and yet be able to go back home and do exactly the opposite. Plainness, simplicity and restrained elegance are not to be numbered amongst the accomplishments of the rich Houstonian dame. I do not want to sound bitchy, however. They welcome me with charm and warmth. The price for my supper is a small speech, which they receive very kindly.

The ladies I sit with attend a dinner/ball/rout/gala of this kind at least once a week in the season. Endowment and philanthropy are enormously important. The rich are expected to choose at least three or four pet charities and to be extremely generous to them. The beneficiaries of this evening's party are a large number of institutions directly funded by the Society of Performing Arts. Any assumption that rich Texans are automatically philistine, right-wing and crass is instantly contradicted. These people value culture in all its forms, including a theatre whose practitioners often bite the hands that feed it:

'Honey, I ploughed so much money into a play you would not believe. Wonderful young writer, but oh dear me he does so hate us all.'

Yes, on one level you could look at the sea of dyed hair and blushered cheeks and listen to the tortured vowels of refined Southern speech and cry 'Vulgar! Self-satisfied! Rich! Vain!' but you would be dishonest not to acknowledge also the unconditional generosity, open-mindedness, hard work and charm with which these people live their highly privileged lives.

How much easier America would be to understand

if it conformed simply to all our snootiest, snobbiest and most sneering expectations. Instead it does conform, but not simply. It conforms with ambiguity, contradiction and surprise. Maybe that is why I love it so.

BORDER PATROL

The frontline in America's war against illegal immigrants is the Mexican border. I come to El Paso, where many of the fiercest frontline battles in that war are daily fought. Mexico has influenced Texas hugely; their respective cultures have combined to form a very particular style of Tex-Mex food, drink, music and architecture. But while Mexican music, beer and quesadillas may be welcome in the United States, its people are less so.

There is a class of vigilante volunteer who patrols the southern border off his own bat. Not officially sanctioned or funded, these people's vigils are fuelled entirely by their personally felt enmity towards 'illegals' and by what they would describe as their own patriotism. They call themselves the 'Minutemen', a title borrowed from the militias of the Revolutionary Wars who declared themselves ready to face the enemy (in that case the British) at a minute's notice.

I join Minuteman Shannon, in the frontier town of Fabens, about an hour from El Paso. He drives us along the borderline in his pick-up, pointing out places where illegals are known to try and cross. Every now and again we pass a genuine government Border Patrol vehicle. They are on friendly terms, Shannon assures us, for the Federal Agents know the

Minutemen are law-abiding and would never tackle an illegal immigrant themselves, they would radio the information to the proper authorities. Are there British 'patriots' who are so incensed by illegal immigration into the United Kingdom that they would set up their own border patrols in like manner? Shannon strikes me as more sad and lonely than dangerous. He has that slightly obnoxious and overstated pride in his obedience to the law and his respect for proper authorities characteristic of the self-righteous patriot. I ask him whether he has any sympathy for the Mexicans whose lives are so poor and who look out daily across a river to a land of riches and plenty? He evades the question by referring once more to the law.

Incidentally, I say that the Mexicans look out over a river, and it may be that you already know that I am referring to the Rio Grande, which for much of its course forms the natural border between America and Mexico. Illegal immigrants are often called 'wetbacks' on account of their having had to swim that river. You may imagine my surprise then when Shannon showed me the Rio Grande. Not a river at all, but a drain, a dry ditch. Further along it swells into a small stream, I am told, but here it is no more than a trickle.

The following day I join the official United States Border Patrol in the city of El Paso itself. Agent Romero drives me along the fences on the US side of the border and we see, over the dribble that is the Rio Grande, Mexicans in the city of Juarez gazing across at us. Helicopters fly overhead and we pass dozens and dozens of other Border Patrol vehicles. The budget for this level of security must be colossal.

There were a few moments of high-intensity action when we are sped towards spots where illegals are actually crossing, according to our in-car shortwave radio. We arrive at one place in time to see a pair of elderly Mexicans being led away. Often, Agent Romero tells me, they will be paid to try a bold and ridiculous crossing in order to create a diversion that is cover for a more serious incursion somewhere else along the frontier. As often as people, it is drugs that are smuggled across. I ask him the same question I asked Minuteman Shannon. Does he, as a Latino-American especially, feel any sympathy for those trying to get in? He returns the same answer. It's the law. They must not break the law.

'If the law was different I would feel different,' he eventually confides. A very odd thing for a free human being to say in my opinion, but I suppose a government agent being filmed is not, in the usual sense, free. Illegal immigration has become a huge issue in America, much as it has in Britain, and perhaps he feels that if he is caught on camera expressing even the smallest degree of understanding or fellow-feeling his job will be forfeit.

I climb into a 'sky box', a preposterous, hydraulically lifted mobile sentry box in which the poor agent tasked to it has to stay for eight-hour shifts. Either side of the river lie the two enormous cities of El Paso and Juarez, and I can see them clearly from my high vantage point. The difference in prosperity is all too apparent. The only way to stop people wanting to migrate from Juarez to El Paso, it seems to me, is for Mexico to become as prosperous as the United States. In recent years Mexico's economy has grown, certainly, and it continues to expand at an unprecedented rate. Perhaps the day will come when it is American illegals who try to swim the Rio Grande? Not in my lifetime, I think, but perhaps one day.

Since Montana and the Canadian border I have trailed the Rocky Mountains southwards. It is here that they end, in the pass (El Paso) where their southern journey through Mexico as the Sierra Madre begins. I sit in an old cantina, sipping Mexican beer and being treated to Mexican music and I contemplate the next leg of my journey which will take me back north—as far north as America goes. The frozen seas of the Alaskan Arctic seem a long way away from the warmth of southern Texas.

THE SOUTHWEST, PACIFIC NORTHWEST, CALIFORNIA, ALASKA AND HAWAII

NEW MEXICO
KEY FACTS

Abbreviation:
NM

Nickname:
Land of Enchantment, *Tierra Encantada*

Capital:
Santa Fe

Flower:
Yucca

Tree:
Two-needle piñon pine

Bird:
Great roadrunner (Meep, meep!)

State insect:
Tarantula wasp

Motto:
Crescit eundo ('It grows as it goes')

Well-known residents and natives:
Cochise, Geronimo, Bill Richardson, Pat Garrett,
Billy the Kid, Conrad Hilton,
Clyde 'Pluto' Tombaugh, Georgia O'Keefe,
Ernie Pyle, Bruce Cabot,
William 'Barbera' Hanna, Ronny Cox,
Val Kilmer, Demi Moore.

NEW MEXICO

'There are pueblos in New Mexico as old and as continuously inhabited as the oldest European villages.'

It is something of a surprise to learn that New Mexico, a land that is mostly flat, arid, sparse and scrubby, should also be so ethnically diverse, so culturally rich. America's largest Hispanic and fifth-largest Indian populations bestow unique characteristics upon the state. There is a brand of 'New Mexico Spanish' with its own words, a blend of archaic colonial Castilian and Native American vocabularies. There are pueblos in New Mexico as old and as continuously inhabited as the oldest European villages. This mix of cultural integrity and diversity has attracted over the years hundreds of thousands of countercultural, alternative lifestyle Americans—hippies, peaceniks, eco-warriors, artists and musicians.

SANTA FE AND THE PUEBLOS

I begin my exploration of the state in its capital, Santa Fe, a town that has kept its historic feel like few other American cities. Or has it? In fact it is all very false and more than a little self-conscious. The city was originally laid out by the first Spanish settlers (it had been a series of Indian pueblos since the eleventh century) with streets radiating from a central square, or plaza. By the time New Mexico was admitted to the Union in 1912 (despite the Oscar-winning Judy Garland song, the Atchison, Topeka and the Santa Fe railroad never actually reached Santa Fe, which was served by a branch line) this system had been overrun by standard American architecture and the City Fathers determined that Santa Fe, which had precious few other routes to prosperity, should be made over in the traditional style and become a tourist centre. To that end the city was—wait for a gorgeous new verb—*pueblofied*.

Pueblo is a word which does so much service in so many directions as to need a little clarification. It is the Spanish word for town or village. When the Spanish arrived in *Nuevo México* they saw that the Native American populations lived in villages, unlike their more nomadic brothers and sisters in the Plains for example. The colonists therefore called these tribes *pueblo* Indians. The kinds of house the tribes built—dried mud *adobes*—were called pueblo also. Thus pueblo means:

A Native American people
The villages lived in by the above (there are twenty-one federally recognised pueblos)
The style of architecture of the above

The decision to pueblofy Santa Fe has resulted in an *artful* city. Literally. It is artful in its artifice and it is filled with artists and their work. Indeed it has the third-largest art market in America, after New York and Los Angeles. The adobes are attractive, no question: in a climate like New Mexico's you can dry mud, fill it with a few husks and straws and you have a magnificent building material. The classic pueblo colour is brown, which sounds dull but suits the landscape well. Pinks, yellows and whites are also common, giving a pleasant marzipan and icing-sugar feel.

I spend the morning wandering around. One whole side of the main plaza is taken up by sellers of jewellery and other artefacts: blankets spread out before them are covered in silver and turquoise brooches, belt buckles and hair slides. Many of them are ageing hippies. I find it all very depressing and I am not sure why. I see a woman of sixty with long, long silver hair. She looks a little grouchy and not very well nourished. I picture her coming here with a boyfriend. She is twenty, serene and beautiful. It is 1968. A new life of peace, love, beauty and joy awaits them here. Over the years reality bites. Sexual infidelity, betrayal, desertion, angry children, drugs, money troubles, the dissipation and destruction of a dream. Maybe my imagination is running away with me, but the atmosphere of Santa Fe depresses and distresses me in equal measure.

I am cheered up, perversely, by the sight of a plaque in the back yard of a tourist shop in East Palace Road.

The plaque commemorates the site as being the office out of which grew the Manhattan Project, the code name for the design, construction, testing and delivery to the air force of the world's first atomic bomb. This address was the PO box to which all correspondence was sent for the duration of the Bomb's development. The actual site was too secret to allow its address to be known to anyone. It is well known enough today however: Los Alamos.

LOS ALAMOS

The Los Alamos site, a converted school high up on a mesa twenty miles from Santa Fe, is now even bigger and busier than it was in 1944 when Robert Oppenheimer led his team of physicists and engineers towards the nuclear age.

I said it was perverse of me to be cheered up by the thought of the Manhattan Project, and of course much about it was terrifying, tragic and wholly lamentable. However I have always been excited by Big Science, by the minds, insights and achievements of great physicists. After a morning of faded hippies, bad art and tacky artefacts, it comes as a relief to know that the discipline and hard-headed reality of science have their place in New Mexico too. One of my all-time heroes is the Nobel Prize-winning Richard Feynman: my heart beats faster and my eyelids flutter at the very mention of his name. He worked in Los Alamos in the late forties as a very, very young man. In one of his essays he writes about taking a cab through New York on his way back from Los Alamos to Princeton. He sees men working on new skyscrapers and wants to shout out at them, 'Don't bother! The whole world is going to end soon. There's no point building anything!' These men and women knew what they were creating, but most of them were Jewish and knew what they were fighting too. It was believed by

392

everybody (rightly as it turned out) that Hitler was working on nuclear fission himself. Luckily, the Nazi contempt for Jewish science had led them down the wrong path and the war ended before they could harness the power of the atom.

Los Alamos today remains one of the most important centres for scientific research in the world. I am shown around a piece of incomprehensible testing machinery by Director of Science Terry Wallace. The passion with which he speaks and his pride in the achievements of the laboratory are infectious. He talks to me of self-healing materials for bridges and buildings, of carbon atoms being drawn into cylindrical shapes that can store power . . . ending the capacitance crisis that forces us still to rely on antiquated battery technology. My mouth is open so wide that drool hits the floor.

They still manipulate the atom here, but in less sinister ways than those of Oppenheimer and his colleagues. Terry shows me a series of hydrogen atoms that have been aligned to spell LANL, Los Alamos National Laboratory. How scientists manage to keep their brains straight at this altitude is quite beyond me. We are a mile and half up here and it is beginning to get to me.

There is time to lunch in the Quark Bar (named after a species of subatomic fermion particle) under photographs of Hans Bethe, Edward Teller and Oppenheimer himself.

TAOS AND THE EARTHSHIPS

My next stop is Taos, a place so hippie-shabby that it makes Santa Fe seem like Beverly Hills, which to the

393

average Taos citizen it probably is. There is a certain charm to the town, but I am headed for an area outside it, beyond the pueblos (which are closed to visitors at the moment, it being a holy time of year). I am looking for earthships.

Earthships were first constructed outside Taos in the early seventies, a long time before ecological considerations were as mainstream as they are today.

What are they? Well, they are eco-homes. One side is made of tyres and rammed earth, the other side is open to the sun, which will power solar panels and photovoltaic cells and warm the greenhouses and conservatories. Everything about them is designed to be as self-sustaining and environmentally friendly as possible—and today of course you can add the phrase 'carbon neutral' to that list.

I am shown round an earthship by one of the heroes of the movement, Mike Reynolds. He was the subject of Oliver Hodge's documentary Garbage Warrior, nominated for three British Independent Film Awards. This made Reynolds an easy man to interview, for he was well used to cameras.

A trained architect, Reynolds has built dozens of earthships for rich businessmen, musicians and movie stars as well as for ordinary families. He explains to me how the water in an earthship is used three times, how a family of four can live in a place like this and be off the power grid and never have to go shopping. It is certainly impressive. Absolutely nothing in the village of earthships looks finished, however—the bourgeois in me wishes they weren't so messy, so surrounded by rubble and old cement mixers. For all their new and urgent contemporaneousness the habitations look faintly sad, shambolic and unloved. Skinny dogs lie outside them and growl. Filled with admiration as I am, I will not be ordering an earthship construction kit from Mike's company. I shall continue to be fuelled by grid electricity and guilt.

My final view of Taos is that of the great gorge of the Rio Grande that lies between the earthships and the town itself. A dramatic riot of geology glides below us. I am giddy from the added altitude, but I realise I had better get used to it. It will be a long time before I am at sea level again.

UTAH
KEY FACTS

Abbreviation:
UT

Nickname:
The Beehive State

Capital:
Salt Lake City

Flower:
Sego lily

Tree:
Blue spruce

Bird:
California gull

Snack food:
Jell-O

Motto:
Industry

Well-known residents and natives:
Brigham Young, Warren G. Harding,
Brent Scowcroft, Butch Cassidy,
John Wesley Powell, Philo Farnsworth,
J.W. Marriott, John Gilbert, Loretta Young,
Hal Ashby, Robert Redford, James Woods,
Roseanne Barr, Gary Coleman,
The Osmonds.

UTAH

'My first exclamation on sighting Monument Valley was "Poor Australia!" '

Goulding's Lodge must be a contender for the motel with the best view in the world for it overlooks one of nature's greatest and most insane achievements, Monument Valley.

Utah, southern Utah especially, contains some of America's most dazzling spectacles: Bryce, Moab and Zion national parks and their canyons and gorges are familiar to millions of tourists. If only I had time to visit them all. But Monument Valley will do. It will do very well indeed. I have known it for most of my life without knowing why, as have you in all likelihood: it has been the almost extra-terrestrial background to some of the best films ever made—the westerns of John Ford. The story of how Monument Valley became Ford's personal movie set is a good one.

THE GOULDINGS AND JOHN FORD

In the 1920s Harry Goulding and his wife, Leone 'Mike', established a trading post with the Navajo, which is now the Lodge where I am staying. By the mid- to late thirties the Depression had bitten and, despairing of the plight of the Navajo and of his business, Harry went to Hollywood. The story goes he couldn't get anyone interested in coming to Monument Valley. Couldn't even get a meeting with a young director called John Ford, who was about to start a big new western. Harry resorted to pushing photos of Monument Valley under Ford's office door. It worked. That year, 1938, Ford came to make the movie *Stagecoach* with his new young star, John 'Duke' Wayne. It was the beginning, as they say, of a beautiful friendship: Ford and Wayne made nine pictures in all at Monument Valley and today Goulding's Lodge offers tours around John Wayne's cabin ('dressing room' sounds a bit mincey for the Duke).

Out in the valley, the location of the attack on an Indian village in Ford's masterpiece *The Searchers* is now officially designated John Ford Point. The stone, the red dust and those monumental geological elements are a part of America's iconography.

We toyed with all kinds of ideas for a cover for this book, but in the end the epic grandeur of Monument Valley was irresistible; nothing else says 'America' in quite so loud and clear a voice. Nowhere else on earth looks anything like this.

MONUMENT VALLEY

Actually, my first exclamation on sighting Monument

Valley was 'Poor Australia!' The whole landmass of Australia has one big rock which they regard as a great attraction, but which would be rejected from Monument Valley as being too small, feeble and uninteresting. Most dispiriting for a proud people like the Australians, I should imagine.

But how do the elements of nature come together to create these Gothic cathedrals, Norman keeps, Moghul palaces, Cambodian towers, modernist statues, elegant terraces and alien settlements, all marooned in a parched red desert? The answer, although ultimately convincing, is as mad and unlikely as the features themselves. We are reduced, as ever, to the geologist's explanation for everything: time and pressure, water and wind.

The first game you play when confronted with the contortions of rock that make up the major pieces of the Valley is to force them to fit something we know. It is an irresistible part of being human, we can't help looking for the familiar even in random abstract wind formations. The Indians got there first of course, and then the Christian missionaries and other Europeans. Hence there is the Totem Pole, the Ear of the Wind, the Three Sisters, the Thumb, the Mittens, Elephant Butte, a 'Saviour' which looks like Jesus and a great system of rocks in the shape of the letters W and V, the W of which has also been interpreted as Mary, Jesus and Joseph. Now there is a Lisa Simpson formation and a computer keyboard butte.

The whole site belongs to the Navajo and I feel extremely honoured to be invited to be their guest, right down on the floor of the valley, with the WV behind us.

WEAVING IN THE HOGAN

The taxi makes its way down past John Ford Point to a corral where twenty horses skitter and frisk. Tourists can come down and do some riding here: the man who runs the corral is Jamieson, a middle-aged Navajo man of great charm and sweetness of manner. He smiles at the taxi and bids me join him in his hogan, a kind of round, earth-topped hut, warm in winter, cool in summer. He smiles with some amusement at my ravings: What a place to live! Imagine waking up every morning in scenery like this! He loves it of course, but it is all he has known.

We are joined by his sister Sally, who is an expert weaver, specialising in traditional Navajo basketware. When I say expert, I mean expert, her baskets are not just charming and desirable ethnic craftwork, they fetch thousands and thousands of pounds from avid collectors around the world. One of them, she tells me proudly, is in the White House in Washington, DC. A weaver is responsible for everything: she picks the sumac twigs (involving a journey of hundreds of miles, for sumac does not grow locally), slices them, soaks them and dyes them. Sally's daughter is learning the craft and I buy two delightful tightly coiled little bowls from her. She explains the iconography of the patterns: the centre, like a navel, symbolises the beginning of the world, and is surrounded by the mountains, the rainbow (where dreams and thoughts dwell) and then the clouds and sky. There is a gap between the navel and the edge which is how man is able to mediate the differing zones. Pleasing. But nothing like as pleasing as the smell emanating from a barbecue grill outside the hogan.

400

Jamieson has invited most of his family to this Sunday morning brunch. I watch as his sister-in-law Lorraine makes frybread, a Navajo speciality, not unlike a fluffy naan. The fluffiness comes from the addition of milk powder, Lorraine tells me. Meanwhile, as with barbecues the world over, the men are scorching the steak, the ribs and the sausages.

This trip has given me many happy moments, but stuffing down real, freshly made Navajo frybread in the shadow of Monument Valley is high in the top ten.

Jamieson turns me round to look at the formation behind us and he says to me, and I know this sounds sentimental and made-up and corny, but he says it to me and I can see in his eyes that he means it, he says, 'See that? WV. It stands for "Welcome, Visitor."'

THE SILVER RIBBON OF TIME . . .

Utah's Mormon settlers had wanted to call the territory deseret, which in their founder Joseph Smith's sad, silly madey-uppy language meant 'honey-bee', hence the nickname The Beehive State and the motto 'Industry'. Wiser counsels prevailed: the name Utah is derived from the Ute, a tribe of Shoshone-speaking Indians once resident in the area around the Colorado River. I remember when I was about nine years old a National Geographic film was played to my class. The American commentator spoke in that peculiar way that took off a be- suffix if there was one and added one where there wasn't: ' 'Neath the be-dappled sagebrush prairie-lands' . . . that sort of thing. He also came up with this rare jewel: 'the silver river of time that is the Colorado River . . . ' My friends and I went round for weeks

401

talking about 'the emerald blanket of love that is the cricket pitch' and 'the golden staff of hate that is this hockey stick'.

The silver river of time that is the Colorado River, it might be argued, has done more wonders than any other river in the world. It carved out the Grand Canyon, that alone is achievement enough. As a reward it has been staunched and stemmed on a scale like no other. It all began with the Hoover Dam in 1930 and it ended with the completion of Lake Powell in 1980. Poor silver ribbon of time that was the Colorado River, be-dammed and diverted to be-buggery.

Imagine that someone was so profligate and peculiar as to seal up the ends of the Grand Canyon and then fill it with water. Well, that is more or less what has happened in the case of Lake Powell, a vast artificial reservoir created in 1956. That is to say, the damming started in 1956—it actually took almost a quarter of a century to fill Glen Canyon and create Lake Powell.

It was considered by many at the time to be a disaster, a wanton act of greedy, brutal destruction. Glen Canyon, though less well known than the Grand Canyon, was held by many to be more beautiful. Never having seen any of it except the parts that rise above the water level, I can believe them. The colourful layered Navajo sandstone on all sides of the lake is exquisite. I cannot deny that the effect of the water is beautiful too. It allows a special kind of tourism—the houseboat holiday. I travel with Rob Bighorse, a Navajo man now employed as a guide by the boat company. I look around the boat. There is a kitchen, the largest plasma screen TV I have ever seen and, above, a jacuzzi.

Vulgar, yes. Ecologically disgraceful, certainly. Bloated and obscene, no doubt. But the houseboat is damned good fun too, I just cannot deny it. We glide along these clear, tranquil waters with the rays of the dying sun setting on fire the rocks around us before anchoring on a kind of beach. We dine and I fall into bed a very happy Stephen indeed.

The next day we glide for another few hours. I wonder when we will come to the end, but Rob tells me that we haven't yet circumnavigated a fiftieth of the lake's 1,900 miles of shoreline. Another hour of gliding passes, during which I take a jacuzzi, and then we put in to land once more. Rob escorts me off the boat, up a path for a mile or so until we reach the Rainbow Bridge, a natural sandstone arch of surpassing beauty, large enough comfortably to accommodate the Statue of Liberty. They say it is the largest natural bridge in the world. Whether or not that is true, it is certainly sacred to the Navajo and we absolutely cannot walk under it or approach it too near. Rob is annoyed that he forgot to bring corn pollen, with which he could have blessed it. In the legend as told to Rob by his grandfather, a Navajo boy was caught once on the rocks in the wind and rain, with no way to turn. Suddenly a rainbow appeared before him and he crossed it to safety. After he had crossed, the bridge turned to stone.

It seems highly wrong that our return to our land vehicles should be by speedboat, but we have a schedule to keep and so, ripping a great wake in the water and a great roar in the air, we power back to land, the hull slapping down so hard that it jars my arm terribly. I fear that it may open up the fracture, so violent is our passage. From a mood of serenity I am reduced to misery, rage and distress. I make a vow that

403

I shall never travel on a speedboat again. So that's horses and speedboats. I shall hold myself to both pledges.

The memory of pain soon goes, the memory of pleasure lingers, that is one of life's happier truths.

If there is one state you should visit for physical beauty alone, let that state be Utah.

ARIZONA
KEY FACTS

Abbreviation:
AZ

Nicknames:
The Grand Canyon State, the Copper State

Capital:
Phoenix

Flower:
Saguaro blossom

Tree:
Blue palo verde

Bird:
Cactus wren

Neckwear:
Bolo tie

Motto:
Ditat deus ('God enriches')

Well-known residents and natives:
Doc Holliday, Barry Goldwater, John McCain,
Sandra Day O'Connor, Wiliam Rehnquist,
Zane Grey, Frank Lloyd Wright, Steven Spielberg,
Lynda Carter, Michael 'Terminator' Biehn,
Ted Danson, Steve Allen, Sandra Bernhard,

Gary Shandling, Greg Proops, Charlie Mingus,
Wayne Newton, Alice Cooper,
Stevie Nicks, Linda Ronstadt.

ARIZONA

'The saguaro ... is the iconic, tall, comically limbed giant beloved of cartoonists.'

'Arizona official state neckwear' indeed. You think I'm making it up, don't you? Absolutely not. Arizona's state bird is the cactus wren, and since 1971 its state neckwear has been the bolo ('bootlace', we call it in Britain) tie. Yep, Arizona's a western state all right. The name derives from the Spanish *arida zona*—'arid zone' ... or at least so people used to think. But it now seems that this is what etymologists call a false friend, for a Spaniard would always say *zona arida*. The more likely derivation is from the Basque *aritz onac* meaning 'good oaks'. Apparently the first silver camp in the territory was called Arizonac, later shortened to Arizona, which seems to clinch it.

For once, the state capital here is also the largest city. Arizonans will tell you that the city of Mesa, part of the 'Phoenix Metropolitan Area', is the fastest-growing city in America. There is Scottsdale too, the ritzy resort part of Phoenix, and Chandler and Glendale and Peoria—over four million people in an area which is growing too fast for statisticians to keep count. Interestingly, the only state with a comparable rate of growth is also a desert state—Nevada. I suppose the explanation is the huge ageing population . . . all those baby-boomers hitting retirement age and wanting to end their days somewhere warm and dry.

As it happens I meet someone much older than a mere baby-boomer in Mesa . . .

SENTIMENTAL JOURNEY

The Commemorative Air Force is an organisation dedicated to preserving and exhibiting historical military aircraft. While we have RAF museums in Hendon and Cosford and the Imperial War Museum has its site in Duxford, the CAF can boast, aside from its headquarters in Midland, Texas, seventy affiliated groups in twenty-seven states and four other countries. One of their most popular bases, or 'wings', is in Mesa, AZ. I fall into conversation with a splendid old-timer who serves as a docent (guide) here. He was based in East Anglia during the war, in Lincoln and then in Norfolk, which is very much my part of the world, and he was pleased to be able to point out on a map just where he had been and to speak to someone from a place he still remembers fondly. The opportunity to talk with real Second World War combatants is naturally diminishing, so I am deliriously happy to meet him. He served with James Stewart, my favourite Hollywood actor, and

408

still refers to him as Colonel Stewart, for the man was a genuine flyer and a senior officer in the USAAF.

Since starting work last year on a screenplay for a new film about the Dambusters raid, I have had the opportunity to talk to a small number of survivors of that operation and even to clamber around inside a Lancaster bomber. A Boeing B-17 bomber isn't quite a Lancaster, it doesn't have the nape-bristling roar of Rolls-Royce Merlin engines or the elegantly gigantic profile that stirs the soul of every Briton who once glued together a model version, but for all that the Boeing is a beautiful machine. Americans do know how to present an aircraft—all polished metal and rivets. How these machines must have dazzled the German fighter pilots when they began their tour in Europe as daylight bombers. 'Ten thousand nuts and bolts flying in close formation', is what the air-crews called the aircraft also known as the 'Flying Fortress', the bomber that more than any other became a symbol of the USAAF. The *Memphis Belle*, the *Sally B* and the *Swoose* are some of the best-known individuals, but here at the Arizona Wing of the CAF they have a beauty, a B-17G called *Sentimental Journey*. For those who care about things she's something of a hybrid when it comes to power, as two of her engines are Studebakers and the other two are Wright Cyclones. A decal of America's sweetheart Betty Grable peeps coyly and provocatively over her shoulder, the backs of her million-dollar legs as straight as classical columns.

I climb up into the front bubble, taking the bombardier's position. A volunteer crew of enthusiasts in blue uniforms take their places and the engines start. We are flying to Tucson, a journey of 116 miles, to take a look at one of the most bizarre sights in America. The crew have done this many times before but they still can't resist playing with the guns and making Walter Mitty 'tapocketa-pocketa-pocketa' noises.

It's a magnificent flight: the thrum of those four engines, the clear blue of the sky, the sagebrush and sand of the desert racing beneath us. How lucky I am. Lucky to be doing this at all, especially lucky to be doing it in a heritage flight, not as a bombardier in a shooting war.

Approaching Tucson people look up and wave as American history roars above them, and then . . . we are on it! I see it! There it is! Row after row after row of aircraft glinting in the sun: jet fighters, stealth bombers, surveillance planes, spy planes, transport planes, helicopters. All so neatly arranged on grass and tarmac, more aeroplanes than are in the air forces of just about every country you can think of, combined. An astounding arsenal. Silent. Sinister. Asleep.

Why are they there? What are they doing? Well, this is Davis-Monthan Air Force Base, once the largest municipal airport in the world, and now the home of the United States government's Boneyard, the place where decommissioned aircraft come to lie down. The low humidity, infrequent rainfall, and alkaline soil of Tucson make this the perfect place to keep all that metal from rusting.

We land and I say goodbye to *Sentimental Journey*. The taxi has cleverly arrived here ahead of me and I get in and drive up and down the rows, goggling in amazement. 707s, Phantoms, B-52s and B-1s. There are four and a half thousand aircraft here, I am told, worth around $30 billion.

Each one, on arrival, has its guns, ejection seat

charges and all 'pilferable and classified objects' removed. The fuel system is drained, refilled with lightweight oil and then drained again. This protects the tanks and lines with a film of oil. The whole plane is then shielded from dust, UV and scorching temperatures by spraying it with a kind of synthetic latex vinyl compound called 'spraylat', or, in less dignified cases, it is dressed in a garbage sack, what we would call a bin-liner. For some aircraft this is the end of the line, their spare parts will be cannibalised and sold on. They say this is the only air force base in America that makes a profit. For other aircraft, however, this is not death but a kind of sleep. Once every four years their ignition keys will be turned and engines fired. For one day, one day, my guide assures me, these slumbering dragons may be called upon to serve their country again.

CACTUS AND COWBOYS

This is one of the most beautiful parts of the world I have ever visited. I want to stay here. I want to build a house here and live here for the rest of my life. I dare say the feeling will pass, for I am fickle as flame, but for the moment I find myself to be hopelessly in love. You may think a desert would be too hot for comfort, but the heat here is so dry that the atmosphere is entirely pleasant, you can move around easily in temperatures close to 100° without sweating. Very different from the swampy, sultry south in Louisiana and Alabama or the humid summers of New York and Chicago.

Tucson's Mountain Park. The Sonora desert. Cactus. The saguaro, pronounced 'sa-uaro', is the

411

iconic, tall, comically limbed giant beloved of cartoonists. They often have holes in them where dedicated woodpeckers, finches and a bird called the Golden Flicker make their homes. Their stunning blossom is the state flower of Arizona and produces millions and millions of seeds, one of which, if it is lucky, will sprout in the summer rain and, over fifty to eighty years, grow a side arm and be tall enough to hit a ceiling. They have been known to live for a hundred and seventy-five years and achieve heights above forty feet. They are funny and noble and beautiful and silly and grand all at the same time. Rather like America, come to think of it.

If you see a saguaro in a western then the chances are that western was made in the Old Tucson Studios, 'Arizona's Hollywood in the desert'. Saguaros don't grow in Texas, or California or anywhere else really. Just around here and in parts of Mexico.

I am introduced to an actor named Travis, for I have been invited to take part in a shoot-out with some of the team who daily put on Wild West shows. I had expected to be slightly embarrassed by naffness and tackiness. I should have known better. Travis and his colleagues are smart, committed, clever and funny performers. We devise and play out a small and absurd scenario. I bite the dust, pick myself up and mosey over to the old Mexican church where, after a pause for costume changes, my erstwhile colleagues all emerge and perform a show based on the Steve Martin, Chevy Chase, Martin Short comedy classic *¡Three Amigos!* It is delightfully funny and filled with physically terrifying stunts and dreadful jokes exquisitely performed.

I suck down a bottle of suds. Yep, this really could be it. This could be the place where I spend the

412

evening of my life. Not the studios, but somewhere near the Saguaro Park, somewhere west of Tuscon within sight of the mountains and the cactus.

NEVADA
KEY FACTS

Abbreviation:
NE

Nicknames:
The Silver State, The Sagebrush State,
The Battle Born State

Capital:
Carson City

Flower:
Sagebrush

Trees:
Single-leafed piñon pine, bristlecone pine

Bird:
Mountain bluebird

Fossil:
Ichthyosaur

Motto:
All For Our Country

Well-known residents and natives:
Pat Nixon, Edna Purviance, Steve Wynn,
Michael Chang, Andre Agassi.

NEVADA

'Where are the representations of casinos, lowlifes, strippers, losers, Elvis impersonators and hookers?'

They have tried to cram into Nevada's state seal just about as much imagery as it can take. Trains, silver-mining, a quartz mill, snow-capped peaks, telegraph poles, a wheat sheaf, a sickle and a plough in the foreground. Mineral resources, agriculture, natural beauty, transportation and communications. Sounds like quite a state. Hang on. This is Nevada. Where are the representations of casinos, lowlifes, strippers, losers, Elvis impersonators and hookers?

Early settlers on the Old Spanish Trail from Santa Fe to California liked to stop off at a pleasant area in Nevada, a kind of oasis, naturally greened by its underground artesian wells. The Meadows, they called it, Las Vegas. And what is it now?

The extremity of Sin City, as it used proudly to call itself, is itself extreme. A symbol of human kind's perverse and remorseless will, a symbol of cupidity exploiting stupidity, of capitalism taken to its furthest limits, of gullibility, fallibility, optimism, cruelty, vulgarity and greed. Some find themselves so grossed out, so appalled and frightened by what Las Vegas is that they turn tail and run, never to return. Some are so instantly grossed in, so entranced and seduced, that they dive headfirst into it all, never to leave. Most, like me, are in more or less equal turns amused, repelled, outraged and enraptured.

A phrase that Europeans and Americans alike were fond of using in the early days of the twentieth century was 'the Can Do spirit'. America's ability to solve problems of civil engineering by designing bridges, roads and tunnels bigger and better than any seen before, its habit of throwing up enormous skyscrapers, inventing new gadgets, building whole new cities, devising new ways to serve food, to entertain, to sell, to charm . . . this brand of energy, optimism, drive and ingenuity was something quite new in the world. It is a quality still alive and nowhere more so than in Las Vegas, where they prove every year that they Can Do just about anything.

Vegas depends for its survival on the new, on ever more preposterous and eye-popping achievements in resort-building. They have had no compunction, for instance, in pulling down such historic landmarks as the Sands and the Desert Inn: in fact almost all the great casinos and hotels of the Rat Pack days of the fifties and sixties are now rubble in the foundations of the new. The craze a few years ago was for building cities: New York, Paris and Venice—with all the boring bits left out and all the famous attractions conveniently close to each other. We laugh, of course we do, but most of us cannot but suck in a secret

416

whistle of admiration too. If only all this ingenuity, energy, determination, vision and courage were aimed at something a little less screwy, a little less nakedly concupiscent, a little less pervertedly bogus.

SPY GAMES

I sit in my slate grey and chromium hotel suite fretting about the fact that I haven't found a way to turn off its real-flame fireplace, but European eco-guilt has as much place in Las Vegas as a stripper at a synod. Less.

The doorbell rings and within seconds I am embroiled in a nightmare of identity, treachery and betrayal. She calls herself Trixie. She wears a raincoat and a fedora. She tells me that I have been selected to act as a double-agent, a mole: my mission is to infiltrate myself within . . . well, to be perfectly honest with you, quite what I have to infiltrate myself into is for the moment beyond me. Dark powers working against the common good have conspired, that much is clear. What they have conspired to do is less apparent. The forces of good must be marshalled and the marshalling place is somewhere, it seems, on Howard Hughes Parkway. I have five minutes to get there. Your country needs you.

'Britain?'

'America!' whispers Trixie.

'Ah.'

'Remember. At each place you visit there will be a contact. You must give them each one of these tokens. The others cannot know. You must keep your double-agent status secret from them.'

'The others?'

417

Trixie and I zip down to the rendezvous in the taxi. I have to let her out before I meet the others, for they must not know that I have been contacted by her. The others, it turns out, are the Chippendales. Yes, the bow-tied male-stripping combo that has for years delighted hen nights and Christmas parties the world over.

I am soon plunged into the guts of this 'Spy Game'. From first to last I have no idea what is going on, but some quality of American-ness seems to allow the Chippendales to be absolutely clear about the whole proceeding. They accept the spy packs, cell phones and cameras handed to them as if they do this every day.

Spy games have become all the rage in Las Vegas. They are a structured, if expensive, way of seeing the town, and companies also use them for team-building exercises and the like. The players are sent from venue to venue, mostly via the city's monorail. From Caesar's Palace to the Mirage, from the MGM Grand to the Flamingo we flit, meeting 'contacts'—who turn out to be obvious rain-coated, sun-glassed spooks. I manage to offload two of my mole-tokens before the smartest and most mouthy Chippendale, the 'team-leader', stops me, bids me empty my pockets and exposes me to all as the mole. Naturally I change sides immediately and am now a triple-agent.

It is all most confusing, but by the end of the afternoon I at least know Las Vegas better than I ever could have done otherwise.

MORMON CALENDAR BOYS

The unique moral outlook of Las Vegas seem

418

somehow to have penetrated even the fastnesses of the Church of Latter Day Saints. The morning after my adventures in espionage, I arrive at a photo studio somewhere off the Strip to find myself surrounded by semi-naked young men whose more than ordinarily sparkling eyes, unblemished skin, gleaming teeth and air of sexless perfection tell me that they are Mormons, members of a church that forswears sex before marriage and stimulants or narcotics of any kind, from caffeine to nicotine and cocaine. These are all good Mormon boys who have done their 'missionary work', in other words they have travelled within America, or beyond, wearing white shirts and dark suits and spreading the word of Mormon. This is the second year of their (strictly topless and genital-free) calendar. It raises money for charity and seems to have won the reluctant acceptance of the Church Elders back in Salt Lake City.

I chat to Cody, a personable nineteen-year-old who is happy to discuss any part of his religion to me. He is surprised and pleased, I think, to learn that I do not find his faith particularly absurd, in the way many mainstream Christians do. I forbear telling him that the reason I do not find Mormonism especially ridiculous is because I find all pretend invisible friends, Special Books and their rules *equally* ridiculous. Mormon ideas about realms of crystal rebirthing and special underpants are no weirder than the enforcing of wigs and woollen tights on orthodox Jewish women or laws and dogmas about burkhas and Virgin Births. The religion of the Latter Day Saints is not deserving of especial contempt simply because it is newer. It is as barmy as the rest and I cheerfully treat it as such. It has the same impertinent views concerning women and gays, of course, but Cody is

419

clearly embarrassed about this and says with a touch of defensiveness, 'We aren't as bigoted as some fundamental Christians.' Mm. Yes. Well. I bid my farewells and head for Reno and some good old-fashioned hookers.

Stop press: apparently the man who arranged this calendar shoot, himself a devout Mormon, has been excommunicated, or whatever the saintly Latter Day equivalent is, for bringing the church into disrepute. Seems to me the elders have done that by making arses of themselves once again.

THE WILD HORSE RANCH

All my large, lazy, liberal contempt for religious codes of behaviour seeps away from me as I approach the town of Sparks, NV and face the prospect of hanging around a brothel. Suddenly I am a model of moral disapproval and prudish distaste. Must I really do this?

The first legalised brothel in Nevada was opened by one Joe Conforte in the 1950s. The Mustang Ranch became famous the world over. Conforte ran into trouble over taxes however and skipped the country. The federal government, as a way of 'garnishing' and reclaiming moneys, ran the outfit themselves. Perhaps unsurprisingly, the feds didn't have the first idea how to run a cat house so they closed the Mustang and sold it, I kid you not, on e-Bay. There's a film there, surely?

We fast forward to the present day: the Mustang has been bought and moved, brick by brick and beam by beam, to the compound where the Wild Horse Ranch stands, both now owned and run by Susan Austin. In honour of Joe Conforte she has redecorated the lobby of the Mustang in an Italian villa style.

Susan was herself a working girl before she met and fell for Lance Gilman, a local businessman. His money and her experience in the field have propelled the Wild Horse and Mustang to the forefront. I sit and lunch with her in the 'viewing room' of the Wild Horse. This is a place where clients come to pick out the girl of their choice from a line-up.

Susan is a passionate advocate for legalised prostitution. As a working Madam, she believes that a safe, pimp-free environment where drugs are not tolerated and safe sexual practices are obligatory is infinitely preferable to the predatory, dangerous, disease and drug-ridden world Out There.

When she was a 'working girl', Susan had a great time, she says. She loved sex, so she loved her work. She inculcates the same enthusiasm in her girls. Doctors and shoulders to cry on are always available. The girls are healthy and happy.

Hm. I agree with her that this legalised situation is infinitely preferable to prostitution on the streets, where there is no licensing and there are no safeguards. But none of that makes it a pleasant or attractive profession in my eyes. I am shocked at how old-fashioned I am. More shocks are to come.

Susan shows me a room where the girls ride a vibrating toy. She claims that they gush and splash so much at their moment of climax that the watching men get soaked. This is of course all a way of trying to persuade me (and the BBC audience of potential customers) that the girls *enjoy* themselves and that their orgasms are not only genuine, but overpowering and spectacular. I am not so innocent that I do not know that believing this is, for some reason, important to many men. I believe it slightly less than I believe good Mormons are rebirthed in crystal realms.

Another room is used for DCs. The men and their chosen girl/s go in there to negotiate. Once practices and pricing are agreed the man has to submit his penis to health inspection. DC stands for Dick Check.

Mandy, one of the girls, is wheeled out to tell me how much she enjoys her work, how much she loves the sex. Hm.

Next I am shown the 'premium' suites, which are decorated in Italian, Hawaiian and Chinese style, all very *faux*, but to be fair no *faux*-er than most three or four star hotels. Tantric chairs are a feature of all the suites. I can't help observing how gleamingly clean everything is. Susan tells me that the girls know that they absolutely *must* lay down sheets, so that the expensive furniture and decorations in the suites are protected from the smears and skid marks of juiced-up and lubricated love-makers. Ah. Of course. How romantic.

Part of my living is made by doing a TV show that is often adult (in other words childish) in its content, but I have to confess that after four hours in the Wild Horse and Mustang ranches I feel like lying in a bath and listening to a Noddy tape.

Susan is right. I have no business to disapprove. Sex is real. Men want it. Operating a brothel should be no weirder than running a restaurant, where the most outré appetites can also be attended to for money. And yet . . .

VIRGINIA CITY

Susan sits in the back of the cab and directs me up the mountain to Virginia City, an old silver-mining town

422

that has kept its character better than most. This is where the famous Comstock Lode was worked, a massive silver mine that yielded, in today's values, upwards of $600 billion of ore.

I sip a sarsaparilla at the bar, still taking in the shocks of the morning and afternoon. All around me men and women with beards and accents that seem to come right out of a western fling down their whiskeys and sip their beers. A man called Zeke rides into the saloon on a horse. Virginia is that kind of a roughty-toughty place.

I feel perhaps I have had it with Nevada. Charming as she is, her main features are all too much for an innocent East Anglian.

Happily, my final memories of the state are destined to be of dramatic and overwhelming beauty. I say goodbye to Susan and drive further up the mountain, descending at Lake Tahoe. The state line is not far now.

Sometimes clichés are unavoidable so I forgive myself for yelling . . . 'California, here I come . . . '

CALIFORNIA
KEY FACTS

Abbreviation:
CA

Nickname:
The Golden State

Capital:
Sacramento

Flower:
California poppy

Tree:
Sequoia (California redwood)

Bird:
California quail

Reptile:
Desert tortoise

Motto:
Eureka

Well-known natives:
Ansel Adams, Paula Abdul, Gracie Allen,
Jennifer Aniston, Tracy Austin, Drew Barrymore,
Captain Beefheart, Mel Blanc, Jack Black,
Lloyd, Beau and Jeff Bridges, Albert Brooks,
Jerry Brown, Nicholas Cage, David Carradine,

Keith Carradine, Julia Child, Jamie Lee Curtis,
Ted Danson, Cameron Diaz, Leonardo DiCaprio,
Joe DiMaggio, Dr Dre, Micky Dolenz, Snoop Dogg,
Isadora Duncan, Robert Duvall, Clint Eastwood,
Mia Farrow, Will Ferrell, Carrie Fisher,
Dian Fossey, Jodie Foster, Robert Frost,
Edward Furlong, Jerry Garcia, Danny Glover,
Gloria Grahame, Merv Griffin, Jake Gyllenhaal . . .

CALIFORNIA

'The pioneers who had struggled through the sparse deserts of the west screamed with delight when they fell upon this lush, fertile land.'

As you can see from the Key Facts (see page 307), I gave up on the list of well-known natives once I had reached the end of the Gs. There are simply too many. Ahead lie Nixon, Patton, Reagan, Steinbeck, Schwarzenegger and as many film stars and musicians as you can think of, from Marilyn Monroe to Shirley Temple, from Carlos Santana to Tupac Shakur. I will leave you to fill in the gaps. Imagine if I included the well-known residents as well as natives . . . Statistically California has a habit of boggling the mind. At thirty-six and a half million people, only thirty-four countries in the world can claim to have larger populations. Come to that, only eight countries in the world can claim to have a greater gross domestic product or more powerful economy. As the

426

home of Silicon Valley and Hollywood, California probably exerts a greater cultural and technological influence over the world than any nation. With its size, diversity, power and reach California is a state like no other.

The miles of Pacific coastline and the great wildernesses of Sequoia and Yosemite, Death Valley (the hottest place on earth) and the Sierra Nevada Mountains (which contain Mount Whitney, the highest peak in all the forty-eight contiguous states), the giant redwoods, the beaches, the lakes, islands, palms and pastures—you can imagine why the pioneers who had struggled through the sparse deserts of the west screamed with delight when they fell upon this lush, fertile land. That it should have so much gold too . . . no wonder they call it the Eureka State.

You might be surprised to know that I did not stop off at Los Angeles. It is a place I have visited many, many times, but while you may think that this is no reason not to look at it afresh, I felt that British television has seen too many presenters sitting in the backs of convertibles, too many palm trees flashing by at jazzy angles, too many whip-pans of Rodeo Drive and the Beverly Hills sign—every year at Oscar time we are treated to this, and in between there are plenty of documentaries about Tinsel Town and its faults and foibles. Enough already, I felt and still do feel. So you will have to forgive me for skipping America's second-biggest city and starting my Californian tour in only its fourteenth-biggest, San Francisco.

But what a city. I do not share the fashionable disdain for Los Angeles expressed by so many Britons, but love LA as I do, San Francisco is, to my mind, about as perfect a town as there can be. If you can overlook, that is, its habit of being destroyed by earthquakes every two hundred years.

North Beach, the Golden Gate Bridge, Chinatown, the cable cars—I am happy to wander about like the most rubber-necked, wide-eyed tourist, gaping and grinning at the bumps and hills that Steve McQueen made so famous in that car chase in *Bullitt*.

JONY IVE

The first time I met this hero of the western world I was tongue-tied, so it is as well that I have got to know him better in the intervening years. At forty-one years old Jonathan Paul Ive CBE is probably the most influential designer alive. He was only thirty when he unleashed upon the world, under the aegis of the newly returned CEO, Steve Jobs, the Apple iMac, that transparent blue, all-in-one TV-shaped desktop computer that most informed people reckon revived Apple's fortunes, saved it indeed, from going under. There followed in bewilderingly quick succession the iPod in all its generations of Mini, Nano and Touch, new generations too of iMac, the massively influential titanium PowerBook and most recently the all-conquering iPhone.

We drive around San Francisco, his adopted home (Apple's HQ is the fabled 1 Infinite Loop, Cupertino—forty-five miles to the south) and he points out his favourite landmarks. We drive to the Russian Hill District and chat on the roof of the San Francisco Art Institute.

There can be few people on earth who have not seen that iconic, round-cornered white slab of a device, the classic iPod, I say to him. What was it like when he first sat on a bus or cable car and saw someone with

428

the unmistakable white earphones plugged in? Did he instantly know it was a hit?

Ive is so modest that such a question is impossible for him to answer, for it assumes propositions like success, iconic and hit. I allow him to writhe a little, before embarrassing him further. It is wonderful to me to think that a talented young Briton can make such a name for himself in America. Is there a difference in the way Britons and Americans work?

Oh well, you know. Gosh. Actually most of the Apple design team is non-American. Europeans and Asians predominate.

Why?

Golly. Um . . .

I empty my bag on the ledge of the Art Institute roof. Out come iPods and iPhones of various kinds. His face lights up, not at the compliment being paid him, but as he handles an iPod Nano and recalls the issues facing the anodising of the metal and the number of trips he had to make to China to get the process working just right. Jony's perfectionism, mastery of detail and capacity for hard work are as much the secret of his success as his creative flair and his imagination. It was ever thus of course, but it is one of those universal truths, like the swiftness of our passage through life, that cannot be taught often enough.

NAPA VALLEY

Art and Judd Finkelstein are a father and son team who make wines at Judd's Hill Winery just off the Silverado Trail in the very heart of the Napa Valley, one of California's premier wine regions, which lies about an hour north of San Francisco. They make their own Judd's Hill single varietal and blended wines, the latter of which are so highly regarded that many other vineyards now send their grapes to be blended for them by these two passionate and creative wine-makers. The Finkelsteins are one of those families that seem to be able to do everything, paint, make pots, make music, dance, cook and write poetry. But wine comes first.

I sit at a table in their tasting room and together we judiciously sample the 2006 red varietals. The aim is to make a good cabernet sauvignon. Despite its single variety name, the Californian version is almost always a blend of cabernet sauvignon, merlot and cabernet franc grapes. In other words, they make traditional Bordeaux-style wines here—clarets as we call them in Britain.

After much sipping (and, in the case of Art and Judd at least, spitting) we decide that the best glass we can produce is one composed of 75% cabernet sauvignon, 15% merlot and 10% cabernet franc. Many varying proportions are tried before we hit that magic formula, so I am a little dizzy when I rise to join the family for dinner. It is most important that I go to bed sober, for it would not do at all to have a hangover tomorrow. Trembling hands would be a disaster.

BEING AS THIS IS A .44 MAGNUM . . .

Early in the morning I drive to the 'Helldorado Shooting Range' in Ukiah, CA to meet Officer Greg Stefani and his boss, Tom Allman, the Sheriff of Mendocino County. I am going to fire off some handguns. I have never done this before in all my life.

430

I have had to handle prop guns on film sets, but never the real thing. I am feeling as nervous as a kitten but trying not to show it.

Ukiah is ranked California's best small town to live in, and the sixth-best in all America. I can't help noticing that its name is 'haiku' backwards. The Sheriff tells me that on account of this arbitrary fact, the town holds an annual haiku festival.

'Just as well you aren't called Traf,' I say, donning the obligatory goggles and ear defenders.

'How's that?'

'Well, what a terrible festival that would be . . . never mind.'

Greg takes me patiently through the principles, protocols and operating procedures of shooting and then hands me a Glock semi-automatic pistol. Or is it a revolver? I am not quite sure of the difference.

I raise my arms (my right arm, though much better, is still not the limb it was before the fracture) and—as instructed—squeeze the trigger.

I hit the target! I actually hit the target!

Suddenly and inevitably I am transformed from Stephen Tut-Tut, the wise and sensible anti-firearms abolitionist into Stephen Blam-Blam, a narrow-eyed, gun-toting militiaman. Pathetic, I know, but that's what guns do.

And all this is before Greg passes to me a Smith & Wesson Magnum 44. *Dirty Harry* is one of my favourite films and like many of my generation I know much of it off by heart, especially of course Clint's lines:

I know what you're thinking. 'Did he fire six shots or only five?' Well, to tell you the truth, in all this excitement I kind of lost track myself.

431

But being as this is a .44 Magnum, the most powerful handgun in the world, and would blow your head clean off, you've got to ask yourself one question: Do I feel lucky? Well, do ya, punk?

It was naturally impossible for me to fire this terrifyingly heavy handcannon without first delivering myself of that speech.

I did not hit the target. Nor the second time. Nor the third or fourth. My fifth attempt did get through, knocking the target over. I returned the Magnum to Greg. My arm ached like billy-oh but I did not care to admit it.

'Now that you can handle firearms, how d'you like to take part in a drugs bust?' asked Sheriff Allman, who had been watching my small-arms artillery work with gentle amusement.

WEED

It seems that Mendocino County is just about the national centre of cannabis growing. It is not illegal to grow a small amount for personal, medical use, but the law that legitimises this is complicated and Sheriff Allman explains it to me as we drive to the small town of Willets. The police are not interested in citizens growing for personal use a little more than they are allowed; they are after the gangs that hothouse millions of dollars' worth of the drug for sale all around America. Often young Asians with no record, the growers are hired by the bosses to rent a house with land and to cultivate and harvest the plants. If they are raided it is bad luck, but the kids have clean records so it is unlikely that a custodial sentence will be imposed. With so much money to be made for so little risk, it really does seem like a good business to be in. Only ten per cent of these operations, according to the Sheriff, are busted and closed down. Pay young men good money, assure them of top lawyers and no more than probation if they are caught . . . how can the police fight that? All they get are infrequent tip-offs and the frustration of seeing the offenders walk free.

I am kitted out in a Kevlar bulletproof vest, 'just in case', and join a convoy of police vehicles driving up the hill to the suspects' farm.

This tip-off was good and I watch as the suspects (Vietnamese apparently) are led away with bound wrists and cheerful expressions on their faces. Hundreds and hundreds of plants (all female, all cloned from one Mother) are torn up and thrown onto the back of a truck for burial. Burning is a bad way to destroy them for obvious reasons, but burial causes them to heat up underground and lose their THC, the psychoactive cannabis ingredient that is the source of all the trouble.

ARCATA STONERS

I drive up to Arcata, where some of those drug-growers' best customers live. Arcata is an old-fashioned (by which I mean refreshingly free of franchise burger bars and strip malls) college town with a reputation for being something of a centre for slackers and stoners and for being about as politically progressive as an American town can be. It was here that the first ever Green Party council members were elected and here that the USA Patriot Act has been 'nullified' by the City Fathers. Arcata is also the first town to have declared itself a GM Free zone.

I meet Carmen, a bright and twinkly ginger lesbo Jew (as she styles herself) of enormous charm. She shows me the town. It reminds me of the Back to the Future films, a big central square, no Starbucks, no recognisable national chains anywhere that I can see. Plenty of weed-smoking dead-beats though. The smart college students from Humboldt University seem to be outnumbered by the hobos.

I am taken to the Muddy Waters café to watch Carmen's stage act—a mixture of stand-up comedy and self-penned songs, one of which is so harsh a revenge on a female student lover who did her wrong that I am forced to feel pity for the poor girl. Student life is so intense and cannabis seems to make it more so.

I tiptoe away, leaving the fumes and feuds behind me. The drive north through the Giant Redwood Park and towards the Oregon state line is as astoundingly beautiful as any I've taken on this whole trip.

A lifetime's ambition is realised when I find a sequoia I can drive through. Thank you, California.

434

OREGON
KEY FACTS

Abbreviation:
OR

Nickname:
The Beaver State

Capital:
Salem

Flower:
Oregon-grape

Tree:
Douglas fir

Bird:
Western meadowlark

Seashell:
Oregon hairy triton

Motto:
The Union or *Alis volat propriis*
('She flies with her own wings')

Well-known residents and natives:
Herbert Hoover (31st President), Chief Joseph,
Linus Pauling, John Reed, Raymond Carver,
Ursula Le Guin, Ken 'Cuckoo's Nest' Kesey,
Matt Groening, David 'Se7en' Fincher,
River Phoenix, Tonya Harding.

OREGON

'I have to spend hours camping out, listening to completely unconvincing stories of Bigfoot sightings.'

There is something in the Oregon air. On a bright clear day, when the sky is as deep a blue as can be and the fragrant scent of pine invades your nostrils you can tell for sure that this place is different even from neighbouring northern California. We are in the Great Pacific Northwest. The edging of Douglas firs on the hillside gives a hint. Then there is the atmosphere: it is as if you are looking at a world with 500 megapixel resolution. Not a hint of graininess in the air, but the kind of clarity that says larches, lumber and leaping salmon. Why, this could almost be Canada.

Up I go, innumerable lorries loaded with logs pass me driving south; the Pacific is to my left, forests of fir and spruce to my right. The shacks and settlements

I pass are noticeably less prosperous in their appearance than those of California. I am a little shocked to think that a mere state line could reveal so drastic a change. Oregon, after all, is a wine-producing region, its pinot noir especially being world class, it has its 'Silicon Forest' and Intel microchip plants. Yet more than half the states of the Union are more economically powerful than Oregon.

What is prosperity compared to beauty? The streams and rivers are as clear as the air, the mountains in their shawls of ragged spruce and fir reveal lower slopes abundant with both broadleaf and conifer. Oregon, as it happens, produces ninety-five per cent of all America's hazelnuts.

I am headed for the Rogue River, a few miles west of the town of Grants Pass, which makes up for its lack of an apostrophe with an exclamation mark in its motto: 'It's the climate!' Grants Pass is something of a centre for the caving and rafting that attract thousands of people throughout the year, one of whom, it seems, is going to be me.

I make it perfectly clear to anyone who will listen that black water rafting is all I am interested in. The merest hint of froth, foam and bubbling whiteness in the river and I will be screaming to be paddled ashore. The name of the river is worrying enough. Rogue? Why Rogue?

At the riverbank I meet up with Nate and his girlfriend Laura who Velcro up my lifejacket and assure me they will ashore me if things get rough. To be fair, the stretch of water they have chosen does not look especially roguish.

Nate and Laura started life as environmental activists on the fringes of the law who would think nothing of illegally occupying the branches of any valuable trees threatened by loggers. Nate is now a respected member of the environmental community, his history of tree-hugging and arrests being battle scars that earn him respect amongst the younger generation of eco-warriors. I lie back in the raft as he points out the astounding variety around us. There are more species of trees in this part of Oregon than anywhere else, he tells me. Nate loves trees. Laura thinks that if she were a tree he would love her better.

I wonder if they miss the action and excitement of the old days.

'Oh there's plenty of excitement still,' Nate tells me.

'Such as?'

He tells me the story of the red tree vole, a personable little rodent that lives up in the highest branches of the tallest spruces and firs. Nate's life quest, it seems, is to search for its excrement.

'Really? Well . . . each to his own.'

'See, if I can prove there are red tree voles nesting . . .'

'Is it rare then, this red tree vole? Endangered?'

'Not so much. Let's put in here.'

We beach the raft and clamber out. We start to walk through the forest. And walk and walk and walk.

After three or four miles, Nate returns to the subject of his voles. The red tree vole here in the Oregon woods forms the almost exclusive diet of the Spotted Owl. Unlike the vole, the Spotted Owl is federally listed as endangered. Therefore, if Nate can prove that there are red tree voles in a tree, he is effectively proving that the whole area is Spotted Owl habitat and several acres around that tree will be posted as officially protected from logging. That is why most of Nate's days are spent in climbing tall trees and searching for red vole droppings.

We stop beside a lofty Douglas fir. While Nate and Laura attach ropes and pulleys to themselves, I lie down on a soft bank of earth for a well-earned slumber. Three minutes later I am hopping around trying to dislodge ants. Nature really is inexcusably rude and unkind.

I entrust Nate with my iPhone: he will take photographs of any red vole faecal matter or fur.

Up they go, quick as squirrels.

'Yeah!' A cry of triumph from Nate.

'Don't forget to take a picture!' I yell up.

And he does. And that patch of forest is now protected. Pity the poor logger that tries to pit his wits against Nate and Laura.

SASQUATCH

Oh hell. Here I am driving out of Grants Pass with a Sasquatch spotter.

Sasquatch is an alternative name given to Bigfoot, America's very own Yeti, a large humanoid life form unknown to science, common sense or adult human beings. There is, however, a kind of rare (but not rare enough) infantilised western male which collects books on elite Special Services, is attracted by shiny trucks with huge tyres, thinks guns are great, asks only that a female be big-breasted and believes in nonsenses like Bigfoot. These really do exist.

I meet just such a representative of this frightening species in the car park of a McDonald's on the outskirts of Grants Pass. I have heard of them enough times to believe in the rumours about them, but never met one face to face before.

It is at least six-foot-six tall, it is called Matt. It styles itself a 'doctor of psychology' (I should dearly like to know which institution accorded it this academic distinction) and it drives a truck whose bumper sticker 'Oregun' tells us that it is a member of the Oregon branch of the National Rifle Association.

Look, I know I'm being all sneery and contemptuous and mean and snobbish, but really. I have to spend hours camping out with Matt, listening to completely unconvincing stories of Bigfoot sightings, accompanied by weird and inappropriately tearful mentions of his wife and children. His particular blend of aggressive family sentimentality, macho gun-toting and childish superstition is not something I find easy to respect or like.

I mention that there is no evidence whatsoever of apelike creatures aside from Homo sapiens anywhere in North America. No primates but man in the fossil record, no sightings other than those which rank alongside UFO and ghost sightings as unconvincing, uncorroborated or unverifiable. This cuts no ice with Matt.

He has brought a whole basket of fruit along. Bigfoot especially likes bananas apparently, which he opens in the way humans do. We watch Matt leaving a pile of this fruit down in a dell. We continue to wait. Matt makes the cry of the Sasquatch. A noise that is more likely to attract a seal than anything apelike, but never mind.

I would be the first to see the joke if I was squashed, mutilated, raped, eaten or savaged by a Sasquatch. But time passes and we are treated to nothing.

It would be easy to point out that Matt and his ilk are law-abiding citizens who do little harm in the

world. Mm. Perhaps. They do have a vote, however, a
vote in the most powerful democracy in the world. If
that isn't a cause for worry, I don't know what is.

WASHINGTON
KEY FACTS

Abbreviation:
WA

Nickname:
The Evergreen State

Capital:
Olympia

Flower:
Coast rhododendron

Tree:
Western hemlock

Bird:
American goldfinch

Vegetable:
Walla Walla sweet onion

Motto:
Alki (Chinook Wawa Indian for 'eventually'
or 'by and by')

Well-known residents and natives:
Bill Gates, Paul Allen, Mary McCarthy,
Raymond Carver, Frank Herbert, Richard Brautigan,
Tom Robbins, Merce Cunningham,
Gary 'Far Side' Larson, Edward R. Murrow,

Bill 'Science Guy' Nye, Ted Bundy, Chuck Jones,
Frances Farmer, Burl Ives, Adam 'Batman' West,
Carol Channing, James 'Scotty' Doohan,
John 'Cheers' Ratzenberger, Blair Underwood,
James Caviezel, Dyan Cannon, Gypsy Rose Lee,
Bing Crosby, Quincy Jones, Jimi Hendrix,
Steve Miller, Kenny G, Kurt Cobain.

WASHINGTON

'Here in Seattle, the city of Boeing, Microsoft, Starbucks and grunge, I will bid farewell to the taxi.'

At last. Such bitter joy, such happy pain. The forty-eighth and last of the contiguous states. Only disconnected Alaska and Hawaii await me now. Here in Seattle, the city of Boeing, Microsoft, Starbucks and grunge, I will bid farewell to the taxi and to the whole continental USA.

Washington, like the northwest areas of Britain, is known for its rainfall and Seattle does not disappoint. I arrive at the city's Aquarium early on a damp grey morning. It is quite freakish how fortunate we have been in the weather, all the way from Maine. I have had to accuse the director of slaughtering white cockerels, lighting black candles, saying the Lord's Prayer backwards and uttering sacrifices to the Dark One. There can be no other explanation. We have

444

arrived in some states where the weather has bee unprecedentedly cataclysmic until the day we crossed into it, and we have left others just before they were battered by record-breaking hurricanes, tornadoes and blizzards. All the while a zone of serene meteorological perfection has floated above us like a golden aura. On the very few occasions that it has been cloudy or wet it has not signified. Today is a perfect example. If I am to spend a morning in the company of sea otters, seals and fish, it really doesn't matter what the weather is like.

The staff at the aquarium love their marine mammals. Every day, in order to make life more interesting for the otters they package up their daily intake of fish in ice, taking great care to make the frozen meals varied, colourful and striking. This way the otters exercise their paws, claws and ingenuity to eat and don't sink into a slothful expectation of soft, easy protein. In honour of our arrival a special fishy slab of ice in the shape and colour of the Union Jack has been prepared. I am given the responsibility of lobbing it onto the water. Sea otters like to swim on their backs with their food spread out on their tummy, which makes for one of the most appealing sights in nature. I could watch sea otters for hours. The rest of the aquarium offers harbour seals, river otters (I throw them a hard-boiled egg which they make an enormous mess of) and the more traditional underwater creatures like octopus and those fish that look like women who have overdone the makeup.

Seattle is a city in which so many disparate American threads come together. Boeing and Microsoft typify as much as any two institutions could the astounding power of American technology and corporate muscle. Without the jumbo jet and indows the world would be, for good or ill, a very ifferent place.

And then there is Pike Place Market, one of the finest food markets in the world where every horrible tenet of the American supermarket is disregarded: processed, packaged and homogenised food has no place here; here all is freshly and locally produced, laid out in European style stalls and free from the national branding and corporate badging that prevails in the rest of America. The sight of proper cheese and bread sends me wild with delirium. There are other street markets in the USA, but mostly they are either ethnically specific or species of small farmers' market which, while growing yearly in popularity, do not come close to Pike Place in permanence or quality. Pike Place Market alone is, according to Seattle resident and media impresario Christoph Snell, reason enough to live in Seattle.

A little way along the street facing the market Chris takes me to a coffee shop. It is called 'Starbucks'. Crowds of tourists outside gibber excitedly and take photographs. For this is the first Starbucks coffee shop there ever was: the first of thousands. Well, in truth, the very first one perished in a fire, so this is 'kind of the first', as Chris puts it.

Founded with the best of motives, to offer high-quality, freshly brewed coffee in a friendly, welcoming atmosphere, Starbucks would appear to have moved from being the solution to being the problem. Once the hero of students and those who value quality and atmosphere over sameness and sterility, Starbucks has become the defining sight in Everystreet, America and Everystreet Europe too; like Coca-Cola and Disney, Starbucks is now a metonym for the perceived evils of globalisation and American

446

cultural imperialism.

Chris moves me on and we talk of music. The band Nirvana, led by the doomed Kurt Cobain, poster child of grunge, came to stand for a wholesale rejection of the bourgeois comforts of American corporate life. Cobain committed suicide before he could see the full flowering of the success he could never cope with. His estate overtook that of Elvis in earnings last year. 'Smells Like Teen Spirit', once an anthem for the alienated, disaffected, dispossessed and angry, is now, in original and covered versions, a routine soundtrack to the modern world in all its crass and comfortable venality.

Seattle might be said to lay bare the self-contradictions that define America. Great conservative corporations, bullying, monopolistic, grey, disconnected and as capitalist as capitalist can be. Innovative, progressive, new and alternative businesses and movements that can recharge and revitalise the culture but which themselves transform over time into great conservative corporations, bullying, monopolistic, grey . . .

I suppose America, above all is about change— progress and growth and change. Never sitting still. The majority of the population can claim ancestors who refused to stand still . . . they upped and left their shtetls and villages and their risk-taking restlessness seems still to reside in the American gene pool.

You can bet that a new cultural energy will soon be with us, a new youth movement of one kind or another, and it will bring in its train a recrudescence in styles of music, eating, dressing and behaving. Those styles may not originate in Seattle, or even in America, but I should imagine that it is in American towns like Seattle that they will be transformed into small corporate entities, one or two of which will grow and grow and grow . . . and the whole weary work will need to be done again. Grow, mature, age, slash and burn, refresh, grow, mature, age, slash and burn, refresh, grow, mature . . .

CABARET

Christoph, besides being an able and articulate companion for a walk around Seattle, is also a mover and shaker in the lively world of music and performance here. He runs a club called the Can Can which nightly offers European-style cabaret of the highest standard. Set on a tiny stage, witty, spiky, decadent, peopled by a chorus of jolies laides and muscular, athletic boys, the Can Can shows are a world more sophisticated, smart and intelligent than anything available in London. Expertly and amusingly MC-ed by Chris himself, the shows sell out every night to audiences who are clearly enraptured by the chance to sit and watch something strange and different while eating and drinking.

All you need is a small stage and a group of talented people, Chris says. The audience will come because people are greedy for high-quality entertainment that challenges the sameness of pop and television. I urge him to come to London and sprinkle a little cabaret water in the dry desert of the West End. He smiles the smile of a man who is quite happy where he is.

FAREWELL TAXI

Finally, then, the ceremony of farewell. We are on

the wooden boards of a pier facing Puget Sound and the Pacific Ocean. We can go no further north or west and still be in the United States.

Over the months I have collected fridge magnets in the shape of every mainland state in the union. They are not all to the same scale, unfortunately, but nonetheless I manage to put them together on the taxi bonnet in a shape that more or less resembles America. I gaze down at them unable to believe that there is not one I have not visited. In a fortnight's time I will have said goodbye to Hawaii and be back in Britain. That chill end-of-holiday feeling is beginning to grip me.

And speaking of chill, I return to my Pike Place hotel and pack the warmest clothes I can find. Alaska, I am reliably informed, is cold.

ALASKA
KEY FACTS

Abbreviation:
AK

Nickname:
The Last Frontier

Capital:
Juneau

Flower:
Forget-me-not

Tree:
Sitka spruce

Bird:
Willow ptarmigan

Insect:
Four-spot skimmer dragonfly

Motto:
North to the Future

Well-known residents and natives:
Herman of Alaska (Saint),
Jacob of Alaska (Saint),
a great many dog sledders and mushers.

ALASKA

'None of us has ever experienced cold like it. I am beginning to revise my oft-repeated assertion that I would rather be too cold than too hot.'

Texas is huge. From Amarillo in the northwest to Brownsville in the southeast is a distance of over eight hundred miles. Yep, Texas is mighty big. Yet Alaska is two and half times the size. The next two largest states in America are California and Montana. Alaska is bigger than both of them and Texas combined. Alaska is too enormous for the sane mind to grasp. You could comfortably fit seven United Kingdoms inside, or thirteen Englands. You may remember that Maine, the first state I visited on this trip, has three and half thousand miles of coastline. Well, Alaska has more coastline than Maine and all the other American states combined. Alaska is unexplorably big. The capital city Juneau is inaccessible by road: you have to take a ferry to get

451

there. The interior regions in winter regularly dip below –52°C.

It is a three-and-half-hour flight from Seattle, Washington to Anchorage, Alaska. We fly over British Columbia, Canada, a reminder that Alaska, alone with Hawaii, does not border any other American state. It is technically an exclave of the United States. At Anchorage we catch a small plane to Kodiak. I have wanted to visit Kodiak Island for years. An arctophile like me is always keen to meet a new kind of bear and the Kodiak, a huge subspecies of brown bear, is well worth any trip. I have a bad feeling however, reinforced by reading up on the subject, that we may have arrived a little too early. It is the twentieth of April and the island of Kodiak has endured a hard winter. The bears time their hibernation carefully, ending it to coincide with the running of the salmon which, I am told authoritatively, are late this year.

I manage at least to shake hands with the life-sized specimen that guards the harbour. The port of Kodiak is beautiful in a serene and surreal way I have never quite experienced before. Imperiously gigantic mountains loom above the brightly coloured wooden houses and a harbour filled with hundreds of boats, burgees tinkling and hulls slapping; dozens of bald eagles perch on the lamp-posts and eaves, gulls and gannets screech like witches as they follow the fishing boats home. All the riches, all the nutrient, protein and fat that exists in this part of the world can be said to come from the sea. It is true everywhere that colder water makes for tastier fish. Anyone who has visited Southern Spain and then followed the coast to Portugal will know of the extraordinary rise in quality when you turn from Mediterranean to Atlantic

452

seafood. I have this proved to me here with the halibut I taste in a small restaurant overlooking the water. I have never tasted a better fish in all my life.

It is eight-thirty in the evening but as bright as three in the afternoon, all very confusing. A long-haired, bearded young man in a black cassock sits down at the table next to me. He introduces himself as Father Innocent, Orthodox priest and enthusiastic Jeeves and Wooster fan. Would I like to come to a Palm Sunday service tomorrow evening?

'Palm Sunday? But surely that was weeks ago?'

'On your Gregorian Calendar, maybe. But our church is still on the Julian Calendar.'

'Fair enough.'

RASPBERRY ISLAND

A float plane to Big Timber Lodge on Raspberry Island next morning. I suffer the indignity of being lifted bodily over the freezing waters that fringe the beach by Lee, our host. Lee then suffers the back spasms attendant on having lifted me. No one told me to bring waders. No one told him that I am over 250 pounds in weight.

Lee's wife, Lucinda, fills us with sandwiches and sends us on our adventure. The Lady L, named in her honour, is a customised boat that Lee uses to take tourists and adventurers around the islands on fishing and hunting trips. The plan is to scan the islands and look for signs of Kodiak Bear.

'You never know,' Lee says, 'they might be waking up today. It's a warm day.' (This is a black lie. It is so cold that my eyeballs make crispy noises when I blink.)

As we chug through the channels and straits between islands we encounter wild sea otters swimming around (on their backs of course) in large groups called 'rafts'. They pop up vertically out of the water to check us out, rather in the manner of meercats. Once they are sure that we offer neither threat nor calorific content, they cheerfully ignore us. Instead of brightly coloured Union Jacks made of ice on their tummies, some of them are carrying cubs. It seems extraordinary that a warm-blooded mammal, basically a giant weasel, can spend its whole life in freezing waters; aren't they, I wonder, attracted by the warmth of human habitations? Lee tells me that the sea otter's coat, once greatly prized by hunters and trappers, is the thickest in the whole animal kingdom.

'It likes it here.'

He is right of course, but it is hard not to transfer your own feelings onto fellow creatures: I want to curl up by a fire, so surely any mammal would.

Sea otters are very good at catching fish. Lee thinks it is time I tried to match that skill. He hands me a rod and some bait and I do the usual pessimistic dangling.

I tell him about the enormous fish I caught ice fishing in Minnesota. By now, like all fishermen, I was exaggerating wildly and the Minnetonka sun fish had grown to at least five inches in length. But suddenly . . . a twitch on the line!

I reel and reel and reel and heave and pull and yank until . . . behold! A grotesque creature of the deep arises from the surface. Mushroom and grey in colour, with coffee and caramel highlights, but strangely appealing in a disgustingly ugly way, with orange spines and the widest mouth imaginable.

'What on earth . . . ?'

'That,' says Lee, 'is an Irish Lord.'

'An eater?' I enquire.

'Absolutely not an eater.'

We pose for the obligatory photograph before returning his inedible lordship to the deeps.

No sign of bears, sadly. I survey the tops of hills, where an ursine outline would be easy to spot. Nothing.

'Yes. Maybe you can stay for a week?' Lee suggests. 'They'll be up and about then, for sure.'

'If only,' I sigh. But we have miles to go and promises to keep. Indeed I am promised at Father Innocent's church this very evening.

SURPRISINGLY ORTHODOX

From the mid-eighteenth century onwards Alaska was part of the Russian Empire. By 1869, trappers and traders having brought many fur species to edge of extinction, the Tsar was done with this unprepossessing land and made it known to the United States that he was ready to sell. The American Secretary of State, William Seward got a price of $7,200,000, which worked out at about 1.9¢ an acre. You might think that the American people would be pleased, but the general view at the time was that Seward had been sold a pup, a 'sucked orange' as the New York World put it. 'Seward's Folly' remained a joke until gold was discovered in Alaska just thirty years later (too late for Seward to have the last laugh: he died three years after the purchase). It was not until 1959 however that Alaska, with Hawaii, was finally admitted into the union as a full state.

Signs of the Russian occupation are surprisingly easy to find in Kodiak. Street names ending in -off and

-inski are plentiful, but the most obvious clues are the two Russian Orthodox churches.

Father Innocent is priest of St Herman's, named after Alaska's greatest saint. I slip in the back to find the service already under way. With all due respect to the noble traditions of the Orthodox liturgy, this is just about the dullest service I have ever attended in all my life. So much chanting. So much repetition. They must have asked the Lord to have mercy three thousand times. I am not exaggerating. Either He is going to show mercy or He isn't; simply nagging Him like children who want to be taken to Disneyland isn't going to do the trick, surely?

The smell of incense is pleasant enough, however, and the icons gleam effulgently in the evening light.

BARROW

The next morning we say our farewells to Kodiak and its slumbering bears. We are headed north now. Really, really north. Well within the Arctic Circle. Barrow is the northernmost town in the United States of America.

As we wait at Barrow airport for our luggage to emerge from the plane, we take it in turns to put our heads out of the exit door and we instantly return giggling like schoolchildren. None of us has ever experienced cold like it. The wind is fierce enough to double the discomfort. I am wrapped in the thickest, most professional extreme cold-weather clothing I could find and still it is not enough. I am beginning to revise my oft-repeated assertion that I would rather be too cold than too hot.

At half past ten at night it is still as bright as day. I

456

wander about the town, taking in the sights, such as they are, before submitting to the fact that it will never be dark. The curtains in my hotel room are not thick enough to keep out the white light and I pass a fitful night.

WHALING

In the height of Barrow's summer it sometimes gets above freezing. That is the best they have to look forward to. The majority of the town's population is made up of Inupiat Eskimos who subsist by hunting caribou, fish and whale. The federal and international authorities who govern these issues allow the Eskimos of Barrow (and yes, they do prefer to be called Eskimo here, not Inuit) to hunt twenty-two whales a year. The whales, principally bowhead and beluga, are shared amongst the whole community. In a land where fruit and fresh vegetables are not indigenous and hard to come by even today, whale meat, and especially the muktuk or skin and nasty bits, provide all the vitamins and nutrition that the Inupiat need. I have an appointment with whaling captain Henry, who invites me into his home to meet his bouncy and boisterous family. Henry is delightful: a warm, friendly and very proud Inupiat. He makes his own drums, he fashions his own tools, and he tries to live a life that his ancestors would approve of. He agrees to take us to see his whaling boat. The season is nearly upon us and it may be that whales will be spotted in the open seas. I am quite happy if we don't see a whale, for it would mean a killing. While I fully respect the Inupiat's traditional rights and while I recognise that their hunting techniques on oar-powered boats have never endangered the bowhead or the beluga, I am still reluctant to watch the slaughter of any whale, no matter how traditionally done it might be. As with the Kodiak, however, it seems we are a matter of days too early.

Barrow is a coastal town, which is hard to verify when the sea is frozen. Henry's whaler is actually a mile or so out on the frozen Chuckte (as the Arctic Ocean is called hereabouts). He pulls us along on sleds, driving a Ski-doo. The blueness of the ice comes as a shock to me. I had not thought frozen sea-water could be so hauntingly lovely.

We arrive at the whaler, which is not much bigger than an average suburban dining-table. A crew of eight, at a moment's notice, can run the boat off the ice and jump into it just as it hits the water—water in which a human, no matter how fully dressed, could not survive for more than three minutes. They practise so hard that no one ever falls in. Once they are afloat, however, the real work begins, for they have no source of power other than their own calories: the paddle power of eight land animals against a marine animal more than eight times bigger. At least it seems like a fair fight.

The boat is handbuilt and made waterproof by stretching over it the skin of the Bearded Seal. It is very important, Henry tells me, to cure the hide of the seal for over a year. If not the polar bears will sniff it out as meat. A polar bear can reduce a whaling boat to a splintered ruin in minutes.

Henry shows me his harpoons (which are armed with little internal bombs) which he assures me end the life of the whale instantly. The Inupiat take pride in never causing pain or distress to their quarry. Henry hands over a brass whale gun. It weighs sixty pounds, and I can barely lift it to my shoulder.

We stand where the frozen sea ends and watch the horizon. I am glad to say that I see no whales.

I am at the northernmost point in America. Soon I shall be at the southernmost.

HAWAII
KEY FACTS

Abbreviation:
HI

Nickname:
The Aloha State

Capital:
Honolulu

Flower:
Hawaiian hibiscus

Tree:
Kukui nut tree (Candlenut)

Bird:
Hawaiian goose

Motto:
Ua Mau ke Ea o ka Aina i ka Pono
('The life of the land is perpetuated in
righteousness')

Well-known residents and natives:
Duke Kahanamoku, Barack Obama, Jack Lord,
Bette Midler, Nicole Kidman, Jack Johnson.

HAWAII

' "You taste like pork, apparently. 'Long pig', that is what we used to call the white man," says Titus, serving out a second helping.'

Who would have thought Nicole Kidman and Bette Midler were both born in Hawaii? And who would have thought that Keanu Reeves wasn't? It turns out that despite his Hawaiian name (which means something like 'cool ocean breeze') he was born in Beirut. Barack Obama is quite a boast too: he was born in Hawaii and received a private prep-school education here.

I was so looking forward to Honolulu and Waikiki Beach. I grew up on TV shows like *Hawaii Five-O* and *Magnum, P.I.* and for years *From Here to Eternity* was one of my favourite books and films. And now finally I am here.

What a horrible, what a grotesque, what a *shattering* disappointment. Of all the unspeakably vile tourist hells I have ever visited, this has to be one of the worst. At least Alicante and the Costa del Sol know what they are: Waikiki seems to be labouring under the delusion that it is still a glamorous and elite paradise. I dare say it once was, but decades of thoughtless hotel construction have destroyed any beauty, charm or individuality.

From the moment you get on the plane to Honolulu to the moment you leave, the word 'Aloha' is rammed down your throat. It is a greeting of course, but it is supposed too to mean a spirit of welcome and friendliness and warmth. I find no evidence of this Aloha in Honolulu, despite seeing the word everywhere, in neon, plastic and concrete. I go to bed cursing myself for the naïvety with which I expected anything else.

It turns out that I did not need to be quite so disillusioned for the morrow would bring better things.

OAHU NORTH

Honolulu and Waikiki are in the south of the island of Oahu. Perhaps things will look less grisly in the north? They do!

Here at last is the beauty, the paradisiacal splendour, the botanical variety and the genuine warm kindliness of the Aloha spirit. So naturally the first thing I have to do is go out into the sea and swim with sharks.

The purpose of this trip was to make a BBC documentary series and to furnish you, the reader, with a lavish and beautifully presented book that you will treasure and cherish for ever. It was never, so far

462

as I can tell, the aim of this journey to test me, to put me in touch with my lost virility, to explore the limits of my courage and daring, to push me beyond the bounds of endurance until I reached That Place in which I could face my demons and finally call myself a Man. Was it?

I find myself in a boat heading out from the shore to a place where sharks are known to congregate. As someone who recently broke his arm in a clumsy ship-to-ship transfer I am more than usually careful as I move off the back of the boat and manoeuvre myself into a cage around which the sharks will swim. It transpires that this is the most dangerous part of the entire adventure, for the Galapagos Shark, I come to realise, is no threat to humans at all. As they circle the cage in search of food which has been dropped in the water I realise that the only reason this tourist attraction works is because the Galapagos Shark, entirely dopey, harmless and uninterested in human flesh, nonetheless closely resembles that fearsome killer of the deep, the Great White.

Were I less of a manly man of course, I would not have let slip this information and I would have allowed you to live the rest of your lives believing me to be dashing, heroic and valiant in the extreme, but fortunately I have no need to prove my manliness. The only reason I go on to buy an 'I Swam With Sharks!' T-shirt and wear it around the island is because the colours go with my shorts.

SUNSET ELEMENTARY

Next I have a chat with Kim Johnson, wife of the musician Jack, the Hawaiian-born singer-songwriter whose popularity appears to be growing every month. Kim and I sit in the garden of Sunset Elementary School, where Jack went as a boy and where his and Kim's children will soon be going too.

'We started up this foundation,' says Kim. 'The idea is to get the kids to love and understand nature and the unique wildlife that surrounds them.'

'Doesn't that happen naturally?'

'It should. It used to, but the island language, the culture, traditions and identity are all under threat . . . '

'The hypnotic attractions of mainland movies, TV, internet, sport and music?'

'Right. Plus there used to be cash crops like sugar and pineapples which kept people in the countryside here. Not ideal, but they provided job security.'

'And they've gone?'

'Yup. The lower wages and costs in the Philippines were pretty much irresistible to the growers. There's a Dole Pineapple Plantation museum down the road, but that only employs a handful.'

'I passed it on my way here. What about more tourism?'

'Yeah, but at what cost to the island itself? If the north became like the south it would be a disaster. That's why Jack and I think it all starts here . . . ' she points at the school buildings behind us. 'The hearts and minds of Hawaiian children. If they love their islands enough they will stay and the islands will be healthy and prosperous.'

I hope she is right.

TERRY, P.I.

Back in Waikiki, which I like a great deal more now

464

that I know the whole island of Oahu isn't like that, I meet up with Terry, a private investigator. He tells me stories of the seamier side of life here.

'Few years ago it was the policy of certain municipal authorities on the mainland to give their hobos, winos, druggies and dead-beats a one-way ticket to Honolulu.'

'You mean they'd just put them on a plane?'

'Sure. So a bum from Chicago or Little Rock for example, he'd wake up from the flight and find himself in a city where you can sleep outdoors all year round and where rich tourists are—how can I put it?—more kindly disposed to pan-handling than the citizens back home.'

'So they would stay?'

'Wouldn't you?'

We walk on along the beach. The sun is setting behind the silhouettes of surfers riding in the last of the light.

'I was once called by a rich, a very, very, very rich Texan family,' says Terry. 'They had a drug addict son who had suddenly disappeared from the mean streets of Dallas. He used to hang out there with his fellow junkies. His family used to keep a discreet watch on him, using private detectives and one day the detectives call to say the kid's disappeared off the radar. They think he was given one of these one-way tickets to Hawaii. So the family ask me to look for him here. They email over a photo and the boy's aunt calls me. "He may be worth a fortune in his own right," she says, "but he has what the French call nostalgie de la boue. You'll find him wherever lowlifes gather." So I come here straight away. First place I think of.'

We have arrived at a large banyan tree by a bronze statue of Duke Kahanamoku, the Olympic gold

465

medallist who did more than anyone else to popularise surfing. Under it is gathered a collection of street kids and hobos.

'And sure enough, there was the kid, just there, where the lady with the shopping cart is now.'

'What did you say to him?'

'Told him that his parents wanted him back. That because he had turned twenty-one he was now worth fifteen million dollars.'

'Oh my heavens.'

'He knew what he was worth but he refused to return and collect his money. Far as I know he is still here, living on the streets. That's Hawaii, Steve. Being a Honolulu bum is worth more than fifteen million in the bank.'

KAUAI

The farthest north and westmost of all the Hawaiian islands is Kauai. It is also, in real-estate terms, the most desirable. Many moguls, movie stars and musicians have homes in the north of the island, along a stretch called the Na Pali Coast.

The Kalalau Trail is a strenuous eleven miles of clambering and scrambling that attracts thousands of tourists bolder than I am. I meet up at the trailhead with local surfing dude and proud Hawaiian, Titus, one of the men who has popularised the old-fashioned art of long-boarding. We manage about a mile up the hill before coming down again.

'You're out of condition, dude,' he says. 'Shouldn't be out of breath after such a short hike.'

'Nonsense,' I puff, 'I was gasping at the beauty of it all.' Certainly the view of the coastline has

466

convinced me that Na Pali is even more perfect than the north beaches of Oahu.

Next Titus takes me out, with his two young daughters, on an outrigger canoe. The daughters are there, it becomes obvious, to rescue and subdue me if I fall out.

'You have to count strokes,' says Titus. 'Fourteen on the left side of the boat, then "hup!" and fourteen on the right . . . Oh yes, you're looking very native there. But how about you stop humming the *Hawaii Five-O* theme tune?'

'Sorry, I didn't know I was.'

In the evening there is the treat of watching local children doing authentic hula dancing while sipping local beer and eating whole roast pig.

The sun sets on the beach and the children, with serious eyes and nimble feet, perform the dances of their ancestors. A boy blows on a huge conch. And the sun finally drops below the horizon. A good day.

'My ancestors,' says Titus serving out a second helping of pulled pork, 'used to eat your ancestors when we got the chance. You taste like pork, apparently. "Long pig", that is what we used to call the white man.'

BIG ISLAND

Today I drop in on the largest of Hawaii's islands, officially called Hawai'i (note the apostrophe), which is so confusing that everyone calls it Big Island.

Hilo, where we land (the seas are too rough and the distances too great to island-hop any other way but by air) has the most attractive airport I have ever seen, all flower troughs and tropical hardwoods. I spring into an open-topped rented Jeep and head for Mount

Mauna Kea, whose dormant cone I can clearly see in the distance. You could argue that Mauna Kea is the tallest mountain in the world. From its base on the sea floor to the summit is 33,000 feet. Most people, however, even Hawaiians, would concede that since Everest's 29,029 feet are all above sea level it has the right to its status as highest peak. Mauna Kea is 'only' 13,800 feet high by that reckoning—an 'only' that becomes a sick joke as you drive further and further up the mountain's steep and pumice-strewn road and the air gets thinner and thinner.

We are visiting the Keck Observatory, one of more than a dozen (including a British one) perched on the summit. Our host is the astronomer Alex Filippenko of the University of California at Berkley. Professor Filippenko is a natural communicator, the enthusiasm and passion he has for the stars and supernovae in particular, is contagious.

'You know the first generation of stars after the Big Bang consisted only of hydrogen and helium,' he says, 'but did you realise that the heavy elements of which you are made, the carbon in your cells, the calcium in your bones, the oxygen that you breath, the iron in your red blood cells . . . all of these elements were cooked up in the nuclear furnaces deep inside stars and then blown out into the cosmos by these colossal explosions? So you are, as Carl Sagan used to say, made of star stuff. The study of the supernova teaches us the universe is speeding up, instead of slowing down. How cool is that!'

'And what is so special about the Keck?'

'Clear images that come from a place so high above the water vapour and impurities of the atmosphere are of great scientific value.'

Despite Alex's eminence in his field, therefore,

even he and his famous university cannot be guaranteed more than five or six nights a year at this facility. Recent advances, not in astrophysics but in IT, mean that he can at least do the basic tweaking of the telescope during the day and be down at a lower altitude by night, from where he can watch the images come in remotely. Even a brain like his cannot but be somewhat compromised by the thin air two and half miles above sea level.

He takes me through to the dome itself and I gawp, gasp and gurgle as much in oxygen-starved distress as in genuine appreciation at the scale and splendour of the apparatus. Much as I love talking to eminent scientists, and he is one of the most likeable and accessible I have ever met, the conditions are giving me a sick headache and I am pleased to drive down the mountain and feel the oxygen enrich my lungs with every thousand feet we descend.

LAVA FIELDS

A helicopter ride now, and a helicopter ride like no other. We are to overfly the lava fields of Kilauea.

We take off from Hilo and are soon over hardened fields, like frozen toffee in a pan. Ahead I can see smoke. One side of our helicopter is open, to let the cameraman shoot freely. Martin, the pilot, tells us that the 'smoke' is actually sulphur dioxide.

'Not too poisonous, but might make you choke.'

Kilauea has been active since 1983, but recently a few new fumeroles or vents have opened up. We flew over a 'skylight', a hole in the field, glowing red like a door to the underworld. I could feel the heat up in the helicopter.

There was no room on board for Vanda, our beloved photographer, so you will have to make do with the pictures from my iPhone. Not the highest quality, but they give some idea of the drama that takes place when lava meets ocean.

Here the 'smoke' is caused by huge clouds of hydrochloric acid, sent up into the air every time the waves break on the lava which, as perhaps you can tell in my adequate photograph, gushes out in bright red fingers.

'Very poisonous. The hydrochloric acid will burn your skin real bad.' Martin manoeuvres around the shoreline with great care.

Aside from the hiss of hydrochloric acid sent up when the breakers meet the lava, something else happens. The molten lava is frozen into rock. Over the past six weeks alone, Martin tells me, twenty acres of land have been formed by this action of water on lava.

Somehow Martin lands the helicopter and I stand on a fragment of cooling land to present my final piece of the series.

This is the southernmost part of America and behind me new bits of America are being made. It seems the right moment to say goodbye.

Fifty states. Fifty cultures, societies, accents, cuisines, landscapes and more. I shall never be able to think of America in quite the same way again. I cannot claim to have done more than scratch the surface of this enormous land, but the scope of my adventures and the variety of people I have met have convinced me that it is almost as meaningless to call someone American without specifying their state as it is to call them European without specifying their country. The great metropolitan areas stand on their own as unique entities, but journeying through the rest of the United States I found that statehood mattered and that locality and terroir, as the French would say, seared its brand into everything and everyone.

I loved America before this trip and I love it now more than ever. The obvious characteristics that we celebrate and bemoan—the brashness, the vulgarity, the worship of money, the gun obsession, the distressing religiosity, the ignorance of the rest of the world, the deafness to linguistic nuance, the lack of banter, the whining self-regard, the blame culture, the junk food and the strip malls—yes, these are all to be found, but alongside we encounter the hope, the self-belief, the optimism, the warmth, consideration, kindness, sharpness of wits, will power, pride, wry self-awareness, independence, openness, generosity and charm. There is nothing you and I can observe about America that most Americans haven't observed for themselves. I met very few fools on my travels, save perhaps the British I encountered who thought themselves naturally superior: I still shiver with embarrassment at the memory of their imbecile arrogance. America is not perfect, and I do not love Britain any less for loving America more. As all travellers know, the experience of a foreign country teaches about your own.

AMERICAN ENGLISH

A little quiz to mark the end of the book. Most people are aware that American words can be different. Here are some a little less known than 'elevator' and 'sidewalk'. Most, but not all, have a simple one-word British-English equivalent.

1. Amortize
2. Bangs *
3. Barrette
4. Berm
5. Bimini
6. Binky
7. Blacktop
8. Booger
9. Boondocks, boonies
10. Boondoggle
11. Braids
12. Brodie knob
13. Broil
14. Bronx cheer
15. Bullhorn
16. Bureau*
17. Burlap
18. Bus (v)*
19. Caboose
20. Canola oil
21. Casket
22. Chinch
23. Cilantro
24. Cobbler*
25. Conniption
26. Cotton candy
27. Crosswalk
28. Decal
29. Docent
30. Druthers
31. Eggplant
32. Faucet
33. Flatware
34. Fungible
35. Garnish*
36. Glom
37. Granola
38. Gurney
39. Jackhammer
40. Jimmies
41. Jury-rig
42. Keister
43. Kludge/kluge
44. Mononucleosis
45. Muffler*
46. Mugwump

* aside from the obvious . . .

47. Notions
48. Parcheesi
49. Pavement
50. Polliwog/pollywog
51. Popsicle
52. Rutabaga
53. Saltine
54. Scallion
55. Shill
56. Shim
57. Slingshot
58. Spackle
59. Sprinkles*
60. Stogie/stogy
61. Stroller
62. Suds*
63. Thumb tack
64. Tic-tac-toe
65. Ukase
66. Underdrapes
67. Wet willie
68. Wringer

Answers 1. Pay off (a debt) in instalments 2. Fringe
3. Hair slide   4. Verge or roadside strip of grass
5. Canvas canopy for a boat, golf cart, etc.
6. Children's dummy or pacifier   7. Tarmac on the
road   8. Bogey or hardened snot   9. The wilds, the
back of beyond   10. A project which is a waste of
time and money, sometimes for corrupt reasons
11. Plaits   12. That swivelling knob attached to a
steering wheel to make one-handed turns easier
13. Grill   14. To blow a raspberry is to give a Bronx
cheer   15. Megaphone or loud-hailer   16. Chest of
drawers   17. Sacking, hessian   18. To clean tables,
as in bus-boy   19. The extra car at the back of a train
20. Rapeseed oil   21. Coffin   22. Bed bug
23. Coriander   24. Crumble (as in apple crumble)
25. A fit of rage or hysterics   26. Candy floss
27. Pedestrian (zebra, pelican) crossing   28. A
transfer applied to cars, planes, etc.   29. A (usually
voluntary) museum guide   30. Preference, as in 'If I
had my druthers . . .'   31. Aubergine   32. Tap
33. Cutlery   34. Interchangeable   35. To seize
money in settlement of a debt or claim   36. To steal.
Or to stick (to glom onto someone)   37. Muesli
38. Trolley, especially hospital stretcher on wheels
39. Pneumatic drill   40. Hundreds and thousands, see
Sprinkles   41. To lash together temporarily, also
jerry-rig. 42. Arse. Rhymes with 'Easter' 43. Badly
put together machinery   44. Glandular fever
45. Silencer (on car)   46. One who remains aloof
from   party   politics;   also,   a   big   cheese
47. Haberdashery, buttons, pins and hooks, etc.
48. The game of Ludo   49. The hard surface of the
road   50. Tadpole   51. Ice lolly or lollipop
52. Swede (vegetable)   53. Cracker-style biscuit
(popular with soup)   54. Spring onion   55. The

planted accomplice of a salesman or gambler who pretends to bet or buy in order to entice others 56. A thin strip of metal to help parts fit: i.e. a washer, wedge or other filler 57. Catapult 58. Polyfilla-type compound to fill cracks and smooth surfaces 59. See Jimmies 60. A small cigar 61. A pushchair 62. Beer 63. Drawing pin 64. The game of noughts and crosses 65. An edict 66. Net curtains 67. The child's trick of pushing a spit-moistened finger into someone's ear 68. Mangle

ACKNOWLEDGEMENTS

You will notice that for the most part I write in the preceding pages in the first person singular, as if I were travelling around America on my own. In fact I was in the company of film crews, a driver and the entirely adorable Vanda Vucicevic, whose glorious photographs accompany the text of this book. Vanda was the only person who was with me for every step of the way, by my side for every state and every mile of the journey. For technical, logistical film-making reasons, we had two alternating crews. Crew A was with us for Leg 1—Maine to Maryland, Leg 3—Louisiana to Minnesota and Leg 5—New Mexico to Hawaii. Crew B shot Leg 2—Virginia to Florida and Leg 4—Montana to Texas.

My thanks for their unfailing cheerfulness, professionalism and boundless patience go to Crew A: Director and Series Producer J.P. Davidson, Assistant Producers Lucy Wallace and Annie Macnee, Cameraman Simon ffrench and Sound Recordist Tim Hodge and to Crew B: Director Michael Waldman, Assistant Producer Amanda Sealy, Cameraman Paul Otter and Sound Recordist Adam Toy.

Driving the crew vehicle, tending to the taxi's limey eccentricities and making the whole epic possible was the loyal, indefatigable and tireless Transport Captain, Camera Grip and Driver Frank Davis, a New Yorker but now an honorary Londoner.

André Singer of West Park Pictures was behind the project from the first and the benefit of his unexampled experience and wisdom was crucial to the preparation and planning of the whole undertaking. Janina Stamps's calm and efficient presence in the London office and at the end of a phone day and night extricated us from many a near-disaster with hotel rooms and broken equipment.

André and I took the idea of the series to Richard Klein and Peter Fincham at the BBC and they were both passionate in their support—all from a refreshingly and benevolently hands-off distance.

My producing partner at Sprout, Gina Carter, deserves my profound thanks as always, and I am eternally grateful to Katy Carrington and her team at HarperCollins for their professionalism and creative flair in the face of a very short lead time and an author who seemed so often to be doing everything except sitting down and writing.

As ever gratitude and indebtedness beyond computation to my beloved and loyal personal assister, Jo Crocker.

SF—June 2008